Transformative Science Teaching

A Catalyst for Justice and Sustainability

DANIEL MORALES-DOYLE

HARVARD EDUCATION PRESS
CAMBRIDGE, MASSACHUSETTS

Copyright © 2024 by the President and Fellows of Harvard College

All rights reserved. No part of this publication may be reproduced or transmitted in any form or by any means, electronic or mechanical, including photocopy, recording, or any information storage and retrieval systems, without permission in writing from the publisher.

Paperback ISBN 9781682538746

Library of Congress Cataloging-in-Publication data is on file.

Published by Harvard Education Press,
an imprint of the Harvard Education Publishing Group

Harvard Education Press
8 Story Street
Cambridge, MA 02138

Cover Design: Endpaper Studio
Cover Photo: Endpaper Studio

The typefaces used in this book are Adobe Garamond Pro and Myriad Pro.

*To Quetzali, Xóchitl, & Xoaquín—who embody
my hope for alternative futures*

Contents

INTRODUCTION		1
CHAPTER 1	Why Teach Science?	17
CHAPTER 2	Teaching Transformative Intellectuals	43
CHAPTER 3	Social Justice Science Issues	67
CHAPTER 4	From SJSI to Curriculum and Assessment	99
CHAPTER 5	Teaching for the Love of Life, Not Biology	121
CHAPTER 6	Teaching Science as a Catalyst for Alternative Futures	139
	Notes	151
	Acknowledgments	167
	About the Author	169
	Index	171

INTRODUCTION

I scribbled in a warped composition book with a black and white marbled cover, the kind that so many science teachers buy in bulk at dollar stores or back-to-school sales for their students to use as laboratory notebooks. The number of composition books in circulation has probably decreased since students turn in so much of their work electronically now, but I keep several around. I use the leftovers from previous back-to-school bulk purchases for recording my thoughts about teaching. I tried recording these thoughts on a phone or computer, but there is something about paper and pencil that works better for capturing my ideas—from curriculum brainstorms to philosophical ponderings. This particular warped composition book was designated for reflections, notes, and stories about what it means to teach for social justice. It became disfigured a few years prior when the room where I was staying during a summer trip was flooded by a torrential rainstorm. The notebook had been in my backpack on the floor. I am still grateful to the family members with whom I was staying for rescuing it and meticulously drying it out, page-by-page, because the book contained several years' worth of notes. During a summer curriculum planning session, I wrote one of the last entries in the flood-rescued notebook before I ran out of pages: "Entering into my 10th year teaching, nothing continues to perplex me more than the various and multiple demands on science curriculum and teaching."

That sentence, scribbled into a water-damaged composition book expresses the conundrum that drives this book: What should be our priorities as science teachers? And how do we teach in a way that reflects our priorities? If you picked up this book, you likely agree that equity and justice must be central. You also likely believe that science education plays a central role in achieving broader societal goals like public health and sustainability. But in two decades as a science educator, I have learned that exactly what equity, justice, and sustainability mean and how these relate to the day-to-day work of science teaching are not as clear-cut as I thought they were when I started as a young teacher. This book encourages science teachers to challenge dominant ways of thinking about equity in education through reconsiderations of why we teach, who we teach, and what we teach. It also addresses not only how we teach, but how we continue to learn. This introduction provides a different way of thinking about how the concepts of equity, justice, and sustainability relate to each other. Subsequent chapters weave together research, stories, examples from practice, and questions to guide and inspire science teachers to link equitable science learning activities in their classroom with justice and sustainability in larger society.

THE UBIQUITOUS PIPELINE METAPHOR

For as long as science has been a subject in schools, there has been a singular goal dominating the discussion about the priorities of science teachers: to prepare future scientists. In recent decades, this goal merged with goals for other technical disciplines and came to be represented by a metaphoric pipeline for the preparation of science, technology, engineering, and mathematics (STEM) workforce. Politicians, corporate executives, and various reports they commission frequently emphasize the importance of this workforce for the purposes of economic competitiveness and national defense. This book provides an alternative perspective about science education: that it may promote values of equity, social justice, and sustainability instead. Then it provides science teachers with guidance about how to align their curriculum and instruction with these alternate values—guidance that begins with challenging the value of the STEM pipeline.

For those educators who Glen Aikenhead labeled "pipeline enthusiasts," equity is defined simply as "broadening participation" in STEM.[1] But Aikenhead also pointed out that even as the preparation of future scientists has dominated the discussion about why we teach science, there have always been science educators who rejected these goals and pushed for alternatives. The most visible and persistent alternative vision for the goals of science education has been scientific literacy, which has been defined in myriad ways. The framework that guided the development of the Next Generation Science Standards (NGSS) put it this way: "A major goal for science education should be to provide all students with the background to systematically investigate issues related to their personal and community priorities."[2] It is hard to disagree with this as a major goal for science education. But this book contends that mainstream approaches to equity in science education do not account for how students' personal lives and community priorities are shaped by issues of inequality, exploitation, and oppression.

Efforts to broaden the goals of science education beyond the pipeline and to broaden participation in the pipeline are both important. These efforts may push science education beyond the elitist, exclusionary ways in which the pipeline model has always functioned. But despite good intentions, relatively little progress has been made on either front. In terms of broadening participation, this can be observed in the ways that the opportunities and resources of the STEM pipeline continue to be hoarded by privileged white men. Right-wing manipulation of public opinion on issues like climate change or vaccination are indicators of where we stand as a society regarding the development of widespread and robust scientific literacy. This book argues that what prevents progress in these directions is our failure to recognize that inequity in science education is not an isolated or technical problem. Inequity in science education is interwoven in deep and reciprocal ways with inequities throughout our society. In other words, we cannot radically change science education without changing the world. But this book is about the other side of that coin: science education can be an important strategy for changing the world. Broadly speaking, current relationships between human societies and other organisms and systems on Earth are neither just nor sustainable. This is also true for the relationships within human societies. To the extent that science education can be about teaching students to recognize, appreciate, understand, and reimagine these relationships, it has a key role to play in building alternate pathways to futures that are more just and more sustainable. Within this frame, equity in science education must involve marginalized communities seizing their power to determine their futures. The first step toward reimagining science education as a strategy for social change is to leave behind the tired and problematic pipeline metaphor.

THE PIPELINE LIMITS TEACHERS' ROLES

The pipeline model of science education positions teachers as promoters of the scientific enterprise. This role is apparent in seemingly endless t-shirts and coffee mugs with cheesy slogans like, "Chem-is-try" or "I ♥ science." There is nothing wrong with enthusiastically encouraging our students to engage with our disciplines, but what kind of engagement do we promote? Because the history of many scientific institutions is rooted in European colonialism and US imperialism, there are problematic ideologies just under the surface of biology, chemistry, and physics curricula. As teachers, we need to pause and consider what kinds of messages our students are receiving by our inclusion or omission of key questions and concepts in the curriculum. For example, as we teach about genetics, do we accidentally reinforce widely held false beliefs about racial differences or gender binaries? As we teach about the useful properties of chemicals, do we also teach about their environmental consequences that hit some communities harder than others? Do we acknowledge the role that physics plays in waging violent and unjust wars? Does our curriculum imply that our Earth is a rock full of materials for our consumption or perhaps something more sacred and valuable? As we marvel at the effectiveness of vaccines, do we also caution about the disaster of synthetic opioids developed and promoted by the same pharmaceutical companies? Chapter 1, Why Teach Science?, offers teachers an opportunity to wrestle with why they teach science as the first step in realigning their values and principles with their pedagogies.

THE PIPELINE IS RACIST AND SEXIST

For decades, educational researchers have documented and critiqued inequitable access to science learning resources, opportunities, and experiences for students marginalized by racism, sexism, ableism, and economic dispossession.[3] In recent years, there have been critically important studies that provide insight into the ways in which racialized and gendered environments and expectations are linked to stereotypes and create inequitable and harmful pathways to and through the STEM pipeline.[4] Science educators have also demonstrated that how teachers deal with students' culture, language, and identities *vis-à-vis* the institutional language and culture of science matters.[5] There is a stark contrast between teachers who begin from the assumption that their students enter the classroom with a wealth of experiences and intellectual resources and those who see only deficits and misconceptions. For example, in science classrooms throughout the US, students whose first language is not English are often treated as if their home language is a deficit rather than understanding their emerging bilingualism to be an incredible asset for learning.[6] This is just one way in which some classrooms insist that students fit into narrow definitions of what it means to be smart or scientific while others invite students to participate in scientific communities as their full authentic selves. These assumptions about students and what counts as scientific consistently uphold white supremacy and patriarchy—except in classrooms where teachers explicitly and consciously challenge these forms of oppression. This book contains numerous examples to illustrate how this can play out. Teaching practices always involve language, culture, and identity, and they can significantly enhance or damage students' learning experiences. If teachers value their students' ways of being and understanding the world, then they can create opportunities for students to consider how the practices and ideas of the sciences may be inspiring and useful.

Even as there has been substantial progress with respect to identifying the sources and consequences of inequity in science education, the notion of STEM access has been perverted to reinforce these existing inequalities. Low standardized test scores in mathematics or limited resources for science materials are often used as justification for rote and simplistic learning activities that deny students rich and meaningful learning opportunities. The promise of economic opportunity associated with STEM has also allowed corporations to co-opt schools for their own workforce development purposes. For example, there is a corporate model of STEM schools that has proliferated through urban school districts that offers mostly Black and Latine students a pipeline into so-called "middle skill" jobs rather than into graduate or medical school.[7] Indeed, the "playbook" that describes the blueprint for these schools prioritizes English language arts, mathematics, and workplace learning. In other words, these are STEM schools where learning science takes a backseat to instilling "workplace values" as defined by the large technology corporation that wrote the playbook. While these STEM schools are promoted as beacons of equity, they show how the STEM pipeline model continues to be most effective at discriminating between students by sorting them into bins based on their perceived value to the workforce. The pipeline approach is less effective at promoting growth, opportunity, and critical thinking. Abandoning the pipeline metaphor allows us to ask instead: *science education for whom?* Chapter 2, Teaching Transformative Intellectuals, models for science teachers how we can begin to answer that question by changing the way we view our students, our disciplines, and the relationships between them.

THE PIPELINE CONSTRAINS STUDENT THINKING

There is another dimension of equity and justice in the research on science curriculum that has been less prominent in both research literature and public discussions but is equally important: the ways in which science curriculum often limits and constrains how students understand the world and all its complexity. For decades, science teaching has focused on how closely students' explanations of phenomena resemble simplified scientific consensus articulated in textbooks and learning standards. But students are capable of so much more than that! This book offers an approach to science teaching that engages them with issues that matter and questions to which teachers do not have the answers. Sometimes students already care deeply about these problems; other times they may have never considered them before. Either way, the focus of science class becomes figuring out how scientific ideas and practices might be helpful in our lives and communities rather than coaching students to reproduce a standard explanation for why iron rusts or how energy flows through an ecosystem.

When school boards, state legislatures, or groups of experts deliberate what is worthwhile to teach in science class, two concepts tend to spark debates that show up in the news: climate change and evolution. The third recent lightning rod of science and society—vaccines—are often not even addressed in science curricula. These highly visible examples are extremely important topics to teach. But even beyond them, ideology informs *every* decision about what we teach in science class. Our cultures, our values, and our politics shape what we consider to be worthwhile for our limited time with students. And, in turn, these decisions have the power to expand or constrain possibilities for our students, including not only their career paths, but also their community involvement and their worldviews. Unfortunately, these decisions about what is worth teaching in science class too often reflect views that are outdated, discriminatory, or overdetermined by the most powerful people in our society. Most of the time teachers do not even get a chance to consider whose priorities are guiding their curriculum.[8]

I am not very active on social media, but a viral post recently caught my attention for its concise analysis of how this plays out in social studies curriculum. The post stated that the US education system makes sure that students know the names of the boats that Columbus brought to this continent better than the names of the Indigenous peoples who were already here. Of course, this is a point that educational researchers have made in much greater depth and nuance.[9] When science teachers are confronted with this kind of analysis, many shrug it off, assuming that our content areas are incapable of such bias or oversight. But as our colleagues down the school hallway repeat false and tired narratives about Columbus or the so-called founding fathers, we emphasize Newton's laws, Darwin's theory of evolution, or the Born-Haber cycle. Together, what do these curricular decisions implicitly teach our students about the *who* and the *how* of science? How do we consider the historical context wherein the US and Europe built up institutions of scientific inquiry that were funded by the spoils and informed by the ideologies of slavery, racial capitalism, and settler-colonialism? This book engages science educators with these questions as a way of deepening engagement with the decision about what matters in our classrooms and curriculum. Chapter 3, Social Justice Science Issues, describes a process for teachers to organize their curriculum around social justice science issues (SJSI).

THE PIPELINE IS NOT SUSTAINABLE

As science teachers, we would be wise to encourage *critical* engagement with our content areas. We can promote students' fascination with the processes of life without promoting biotech corporations. We can encourage students' awe about the power embedded in the smallest particles with honesty about the fact that the US government funded the research that constructed that knowledge in pursuit of violence and destruction. We can teach that science and technology have a role in mitigating the climate crisis while also acknowledging that they continue to facilitate the exploitation of fossil fuels that brought us to the point of crisis in the first place. This book provides science teachers with guidance about how to concretely shift our role from promoters of the scientific enterprise to promoters of equity, justice, and sustainability who believe that sciences can play a role in these pursuits. This implies a shift in how we view our content areas from slogans like "science is my superpower" to deeper forms of both appreciation and critique.

Such a shift requires teachers to embrace their role as curriculum developers, so that curriculum can be locally responsive and because mainstream textbooks do not reflect these values. At the same time, it is not feasible for teachers to start from scratch or to take on the work that well-resourced teams of curriculum developers do as full-time jobs. Therefore, chapter 4, From SJSI to Curriculum and Assessment, describes *how* teachers can plan justice-oriented curriculum and assessments within the constraints of schools. These processes begin by designing assessments that seriously consider how learning in our content areas might be authentically meaningful to students beyond our classrooms. Teachers can rely on existing published materials or tried-and-true lessons while taking on manageable redesign or creatively supplementing with activities that ask students to consider the historical contexts and underlying values of scientific ideas and practices.

Perhaps the most dangerous falsehood that we communicate to students is that science is objective and universal. Our schools teach students, not only that there is only one way to do science (the scientific method), but also that it is the universal path to truth. This does not encourage students to understand that even across the various sciences, there are divergences about what constitutes a valid experiment or reliable evidence.[10] Students are not often asked to make connections between how they have already come to understand the world and scientific ways of knowing. They are rarely asked to consider how scientific knowledge might intersect with historical knowledge—let alone artistic, aesthetic, or spiritual views of the universe. Indeed, most science curriculum teaches students that scientists work in isolation from politics and culture. Perhaps it is not surprising that college students who decide to major in STEM fields tend to be less socio-politically engaged than their peers who study other fields.[11]

Just like actual pipelines, which are an important part of the infrastructure that enables the unsustainable exploitation of fossil fuels, the STEM pipeline may be doing more harm than good to our communities and our world. A brilliant student I taught named Cristina explained this to me in an interview. About a year and a half after she took my AP chemistry class, I was talking to Cristina for a research project I was doing about that class. She was telling me about her decision to major in chemistry in college when she described how she viewed the ambivalent relationship between the field of chemistry and her values:

> I could go and get my degree in chemistry and do something horribly, horribly wrong with it....I could work for, like, a polluting industry or, I don't know, a chemical manufacturing industry that exploits workers and dumps their crap on the river....If you get that kind of job, you're probably going to get a lot more money too.

True to her values, Cristina decided to become a community organizer for an environmental justice group instead, explaining her decision in the following way, "Usually when people ask me, without getting into the whole story of it, I say I realized that I liked chemistry and I liked working with my community, so I'm just putting them both together." Every student cannot and should not pursue a career as an environmental activist or a community organizer; nor should every student pursue a career in the STEM pipeline. What's more, K–12 education should not primarily be about career preparation. What is important about Cristina's reasoning is the way she speaks to the lack of political awareness or attention to ethical commitments in the pipeline approach to science education.

In the vision for science education presented in this introduction and elaborated throughout this book, teachers should engage students with sciences not as a singular method, but as a set of communities, tools, practices, and ways of understanding the world. At the same time, teachers should also support students in critiquing the enterprise of science as a set of institutions and norms that have undergirded unjust forms of domination and unsustainable development. Chapter 5, Teaching for the Love of Life, Not Biology, shares examples to concretize what it means to teach students about science as a set of institutions that do not have a monopoly on curiosity. These examples challenge simple binaries to illustrate how science class can focus on serious issues and yet still be a place where students experience fun and joy. By rejecting the alluring appeal of universal "best practices" and "science for all," teachers can cultivate students' imaginations, complex thinking, and commitments to justice and sustainability in both ecological and cultural domains. Students can learn to critique the STEM enterprise while also cultivating their sense of wonder about the world.

IMAGINE A WORLD WITHOUT PIPELINES

A 2018 advertisement for a company that builds and maintains petroleum pipelines cynically asks us to imagine "a world without pipelines." The booming voice of the narrator gives its audience three options for meeting our energy needs, "Do you want this…this…or this?" In the video version of the ad, the first option is represented by tanker trucks maneuvering through traffic with blaring horns and hissing air brakes; the second option shows a long freight train of matte black tanker cars barreling down a railway. The third option shows a birds-eye view of a serene green countryside with the narrator's voice accompanied by chirping birds. Who would choose anything but option three? This advertisement, for a company founded by two billionaires, argues that without pipelines, we would be stuck with more oil tankers clogging highways or roaring down railroads whereas pipelines preserve and conserve the pristine landscapes they traverse. This is a false and unimaginative choice. Just like this ad for literal pipelines, the metaphoric STEM pipeline offers students a limited, unsustainable, and unjust range of possibilities for our future.

Our science classes should provide space for students to imagine alternative futures. It should not be so difficult to imagine a world that is not only without pipelines, but without burning fossil fuels. However, encouraging imagination can be hard for STEM teachers. We often feel more comfortable teaching students to engineer technical solutions to problems; indeed this is what the learning standards ask us to do. I am not arguing that we should not teach principles of engineering. It is an important part of our role as science teachers to support students' thinking about the technical components of problems. But it is equally important that we do not isolate the technical from the social and political and that we take what Kristen Gunkel and Sara Tolbert call a dimension of care into engineering.[12] But if we are focused on engineering electric trucks as a solution to air pollution and climate change, we forget to ask whether it is sustainable, just, or even possible to mine the amount of lithium required to simply swap fossil fuels for battery power. More importantly, we may miss an opportunity to focus on reducing the amount of unsustainable consumer products or the distances they are transported across the world. If young people do not learn to question our relationships with the Earth in science class, where will these questions arise? What better place to problematize the way our economy is structured around never-ending increases in production and consumption than in the class where they learn the law of conservation of matter? Yes, we need students to apply principles of engineering, when appropriate. But we also need them to recognize when a problem may require a political solution and even more importantly, to dream about ways of interacting with each other and the Earth that are not extractive and exploitative.

This book describes approaches to science teaching that are likely much different from the way that science teachers learned their disciplines. Such a dramatic shift requires teachers to unlearn and relearn much of what we think we know, and it requires learning in new directions. Therefore, this will not be the only or the last book teachers must read to align their teaching with the goals of equity, justice, and sustainability. Suggestions for other books, articles, websites, and resources are sprinkled throughout the text and also in the endnotes.

THE SCIENCE QUESTION IN SOCIAL JUSTICE EDUCATION

Educators and organizers have developed rich traditions of teaching students to imagine—and work toward—a different world. But science teachers are often unfamiliar with these theories. The field of science education has mostly ignored the transformative possibilities they represent. As science educators, it behooves us to learn from these traditions by asking what I call "the science question in social justice education" —a way of thinking about our work that was inspired by Sandra Harding's "science question in feminism."[13] For example, Bettina Love, drawing on W. E. B. DuBois and Angela Davis, may encourage us to abolish pipelines (of the STEM and petroleum variety),[14] so that we can "do more than survive" the climate crisis and pandemics we face.[15] Indeed, LaToya Strong and Atas Das provide a vision for *Abolition Science* in a brilliant podcast for STEM teachers.

Maxine Greene believed that cultivating social imagination was at the heart of education.[16] Indeed, reimagining our disciplines is an important step in answering the *science question in social justice education*. Chemistry is the study of materials, but we cannot limit our considerations to simple reactions and properties. We cannot take a view of understanding materials that prioritizes what is to be gained from new synthetic chemicals over questioning their long-term ecological and health impacts. We must encourage students to think critically about the materials they use or consume and teach them to consider the benefits and harms that arise from human manipulation of materials. In high school, physics is too often reduced to the study of simple forces and motion. Of course, the actual field of physics is much broader and more exciting, but we should push students even beyond those boundaries to understand the study of the physical world in broader contexts. Nuclear physicists are not simply curious about the energy stored in the forces between subatomic particles. Their curiosities are driven, or at least funded, because of the potential implications for power—and not the derivative of energy over time, but *political* power. These are the kinds of contextual considerations that we need to move into the physics classroom.

Biology is the scientific study of living systems, but Brazilian educator, Paulo Freire, encouraged biology teachers to view life more expansively than is typically the case in classrooms:

> And let it not be said that, if I am a biology teacher, I must not "go off into other considerations" —that I must only teach biology, as if the phenomenon of life could be understood apart from the historico-social, cultural, and political

framework. As if life, just life, could be lived in the same way, in all of its dimensions, in a favela (slum) or cortiço (beehive—slum tenement building) as in a prosperous area of São Paulo's "Gardens"! If I am a biology teacher, obviously I must teach biology. But in doing so, I must not cut it off from the framework of the whole.[17]

Freire insightfully argues that we cannot understand human life as if it were experienced the same way by people in extremely different socioeconomic circumstances, and we could add that the same is true for people who experience other forms of oppression like racism, sexism, and ableism. But expanding the boundaries of the curriculum to consider social context, as Freire's quote suggests, it not simple. Research documents that boundary-expanding teaching is challenging and rife with complexity. In my own work, my colleagues and I have found that new science teachers have a very difficult time figuring out how to address issues of structural racism or other forms of social inequality in science classrooms.[18] More experienced science teachers often avoid these issues too.[19]

Questioning the larger contexts of knowing and learning is at the heart of critical pedagogy, a tradition most often associated with Freire and Latin American revolutionary movements. But this type of challenge to the status quo of schooling also resonates with the role that education has played in the Black freedom struggle in the US. Culturally relevant pedagogy and its remix, culturally sustaining pedagogy, follow in the spirit of that struggle and resonate in important ways with the transformative goals of critical pedagogy.[20] Ideas about teaching to change the world have been historically intertwined with popular education, citizenship schools, freedom schools, and other grassroots efforts led by teacher-organizers like Septima Clark, Bob Moses, Myles Horton, and many others. But science educators have largely avoided connections with grassroots organizing or conversations about oppression. Science education has mostly eschewed these powerful visions of teaching for justice. As a result, the role of science class in social justice education remains unclear for many teachers. The goal of this book is to equip science teachers with some ideas, structures, and principles for engaging in boundary-expanding science teaching. Chapter 6, Teaching Science as a Catalyst for Alternative Futures, pulls together these ideas, structures, and principles to offer a better metaphor for science education: a catalyst for alternative futures.

OVERVIEW OF THE BOOK

This book asks, and provides some answers, to the question of how teaching and learning science can contribute to what Eve Tuck and K. Wayne call "diverse dreams of justice in education."[21] These "answers" are based on what I have learned over two decades as a science educator, but they are not meant to be universal or definitive. Rather they are an articulation of principles and possibilities. The principles articulated by the book are based on research that I have done with colleagues about what it means to teach science for justice and how teachers can learn to teach toward those ends. Throughout the book, there will be quotes and examples from students and teachers who have participated in those research projects to illustrate and provide evidence for these principles. The book also includes numerous examples from my practice as a high school science teacher as a way of making the possibilities concrete and visible so teachers can imagine reinventions for their own classrooms. The book is organized around key questions that teachers often ask about shifting their teaching to align with their values. Chapters 1, 2, and 3 focus on why we teach, who we teach, and what we teach, respectively. Chapter 4 takes up the *how* of teaching for equity, justice, and sustainability, not by prescribing core practices, but by suggesting changes in teachers' stances and priorities in classroom decision-making. The penultimate chapter shifts from the why, who, what, and how of teaching to focus instead on *teacher learning*. And the final chapter brings the possibilities and principles of the book together to suggest a different metaphor for the role of science education: a catalyst for change rather than a pre-professional pipeline. The remainder of this introductory chapter provides more detail about how each of the chapters ahead supports science teachers in joining this collective project of dismantling the pipeline and developing science education as a catalyst for change.

Chapter 1 invites readers to interrogate why they chose to teach science. It also prompts them to consider the problematic ideologies that are sometimes inadvertently communicated in mainstream biology, chemistry, and physics curricula. For example, there are implicit and explicit ways in which traditional science curricula communicate Eurocentric and patriarchal ideas about who does science. The first chapter suggests that science education has a problematic canon wherein Newton and Einstein in physics class are akin to Shakespeare and Hemmingway in English class. The first chapter contains examples of relatively easy changes that science teachers can make in their lessons to challenge problematic ideologies. The recent shift in our field toward focusing on the practices of science has made some progress on this issue, but it still does not equip teachers or students to take up authentic local problems or expand the boundaries of the content areas in the ways suggested by this introduction. To that point, the first chapter debunks the commonly held notion that social justice curriculum compromises the academic richness of science class with research that documents the deep and sophisticated learning students have done in justice-centered chemistry classes. Through examples in chapter 1, teachers can see the possibilities for drawing connections between the science they are accountable to teach and the issues that matter outside of the school.

Chapter 2 invites readers to remember and revisit why they chose to teach young people. It includes an exercise for teachers to rethink some of the frustrations they encounter in the classroom and reminds teachers to consider who they are and what they bring into the classroom. Chapter 2 suggests that it is normal (and good) for students to respond in different ways to justice-centered science teaching. Some students, who already view themselves as aligned with science, push social justice issues to the background so that they can focus on the technical learning. Other students are only willing to learn the science when there are clear connections with social justice issues. And some students fully embrace the notion that we can use science to change the world and change science itself in the process. This chapter advocates positioning students as transformative intellectuals, which means valuing the experience and viewpoints they bring into the classroom and believing in their power to change the world beyond the classroom. When we view students as producers of knowledge and culture, we are compelled to teach differently.

Chapter 3 describes a process that teachers can use to identify "social justice science issues" (SJSI) which are issues that sit at the intersection of the science we are asked to teach and the issues to which students or their communities are committed. Chapter 3 includes examples of SJSI like drug development and coal power plant pollution and considerations about whether they are truly relevant to students and communities. The chapter also includes a process for moving from SJSI to curriculum by designing authentic assessments and then considering the standards. This process is illustrated with an example from my teaching about diamonds where I learned how to combine sociopolitical and historical context with important chemistry concepts in an assessment that was fun for students. This example illustrates how it took several iterations of this assignment and the lessons that led up to it to figure out how to scaffold student work in a way that allowed for this complexity. Chapter 3 also includes advice to avoid common mistakes science teachers make while framing or defining SJSI with their students.

Chapter 4 presents questions that teachers can answer for themselves to reinvent justice-centered pedagogy in their contexts. Answering these questions allows teachers to understand how disciplinary tools and concepts might contribute to social justice pursuits, which facilitates being able to consistently design and enact justice-centered projects and lessons. For example, thinking about chemistry as a science focused on materials allows for expansion of the curriculum to consider how the tools and concepts of chemistry might help students think about consumption, production, and disposal of materials in transformative ways. Even with a focus on transformative thinking, chapter 4 helps teachers to imagine how they can repurpose or modify existing activities or curricula to serve a different set of goals, rather than always starting from scratch. The questions presented in this chapter also help teachers consider how they might prepare their students to push past the boundaries of their discipline or learn to critique some of its oversights.

Changing science teaching in the ways described by this book requires teachers to do a substantial amount of learning. Chapter 5 focuses on how this learning begins by rejecting our presumed role as promoters of our disciplines. Instead, teachers might embrace their role as nurturers of students' natural curiosity and vibrancy. The chapter uses classroom examples to illustrate how teachers can tackle challenging issues while still cultivating feelings like wonder and joy. Through activities that are fun and engaging, teachers can encourage a love of life rather than enculturate students into the field of biology. Chemistry classes can reject both chemophobia and chemophilia. And teachers of physics, Earth, environmental, and space sciences can prompt awe about the universe rather than passion for these disciplines. Such simple shifts make for classes that cultivate appreciation for scientific insights and healthy skepticism of scientific institutions. Our teaching can reinvigorate curiosities that previous courses may have dampened. For example, I describe classroom assessments that can be playful while also challenging students to develop their academic skills. Dealing with serious issues like racism and climate change can be uncomfortable and heavy for both teachers and students. But this penultimate chapter explains how understanding the root causes of these problems can make our collective capacity to address them feel more within reach. For example, a group of science teachers with whom I have work learned to prioritize teaching about grassroots environmental justice victories as a source of hope in the face of substantial local challenges.[22]

Finally, in chapter 6, I revisit this opening critique of the STEM pipeline and offer an alternative metaphor: science education as a catalyst for alternative futures. Drawing on the chemistry of catalysis, I expand the common metaphor, *catalyst for change*, to consider how science education might create mechanisms for social change that require less harsh conditions and allow us to be more selective about the outcomes we want: equity, justice, and sustainability.

CHAPTER 1

Why Teach Science?

It is sometimes said that high school teachers teach science, or math, or history—but elementary school teachers teach *children*. Indeed, science teachers would be well served to remind ourselves that we teach *young people to engage with sciences*. Whether foregrounding the content or the students, if the goal is equity and justice, we must examine the taken-for-granted assumptions about *why* the sciences are core subjects in school. This chapter invites teachers to interrogate why they teach sciences. When posing this question to aspiring science teachers, I often hear stories about falling in love with science as a kid or explanations about how science helps us think critically or understand the world around us. This kind of exploration of our early experiences or motivations for our work is important, but it does not go far enough.

As the introduction of this book explained, science teachers have long been put in the role of promoting the scientific enterprise, both in terms of educating the professionals who work therein or convincing all others of its value and authority. But accepting this role does not encourage critical engagement with the problematics of the scientific enterprise nor with possibilities for more just and expansive scientific communities and practices. We need to think about how our reasons for teaching sciences match up—or not—with our values and politics. As science teachers, an important question to ask ourselves, alongside the question of why we teach science is: *How does my teaching reflect the world in which my students live and project the world they would like to see?*

Through personal stories and classroom examples, this chapter examines possible reasons for teaching sciences. It argues that the sciences, like other disciplines, have a canon, or central topics that have dominated the curriculum for generations. The canon is arbitrary in some ways, but ultimately promotes the scientific enterprise to the detriment of other possibilities for teaching and learning. With each critique of the canon, this chapter also shares an alternative approach. The final part of the chapter uses an example from research to show how teaching science for community health and environmental justice can support rich disciplinary learning that stretches beyond the canon to prompt students to think about relationships between scientific evidence, activism, social change, and their own community involvement.

LEARNING SCIENCE FOR COMMUNITY HEALTH AND ENVIRONMENTAL JUSTICE?

Late one cold winter night when I was a sophomore in high school, my father and I were returning home in the family car when he abruptly pulled over two blocks from home. He grabbed a video camera that was stashed between the front seats and pointed it out his window to capture billows of smoke pouring from a hospital building across the street. The building was not on fire; he was filming one of two medical waste incinerators in the city. My father and several of our neighbors had recently become aware of the potential for these facilities to harm public and ecological health in the neighborhood. He was documenting this late-night emission to refute the hospital's claims that the incinerator operated infrequently and only at certain scheduled times. This documentation was part of a larger community effort to force the closure of these polluting facilities.

Whereas the surrounding college town was predominately white, most of the residents in the neighborhood surrounding the incinerators were Black. The struggle to shut them down was my first exposure to the concept of *environmental racism*, the unequal distribution of environmental conditions that disproportionately benefits white communities and disproportionately harms communities of color.[1] Not being Black myself, I was aware that I experienced privilege that most of my neighbors did not. I also learned that it was not a coincidence that both incinerators in the city were located on our side of town.

My father challenged me to apply knowledge from high school chemistry class to understand the impact of the incinerators on our neighborhood and health. He gave me readings that explained how burning polyvinyl chloride could produce polychlorinated dibenzo dioxins (or dioxins for short), a class of highly toxic and carcinogenic substances—substances which were being emitted by the incinerators. My parents wondered whether the incinerators had anything to do with my younger brother's asthma. This was the first time that I remember science class being potentially relevant in my life and in my community. Chemistry was my favorite class at school, and I had an excellent teacher. But even so, what I was learning at school did not offer much insight into our community's struggle.

This experience had a profound impact on my reasons for teaching the sciences. In my research, I refer to topics like our community's struggle to shut down those medical waste incinerators as *social justice science issues* or SJSI. Besides sitting at the intersection between social justice and scientific or technological understandings, SJSI are locally relevant *and* explicitly situated within broader political and historical contexts. When I became a teacher, I quickly realized that organizing the science curriculum around SJSI is difficult. Teachers, both new and experienced alike, often lament, "I just have too much to cover!" Others express this a different way—like the colleague who commented after a public presentation, "The activism is nice, but students really need to learn the content better." I have heard the other side of that coin too, from colleagues who argue that students need to know the basics first before they can understand scientific concepts in their real-world complexity. And finally, one of the most common explanations for why teachers cannot take up SJSI: "It's just too political." In one way or another, these challenges are all related to our priorities about what matters in science class. Science teachers often have more power than they realize to decide what is worthwhile to teach and learn. They also wield important influence in deciding what and how they communicate with students regarding why learning about sciences may be important.

BLANKETS COVER, TEACHERS TRANSFORM

I have never met a science teacher who pursued the profession out of a deep desire to "cover the curriculum." But so many of the decisions that science teachers make are constrained by the pressure to do exactly that. Some of this pressure is external, driven by departmental mandates or high stakes exams. But teachers also feel a deeper internal responsibility. The inner voice of physics teachers asks: How can students graduate high school without knowing Newton's laws? Biology teachers feel guilty that their students never learned the phases of mitosis. In an interview for a research project about community-based science projects, one of the teachers with whom I collaborate explained this internal pressure to stick to the canon: "I think it's in my head in a lot of ways because I feel like my administration has the confidence in me....I'm just so used to following that book that now if I go off script, it's like, will the city end up in flames?" This teacher's reflection was shared with a laugh, but also captures the fear that many teachers associate with deviating from the canon. Even with protections like tenure and a supportive administration, this teacher felt like the decision to "go off script" could lead to disaster—a city metaphorically burning. These pressures that teachers feel to stick to the script—whether internal or external, real or imagined—are normal. But they often prevent science teachers from aligning their curriculum with their reasons for teaching science. I encourage teachers who feel these pressures to remind themselves that *blankets cover, but teachers transform*. When teachers prioritize covering the curriculum, they are deciding that what matters is the *canon*.

Language arts educators, especially those concerned with issues of equity, often critique the canon, or the set of so-called classic texts or concepts that are considered fundamental to school curriculum. Because the canon was developed in a political and historical context where schooling was organized to advance the interests of a white supremacist and patriarchal power structure, it traditionally included books almost exclusively written by and about dead white men. In response to this racist and sexist cannon, struggles for ethnic studies and gender and women's studies emerged from the social movements of the 1960's and 70's. In the five decades since, multicultural and feminist educators have consistently argued for expanding or abolishing the canon in favor of a more representative and multicultural set of texts that resonate with students' lives and challenge dominant power structures.[2]

In science education, the set of ideas that we teach is often assumed to have been derived from a more objective, practical, or empirical process. But, in fact, *science education has a canon too.* And just like in language arts education, the canon is somewhat arbitrary, but it was also constructed in a particular historical and political context. It therefore reflects the values of influential people and powerful institutions in that context. In this book, the term canonical science refers to this set of concepts and ideas that have come to be accepted as essential to school science.

Other researchers have done deep analyses of how and why different approaches to science education emerged as predominant across history.[3] For our purposes, suffice it to say that the reason science was originally included as a subject in school and the main reason why it has remained a core content area (at least since World War II) has been to promote the enterprise of science through two related strands: (1) the pre-professional education of future scientists and (2) cultivating support among the general public for science. Between these two strands, the education of future scientists has been prioritized and science education has skewed in the direction of the so-called STEM pipeline.[4] But even when policies, approaches, or curricula prioritize 'scientific literacy' or promote 'science for all,' rarely does school science deviate from the overarching aim of promoting the enterprise of science.

This overarching goal seems very sensible in the present political context when powerful politicians minimize the role of scientific evidence even in the face of pandemic and climate crisis. Indeed, science teachers play an important role in educating people who can carefully consider scientific evidence and who treat the advice of experts with appropriate measures of seriousness and skepticism. But this book argues that promoting science—rather than striving for equity, justice, and sustainability—is the wrong approach. This is because science is not just a way of understanding the world; it is an enterprise or a set of institutions with their own politics, values, history, and interests. This set of institutions is complex and has its own internal contradictions, which we should teach students to understand, analyze, —and yes—trust, to some extent. But this trust should not be blind, unconditional, universal or without substantial critiques, questions, and challenges. The following subsections of this chapter point out some of the problems with mainstream science teaching and offer alternative examples that are more aligned with values of social justice and environmental sustainability. These examples and arguments critique curricula and pedagogies that are outdated and yet still common in science classrooms. This chapter also considers some of the important reforms and recent shifts that have moved the field, but not nearly far enough.

WHAT'S IN A NAME? EUROCENTRIC PATRIARCHY

Early each school year, many high school biology teachers ask their students to break down the name of the course into its Greek root words. The goal of this activity is presumably to establish that the course will focus on the branch of study that has to do with life. Some teachers also hope that it might demystify big words and encourage students to engage with the vast and highly specialized vocabulary demands of most biology curricula. Teachers often do not consider that disciplines like fine arts, literature, and even athletics are also ways of interpreting life and the experiences and functions of living organisms. The field of biology is comprised of a particular set of institutions, communities of scholars, and ways of understanding life. The prominent use of Greek and Latin words represents the commitments of those institutions and communities to the Eurocentric narrative of science and reason as emanating from Greece and Rome and later being rediscovered during the enlightenment in Western Europe.

Swedish biologist Carl von Linné or Carolus Linnaeus played an important role in establishing Latin as the language of the sciences with his 18th century book *Systema Naturae*.[5] Linnaeus is often celebrated in high school biology classes for founding the field of taxonomy and binomial nomenclature. His impact on humans' understanding of living beings is likely overstated because diverse peoples around the world independently developed "namings of plants and animals that roughly correspond to what we label as distinct species."[6] The hidden impact of *Systema Naturae* is that Linnaeus also applied his reasoning to divide humans into categories—and then went a step further to arrange these categories into a hierarchy that linked superficial phenotypic features with assumptions about temperament and intelligence.[7] That Linnaeus tried to establish the supremacy of Latin in science and the supremacy of white people in the world is not incidental nor coincidental. These ideas are ideologically consistent, false, and harmful beyond comprehension. In other words, elevating the prominence of Greek and Latin as the languages of science helps to weave a story that justifies white supremacy. But even more egregious and harmful was Linnaeus's pioneering classification of humans into fabricated hierarchical categories. Even the scientific society who named their group after Linnaeus admits that the most well-known (10th) edition of his famous work is one of the first and most impactful efforts to justify ideas of white supremacy and racism with biology.[8] Indeed, our world continues to be haunted by its legacy today even as biology teachers continue to celebrate Linnaeus.

Unlike biology, few chemistry teachers dive into the etymology of their discipline's name. In fact, I already had earned a degree in chemistry and had been teaching the subject for several years without ever being asked to consider where the word "chemistry" came from. Then one year, a tenth-grade student asked me about the etymology not of chemistry, but of *stoichiometry*—one of the most dreaded topics in the chemistry canon. The abstraction and drudgery of stoichiometry is emblematic of rigorous science curriculum, even serving problematically as a line of demarcation between students capable of becoming scientists and those who are not.[9] Having never considered the etymology of stoichiometry before this student asked, I offered him extra credit to find the answer to his question. He came back the next day to explain that *stoich-* is from the Greek word for *element* and that *-metry* is a Greek suffix meaning *measurement*. I was frustrated that my student's extra credit assignment had led us back to the same tired narrative. I was also suddenly curious about the origins and meaning of the word chemistry. I started to do my own research. Not surprisingly, the word is connected to alchemy, which comes from Arabic and ancient Greek before that. But tracing further back, I found that there is no consensus about the etymology of chemistry. The most accepted explanation of the root *chem-* is that it originates with *khem*, which was the name that ancient Egyptians gave to their homeland.[10] The word referred to the rich black soil of the Nile River Delta. One theory is that ancient Greeks learned from Egyptian metallurgists how to manipulate metals and other materials, they referred to this practice as coming from *khem*, giving credit to the people from whom they learned. After I learned this story, I always mentioned this tentative etymology of chemistry in my classes as part of a larger effort to challenge the Eurocentric narrative of science that is still all too prevalent in science textbooks. I also wrote short texts and created activities that asked students to consider the history of science beyond the typical Eurocentric stories. For example, students often learn that the metric system was invented in France and uses prefixes and nomenclature based on Greek and Latin. But it is less common for them to learn that the base ten number system (which makes the metric system and most quantitative components of science possible) originated in India.[11] To make the importance of this contribution clear, teachers can ask students to try to do math using only Roman numerals. Again, the emphasis on Greek and Latin nomenclature in science is part of an effort to tell a narrow Eurocentric story. Another way many teachers challenge this story is to engage students with the sophisticated place-value number system developed by Indigenous peoples of Central America centuries ago.[12] These kinds of lessons can teach how political power and imperialism have driven the spread and suppression of scientific ideas more than the brilliance of the ideas themselves. They can teach students that there are countless different meaningful and effective ways to understand, model, and describe the universe. Or, as I discuss in the next section, lessons can include superficial references to culture that make students feel stereotyped rather than represented. The key is for teachers to treat the development of scientific knowledge as cultural and political and also as dynamic and complex. There is no single method nor origin of science.

Yet, the scientific names for disciplines, relationships, models, theories, and even units of measurement reinforce the misleading narrative that science is a Euro-American and male undertaking. Moreover, they are part of an individualistic and elitist vision of scientific knowledge production. Intentionally or not, we teach students that science is done by geniuses and heroes—almost all of them dead white men. The canon of science celebrates Linnean nomenclature, Newton's laws, Avogadro's number, Darwin's theory of evolution, and countless other examples. These heroes are portrayed as working in virtual isolation, and their stories are told without meaningful historical context. Rather than deifying these heroes of science, we could refer simply to binomial nomenclature, principles of motion, a mole, and evolution. A simple shift to referring to these ideas without their namesakes will not dislodge the Eurocentrism or patriarchy of science education, but it represents a very small and very easy pedagogical change that can make difference in combination with larger shifts, like those described below.

AGAINST TOKENISM: TOWARD ANTI-ELITIST, ANTI-RACIST, ANTI-SEXIST SCIENCE EDUCATION

The most common response to the Eurocentrism and patriarchy embedded in the science curriculum is to include profiles or tributes to scientists who are women or people of color. Of course, acknowledging the breadth and depth of contributions to scientific thought made by women and people of color is important. But there are also several common mistakes that teachers make in their attempts to open the canon to acknowledge a broader range of scientists. One common misstep is highlighting an occasional woman or person of color within what is still an overwhelming preponderance of white men in the curriculum. I do not want my words to be misconstrued. I have often taught about the stories of Percy Julian, Mario Molina, Rosalind Franklin, and many others. Their biographies and contributions to science are fascinating and worth telling in our classes. But taken up without care, this practice may end up positioning women scientists or scientists of color as exceptions that prove the rule, thereby reinforcing oppressive ideas about who does science while still mostly ignoring historical contexts of structural racism and sexism. This mistake is often called tokenism and it can have the opposite of the intended impact. The second oversight that teachers often make in these efforts is reinforcing the notion that scientists are heroes who work individually to produce knowledge. This scientist-as-hero trope is one way that mainstream science education promotes the scientific enterprise. But this approach is not an accurate representation of scientific work, nor does it encourage students to imagine sciences in anti-elite and democratic ways.

To avoid these problems, teachers may consider three more simple shifts. First, teachers should question what the inclusion of famous scientists' names, biographies, or stories is adding to the curriculum. What implicit and explicit messages are these sidebars or lessons sending to your students about science? How engaging are the stories for students? This kind of reflection often leads teachers to decide that teaching about the life of Robert Boyle or telling the story of Carl von Linné latinizing his own name are not actually worthwhile. Second, if teachers are going to teach the history of science, it should be with appropriate context. Lessons about the history of science should consider the interconnections between the rise of modern Western science and US–European imperialism. Third, teachers should consistently engage students in stories and discussions about the collective character of scientific work and the fraught relationships between science and social justice.

ALTERNATIVE EXAMPLES: CHALLENGING THE DOMINANT NARRATIVES OF SCIENCE

The construction of the institutions of modern Western science (like universities) was often paid for by the spoils of slavery and settler colonialism.[13] These institutions, in turn, produced the ideologies and technologies that facilitated and justified ongoing atrocities.[14] Without this context, the preponderance of white male scientists in the curriculum incorrectly implies that developing sophisticated understandings of the natural world is something that white men do more than other people. But in proper context, students can understand that the scientific endeavors of the most famous scientists in history were funded and shaped by the cruel exploitation of peoples, lands, and animals. Furthermore, students should understand that Indigenous peoples' knowledges has often been, and continue to be, appropriated by Western scientists.[15] The construction of the scientific canon was a much more complex and fraught process than textbooks communicate. Teachers may ask students to analyze their science textbooks with the lenses of Eurocentrism, sexism, and colonialism in mind.

Nixtamalization Challenges Eurocentric Acid-Base Chemistry

Acid-base chemistry provides an example for how to encourage students to recognize the skewed narratives of science presented in textbooks. In my chemistry classes, students learned that one of the most important and earliest applications of acid-base chemistry was invented by Indigenous peoples in Central America. The process of *nixtamalization* uses a basic (high pH) solution traditionally made with water and ashes to process corn by removing its pericarp to unlock its nutritional value. The common addition of crushed seashells to the solution incorporates calcium into the resulting *masa* (corn flour) that is used to make tortillas, tamales, and other Central and South American staples.

To begin a series of lessons on acid-base chemistry, I would ask students to read the ingredients label of a pack of tortillas or tortilla chips. The ingredients of corn tortillas are simple: corn, lime, salt. Students often already understand that "lime" does not refer to the citrus fruit. We learn that lime is a name for what chemists call calcium hydroxide solution, the industrial version of slurries of ashes, seashells, and water. Teachers can save ashes from a campfire or hardwood barbeque and ask students to mix these ashes with distilled water, filter it, and then measure the pH of the distilled water and the resulting filtered solution using red cabbage solution they prepare or any commercially available acid-base indicator. Through this simple activity, students can appreciate the genius of nixtamalization and understand the ancient roots of acid-base chemistry in a way that is still applicable to understanding present-day food systems. Teachers can show students current peer-reviewed studies in food and nutrition science to illustrate that nixtamalization is still an important process taken up by scientists in the twenty-first century. In my classes, we also learned that when European colonizers first appropriated corn as a staple food, they often caused malnutrition because they did not understand that nixtamalization is essential for making the nutrient niacin available for biochemical processes in the human body.[16]

After we learned about nixtamalization, I asked students to consider how chemistry textbooks introduced acid-base chemistry. Invariably, they noticed that textbooks only included the contributions of European or Euro-American men like Sven Arrhenius and Gilbert Lewis. We discussed how the innovation of nixtamalization cannot be traced back to a single hero scientist but was most likely developed by communities of Indigenous women over long periods of time. This communicates a different, and more accurate, vision of how sophisticated knowledge about the universe has been developed by humans.

Historicized and critical views of scientific knowledge production can equip students to better understand numerous important intersections between science and society. This is a Science Technology and Society (STS) approach that has been practiced by science teachers for a long time.[17] STS scholars like Ruha Benjamin, Sandra Harding, Safiyah Noble, and Kim TallBear, among others, bring critical theories of race, gender, and colonization into STS in ways that are likely to be helpful for science teachers committed to equity, justice, and sustainability. In the context of anti-vaccine sentiments, Liliana Valladares points out that an STS approach to science teaching can serve as a metaphorical vaccine against misinformation.[18] I would add that challenging Eurocentric narratives of science can simultaneously undercut dominant narratives and fringe conspiracy theories. For example, it may be important to teach students that China is the likely place where the principles and techniques underlying inoculation originated, and those principles were practiced in India and Africa long before they made their way to laboratories in Europe or the United States.[19] Materials scientist Ainissa Ramírez, who writes about the interconnections between chemistry and history, highlights the role of Black scientists in establishing the effectiveness of the polio vaccine.[20] The long and multicultural history of vaccine development provides an important alternative perspective for students who may be skeptical of Western medicine or large pharmaceutical corporations.

Ongoing critical discussions about the production of knowledge can disrupt Eurocentric, patriarchal, and elitist narratives about science that are still common in curricula and popular culture. They avoid the trap of tokenism and the trope of scientist-as-hero. Through this type of science education, students may also be equipped to continue the practice of challenging dominant narratives about science. Here and in the segment that follows, I will draw on examples from a former student named Odette whose learning illustrates the power of justice-centered science pedagogy. Odette is a Mexican woman who grew up in an immigrant community in a large US city. After attending a public neighborhood elementary school, she was a student in one of my tenth-grade chemistry classes and later took advanced placement (AP) chemistry with me at a neighborhood high school focused on themes of social justice. Odette went on to study environmental science at an elite liberal arts college and told me during an interview about several ways that she challenged Eurocentrism and patriarchy in the science curriculum there. For example, she wrote an essay for a college seminar about the global and multicultural origins of science to explicitly push back against one of the course readings that positioned science as emanating only from Greece. Reflecting on one of her college classes, Odette said:

> In my chemistry class, there was a lot of emphasis on the old dead white guys, and when I would do my readings in the book, I kind of ignored those parts because they would introduce each chapter talking about a certain guy and his law. And even in some of the exams, it was like "describe this guy's findings." And I'm like I don't know what he found. I didn't focus on that. I know the concepts in the chapter, I just don't know who they 'belong' to [makes air quotations with her fingers]...The professor definitely did emphasize [historical figures in chemistry] —like he was in awe with those guys. And I totally understand because it was cool the things they found out. It definitely is. But—other people should also be credited for their science when it's not Western science.

Odette also mentioned that her essay and comments in class created some temporary hostility with her professor and may also have cost her some points on an exam because of her choice to focus on "the concepts in the chapter" instead of "who they 'belong' to." Notably, Odette was not dismissive of the accomplishments of the heroes of science, but she advocated for more honest and expansive narratives about the origins of scientific knowledge.

Activism Challenges Radioactive Pollution and Weapons

Besides troubling and expanding the history of science, discussions about the relationships between science and social justice should be situated in present-day circumstances. One example from my chemistry class involved showing a documentary film called *Homeland: Four Portraits of Native Action*.[21] In one of these portraits, a Navajo community successfully prevented an energy corporation from mining for uranium on their land.[22] One of the leaders of this struggle, Mitchel Capitan, was a member of the Eastern Navajo community who had worked on an engineering project for a different company. He was involved in laboratory work where they determined that it was impossible to use the proposed mining technique without contaminating the ground water with radioactive uranium. My classes discussed how this Indigenous community used their collective scientific, historical, and social knowledge to protect their community from dangerous extractive applications of science and engineering. This example also pushes back against the erasure of Indigenous people in the modern world that happens if Indigenous peoples are only discussed in distant historical context.

In another example, my physics classes read excerpts from the transcript of the Nobel lecture, "The Quest for Peace and Justice" that Dr. Martin Luther King, Jr. gave when he was awarded the 1964 Peace Prize. In the context of learning about nuclear physics, we read and discussed the following excerpt from the first part of his speech, which is now also available as an audio recording on the Nobel Prize website:

> Modern man has brought this whole world to an awe-inspiring threshold of the future. He has reached new and astonishing peaks of scientific success. He has produced machines that think and instruments that peer into the unfathomable ranges of interstellar space. He has built gigantic bridges to span the seas and gargantuan buildings to kiss the skies. His airplanes and spaceships have dwarfed distance, placed time in chains, and carved highways through the stratosphere. This is a dazzling picture of modern man's scientific and technological progress. Yet, in spite of these spectacular strides in science and technology, and still unlimited ones to come, something basic is missing. There is a sort of poverty of the spirit which stands in glaring contrast to our scientific and technological abundance. The richer we have become materially, the poorer we have become morally and spiritually. We have learned to fly the air like birds and swim the sea like fish, but we have not learned the simple art of living together as brothers.[23]

Our discussions of his speech focused on his argument about the relationship between scientific advancement and moral and ethical sensibilities. But we also talked about the sexism in his words (referring repeatedly only to men, mankind, and brothers). I emphasized how he specifically addressed the immorality of war and weapons of mass destruction in the context of nuclear non-proliferation. We discussed whether King understood science and engineering as politically neutral or morally objective and how his analysis of technological advancement connected to his activism against racial injustice, economic exploitation, and war.

While some teachers might argue for Dr. King's Nobel Prize speech to be included in social studies curriculum rather than physics class, I argue that this separation of scientific concepts from their ethical implications in education is partially responsible for the disconnect that Dr. King critiqued. In my own science education, the relationship between the concepts of physics and the technologies of war were often taken for granted in a way that shows that physics is not neutral nor merely abstract. In physics classes that I took as an undergraduate student in the late 1990s and early 2000s, the residue of cold war politics was still visible in the curriculum. As we learned how to model simple two-dimension motion, the examples often focused on a missile traveling between the US and Russia. Indeed, there is a long and intimate relationship between the field of physics and the military.[24] And even diversity, equity, and inclusion initiatives in STEM education are often funded by military sources.[25] This version of equity focuses on including more people who have been marginalized by US racism in the STEM workforce where they might design weapons that kill people who are marginalized by racism around the world. Indeed, science and engineering education that fails to deal explicitly with the relationships between physics and the military is unlikely to challenge the dominant nationalistic ideologies that position some lives as more valuable than others.[26]

Embodied Learning Challenges Separation of Mind and Body

It is important for physics teachers to challenge the relationships between their discipline and the military, but there are also ways to take up kinematics in ways that highlight joy and multiple ways of knowing and being in the world. In a unit that we called "Nerds and Jocks," Alejandra Frausto Aceves and I engaged students in learning physics while challenging stereotypes and the false dichotomy between mind and body. In this unit, students were asked to make a short documentary film using the principles of kinematics to analyze the performance of an athlete in their school community. We encouraged students to think of athletes broadly. Certainly, they could profile members of the school's sports teams, but they were also encouraged to profile dancers or skateboarders. Besides analyzing the athletic performance itself, the short student-produced films were also required to include an interview with the athlete about stereotypes. Our goal was to engage students in explicitly challenging racialized and gendered notions of who does what kinds of activities. Furthermore, we wanted them to challenge the idea that mind and body function separately or that there is a hierarchy or division between physical and mental endeavors (like sports or dance and science). But it was also important to us that this unit emphasized joy and fun.

In one activity, we used motion detectors connected to laptop computers to enact a physics class version of dance battle video games. One pair of students would briefly stand in the hallway while their competitors moved (in planned or improvised ways) in front of the motion sensor. A computer graphed their movements as distance or velocity against time. When the first pair of students re-entered the classroom, their goal was to match the graph created by their competitors. This activity engaged students with understanding the concepts of displacement (or position), velocity, and acceleration and provided an opportunity to practice interpreting graphs—all while having fun. Some students enjoyed taking the idea of a video game dance battle literally, incorporating dance moves into their graph-making. Other students preferred to calmly walk back and forth in front of the motion detectors; both approaches worked. This activity broke down the barriers between knowing and doing—between enacting physical movements and interpreting the associated data. But without the explicit attention to challenging stereotypes and the division between physical and mental activity, this kind of curriculum could risk reinforcing racialized and gendered stereotypes about who is good at dancing or at physics. Students are familiar with these stereotypes and they can show up in student comments or the ways in which they position each other during the activity. Therefore, it was very important that our lesson included readings and discussion about the ways in which scientific racism is responsible for those problematic assumptions and divisions and also that we were prepared as teachers to grapple with racism and sexism in science class.[27]

The examples above illustrate how relatively simple shifts can change the messages science teachers communicate to their students about who does science and for what reasons. These shifts give students the opportunity to be critical of the institutions of science in their historical contexts and to also imagine more expansive, joyful, and participatory scientific communities. These examples require science teachers to resist the pressures they feel to cover the canon and to read and learn in the realms of STS and the history of science. But these examples have all been focused within the science classroom, whereas my experience watching my neighbors and parents shut down the medical waste incinerators suggested to me that science class could potentially be responsive to community concerns outside of the classroom.

Through my first few years as a teacher, I had limited success trying to make this vision for community-responsive science education a reality. One of the barriers I was facing was the canon. Science curricula are set up to teach the big ideas of the disciplines as defined by disciplinary experts.[28] This approach is not likely to support students to deal with local concerns.[29] There might be some overlap between these goals, but mass-produced curricula do not help us find those overlapping areas. Instead, science teachers can connect with community organizations who are already doing the important work to address what matters at the grassroots.[30]

TEACHING SCIENCE FOR ENVIRONMENTAL JUSTICE

The final part of this chapter details a concrete example from an AP chemistry class as a proof-of-concept: *teachers can teach about community concerns in a way that supports sophisticated science learning.* A few years into my career as a teacher, I was fortunate to get a job that had been founded by a grassroots community struggle. This new school was built in one of Chicago's industrial corridors. Unfortunately, it is quite common for schools to be constructed in areas with above average exposure to pollution.[31] In the predominately Mexican neighborhood surrounding this school, there was a small grassroots organization working on issues of environmental racism. As soon as I got the job, I reached out to this organization to learn about their current campaigns. At the top of their list was closing a behemoth coal-fired power plant that was technologically outdated and located less than a mile from the school. Community concerns about air quality and respiratory disease reminded me of what worried my parents and neighbors about the medical waste incinerators in our neighborhood a decade earlier. Based on what we learned from visionary organizers like Kimberly Wasserman Nieto about the campaign to close the plant, my colleague Sue Nelson and I got to work developing curriculum about the coal power plant and the organization's other campaigns. We started with environmental science classes and then moved onto developing justice-centered, locally relevant curriculum for our biology, chemistry, physics, and even AP science courses.

Still, it was not until my seventh year at the school (my tenth full year of teaching) that my classes were able to do authentic science connected to the community-based campaigns for environmental justice. As the introduction to this book points out, I was still struggling to juggle all the priorities of science teaching, but I learned to make decisions by centering what was important to the community, to the students, and to me. The grassroots struggle prevailed, and the coal power plant finally closed that fall. To be crystal clear, our curriculum and our school did *not* play an important role in that victory as we had imagined it might. Science teaching can align with grassroots movements for justice, but so long as schools are structured as they are, there are still important differences between organizing and formal education. Nonetheless, we had built good relationships with the organization that had led the struggle to shut down the plant. Based on our history of collaboration, they invited my AP chemistry class to participate in a larger study taken up by two local professors about whether the coal plant had left behind high levels of heavy metal contamination in the neighborhood soil.

Class began that August by studying the chemistry of coal. Students were engaged with rich and academically challenging science concepts. We wrote chemical reactions for combustion and balanced non-trivial redox reactions that described the acid run-off from coal mines. We made predictions about the secondary reactions in the environment like sulfur dioxide reacting with water in the atmosphere to make acid rain and nitrogen oxides catalyzing the production of ground-level ozone. Students told stories about their experiences and memories related to the coal plant from their childhood. One student said his mom would not let him play outside when large plumes of smoke were coming out of the plant. Another student said that she and her friends played games where they pretended the plant was a giant evil robot. Several students admitted that they had never really noticed or thought much about the plant. A group of students volunteered to collect about three dozen samples of soil from the neighborhood outside of school time. We would later bring these samples to a university lab where all the students in the class would use a laboratory process called digestion to prepare them for analysis.

In the meantime, the chemistry problems we solved in class made connections with struggles for environmental justice, and yet, looked like problems they might see on an exam. As students' understandings of environmental racism deepened, so did their understanding of key chemistry concepts. For example, consider the following trio of problems, originally published in a research article that deal with the solubility of ionic compounds in water and heavy metal contamination as an issue of environmental racism.[32] The first quiz of the year included a two-part problem, shown in Figure 1.1 with a response from Odette, the student quoted earlier as challenging Eurocentrism in her college chemistry courses. This problem was modeled after an item that appeared consistently on the AP chemistry exam at the time. The second part of the question connected the quiz problem to the study of soil contamination we were doing and related to the legacies of industrial pollution that are more likely to harm communities of color and economically dispossessed neighborhoods. Here Odette correctly wrote the net ionic equation for the precipitation of lead (II) carbonate and she connected this reaction with the persistence of lead pollution in soil. She expresses an understanding of common lead compounds as simply insoluble and refers to the mechanism by which ionic compounds would dissolve: "it does not dissociate."

In a problem on a class assignment several months later, students were asked to revisit the same compound, but this time in the context of lead poisoning, a biological problem caused by environmental contamination. In this problem (see Figure 1.2), we also see the limitations of my earlier insistence to avoid using Eurocentric and patriarchal naming practices for scientific concepts. Both the Next Generation Science Standards (NGSS) and the College Board's description of the AP chemistry exam explicitly highlight Le Châtelier's principle, so I felt that it was important for students to know this concept by its canonical name.

Earlier in the year, Odette shared an understanding of compounds as either soluble or insoluble. In her response here, she expresses a more complex understanding of the concept of solubility. In this problem, which uses a physiological

FIGURE 1.1 Example problem with student work from the first quiz in an AP chemistry course

(i) Write a balanced equation for the following reaction: Lead (II) acetate solution reacts with aqueous sodium carbonate.

$$Pb^{2+}(aq) + CO_3^{2-}(aq) \longrightarrow PbCO_3(s)$$

(ii) In our city's soil, lead is usually converted into lead carbonates or lead sulfates. Explain why lead contamination stays in the same place in the soil for decades.

It stays in the same place for decades because it does not dissociate.

FIGURE 1.2 Example problem with student work from a problem set in an AP chemistry course.

One of the treatments for lead poisoning is called chelation therapy. In this therapy, a chemical called EDTA is used to remove lead ions from the blood by forming water-soluble complex ions. While chelation therapy is very effective at removing lead from the blood, it cannot remove lead that has been deposited in bones. The lead in bones is mostly in the form of PbCO₃(s). If we think of blood as an aqueous solution, lead can diffuse from the blood into the bones or from bones into the blood by the following process:

$$PbCO_3(s) \rightleftharpoons Pb^{2+}(aq) + CO_3^{2-}(aq)$$

While chelation therapy decreases the concentration of lead in the blood, it usually rises again as soon as therapy ends. Use Le Châtelier's principle and the reaction above to explain this. In your answer, use the terms: equilibrium, reactants, products, concentration, and chelation therapy.

> Chelation therapy decreases the concentration of lead in the blood decreasing the amount of products. The concentration rises after therapy ends because therapy caused equilibrium to shift to the side of the products. Lead will still be in the bones acting as a reactant making it possible for lead to be concentrated in the blood.

rather than environmental context, Odette applies LeChâtelier's principle, which is a skill and concept emphasized in the NGSS and other science standards and curricula. Her application of this chemical principle makes sense of solubility in a more complex way. She notes that even an insoluble compound like lead (II) carbonate, can dissolve to a lesser or greater extent, depending on the conditions. The context of the problem explains why these very small shifts in solubility can have very important consequences. Still these problems, in and of themselves, are not aligned explicitly with social or environmental justice. But in the context of our ongoing community-based investigation of heavy metal contamination in the soil and our frequent discussions of environmental racism, these problems connected the dots. Problems like these can make important links between what matters in the community, what matters in canonical chemistry, and how scientific concepts can be useful to understanding environmental racism and community health.

About a month after the homework assignment that included the previous problem, students solved another problem related to the minimal solubility of toxic heavy metal compounds. The following problem was designed to push students' thinking in at least two important ways. First, it references a different context. Rather than referring to an urban neighborhood or to human physiology, this problem is situated in a rural Indigenous community. It referenced the documentary film about uranium mining on Navajo land that we had previously discussed. Secondly, this problem asks students to deal with the concept of solubility quantitatively. The problem set presented to the students was as follows, with the sequencing of the problem starting with part (b) due to a typo, which is the kind of thing that happens when teachers design their own curriculum without the help of a publishing team that textbooks employ:

> Earlier in the year, we learned about a group called the Eastern Navajo Dine Against Uranium Mining (ENDAUM) that successfully prevented *in situ* leech mining on their reservation in New Mexico. In the documentary *Homeland* that showed their struggle, one of ENDAUM's founders and leaders named Mitchell Capitan talked about how in experiments he did in his job as a lab technician, all of the uranium could never be extracted from the water in this process.
> (b) In this process, uranium is often precipitated out of ground water as $Na_2U_2O_7$. Write the dissociation equation for this compound as it dissolves in water.
> (c) The K_{sp} for this compound is 8.13×10^{-29}. Calculate the maximum concentration of diuranate ions ($U_2O_7^{2-}$) at equilibrium.
> (d) The EPA limit for uranium is 30 μg/L of drinking water. Complete the calculations necessary to determine if the saturated solution in the previous part of this problem will exceed these limits.
> (e) People often add salt, NaCl, to their cooking water. Use LeChâtelier's principle to explain what this would do to the solubility of $Na_2U_2O_7$ in water. Explain whether this would make the water more or less dangerous in terms of uranium content.
> (f) Calculate the mass of solid that would form if 0.10 moles of NaCl were added to 1 L of the saturated solution from part (b). Assume no volume change.

This would be a difficult problem even in the context of an introductory college chemistry course. But high school students were able to engage with this problem to varying degrees of success. Odette's lightly edited work included in Figure 1.3 includes the dissociation equation as an equilibrium expression, correct calculations for the maximum concentration of diuranate ions with a conversion of the units of concentration. She also correctly interpreted this quantity with respect to EPA regulations and once again applied an understanding of equilibrium often found in college chemistry curricula, the common ion effect. Odette came within an order of magnitude of calculating the mass of solid sodium uranate that would form in the given scenario.

FIGURE 1.3 Example student work from a problem set in an AP chemistry course.

2. b. $Na_2U_2O_7 \rightleftharpoons 2Na^+(aq) + U_2O_7^{2-}(aq)$

c. $K_{sp} = [Na^+]^2[U_2O_7^{2-}]$ $(2x^2)(x) = 8.13 \times 10^{-29}$

$\dfrac{4x^3}{4} = \dfrac{8.13 \times 10^{-29}}{4}$ $\sqrt[3]{x} = \sqrt[3]{2.03 \times 10^{-29}}$

$\boxed{X = 2.7 \times 10^{-10} M}$

d. $30 \dfrac{\mu g}{L}$ $\dfrac{2.7 \times 10^{-10} \text{ mol}}{1 L} \cdot \dfrac{476 g}{1 \text{ mol}} = \dfrac{1.29 \times 10^{-7} g}{1 L}$

476g

$\dfrac{1.29 \times 10 g^{-7}}{1 L} \cdot \dfrac{10^6 \mu g}{1 g} = \boxed{\dfrac{0.129 \mu g}{L} < \dfrac{30 \mu g}{L}}$

so the water does not exceed the EPA limits.

e. $Na_2U_2O_7 = 2Na^+(aq) + U_2O_7^{2-}(aq)$
$K_{sp} = [Na^+]^2[U_2O_7^{2-}]$
NaCl = add more products
Adding NaCl to $Na_2U_2O_7$ in water will be increasing the number of products. According to Le Chatelier's principle, adding more products will increase the number of reactants. Therefore, the water will be less dangerous since there will be less dissociated uranium

f.

	Na^+	U_2O_7
I	0.10 M	0 M
C	2x	x
E		

$0.10 x = 2.7 \times 10^{-10}$ $X = 2.7 \times 10^{-9} M$
      0.10

$2.7 \times 10^{-9} \text{ mol} \cdot \dfrac{634.04 g}{1 \text{ mol}} =$

$() + (x) = 2.7 \times 10^{-9} M$ $\boxed{1.7 \times 10^{-6} g \, Na_2U_2O_7}$

As with the previous problems, this problem, in isolation, does not represent justice-centered teaching. Instead, it is one piece of the bigger puzzle. In this case, the problem explicitly makes a connection with our earlier discussions about communities leveraging scientific knowledge to combat environmental racism. But beyond the connection between the problem and the documentary, this problem was also designed to connect the struggle to close the coal power plant in the school community with related struggles elsewhere through the themes of heavy metal contamination and environmental racism. Making these connections takes a great deal of time and therefore reduces the teacher's ability to *cover* the curriculum. But what is lost in breadth of coverage is gained in depth as both the teacher and the students tend to push harder to understand concepts that have meaning and significance outside of the textbook pages or standardized test items.

Besides providing a scaffold for students to continue deepening their understanding of solubility, this problem also added complexity to how we talked about scientific evidence and community self-determination. Odette and her classmates calculated that the amount of uranium in this problem would not exceed EPA limits. We discussed whether it was equitable or appropriate to intentionally contaminate drinking water with a toxic and radioactive metal, even if EPA regulations theoretically may not have been violated. Our class agreed with Mitchel Capitan that it most certainly was not. We discussed whether the company might be sharing theoretical models like these with government officials while community members like Capitan questioned the safety of their proposal based on his experience in the lab and his concern for his community.

Justice-centered science pedagogy does not assume a simple relationship between scientific knowledge and community activism. Instead, it engages students with the complexities of these intersections. This is something I learned from my students through activities like these. As Odette spoke about her involvement in the project to measure whether the coal power plants had deposited dangerous levels of heavy metal contamination in neighborhood soil, she reflected:

> When people were protesting the coal power plant, the rest of the community and people driving by saw the activism. And science wasn't—I mean, it was obvious, like let's shut this down because it's bad for our health and that's science—but it wasn't really the science that people noticed, it was the activism.

Odette recognizes that there are limits or uncertainties about the role of science in struggles for social or environmental justice. She also recognizes the power of activism and organization. Too often science classes teach students that STEM can solve our problems. Instead, science class should teach students to grapple with the complex role of science in our inequitable society. Justice-centered science pedagogy provides students with opportunities to think about scientific concepts deeply as they relate to their values, their politics, and their commitments—most notably, their commitment to community involvement—as participants in shaping the world.

ALL TEACHING IS POLITICAL

In the summers after my third and fourth years of teaching, I was asked by a curriculum developer to write a series of supplemental readings to accompany an environmental science curriculum that was to be published soon. These supplemental readings would be compiled in a sort of workbook designed to make the curriculum more locally relevant even as it was published for a national audience. One of the first supplemental readings that I wrote was to accompany the section of their energy unit that dealt with coal power. Not surprisingly, I wrote about the struggle to shut down two coal power plants near my school. I framed the reading in terms of environmental racism. The feedback I received from my bosses was that my contribution was "too political" for inclusion in the curriculum supplement. I pushed back on this feedback, noting that my writing connected their section on coal power directly to the local realities of that phenomenon. The curriculum developers' response to my pushback referenced the national audience of the larger curriculum. I was told that securing approval of the curriculum by the Texas state legislature was important and that the fossil fuel lobby has a lot of influence in that process. So, my writing was not too political. The more honest explanation is that it challenged the politics of the fossil fuel industry.

In fact, all teaching and learning is political. I do not mean political in the crude partisan sense that the word is often used in the US. Education is political because teachers inevitably take stances with respect to how power is wielded in society and in government. When teachers try to be neutral about these issues, that is a stance that allows powerful forces (like the fossil fuel lobby) to set teachers' agendas for them. This story illustrates how teachers or curriculum developers claiming political neutrality or objectivity are actually making a concession to the dominant politics and ideology.[33]

Since my experience with the environmental science curriculum supplement, there have been several high-profile battles over the same issue. In 2010, the ubiquitous school publisher Scholastic was contracted by the coal lobby to publish a pro-coal elementary school curriculum. Scholastic backed out of this deal when a movement led by teachers challenged the ethics, politics, and factual accuracy of the curriculum.[34] In 2017, the rightwing Heartland Institute created and disseminated a series of materials to tens of thousands of science teachers that embraced the rhetoric of climate change denial.[35] The oil industry continues to wield substantial power in science education in states like Oklahoma, where they supply teachers with free curriculum that involves a pro-oil cartoon character named Petro Pete.[36] Importantly, these pro-fossil fuel curricula present themselves as apolitical too. The key to an alternate vision for teaching science is not to strive for the impossibility of political neutrality, but instead to be honest about politics. If teachers care about environmental sustainability and mitigating the climate crisis, they cannot be neutral or 'look at both sides' of the exploitation of fossil fuels. They must take a clear stance against the politics of the fossil fuel industry. Of course, this stance is strongly supported by scientific evidence—but that does not make it politically neutral.

TEACHING SCIENCES FOR APPRECIATION AND CRITIQUE

There have been several important shifts in science education recently that make improvements on some of the worst elements of science curriculum critiqued in this chapter. The push toward phenomenon-centered instruction is likely to increase the extent to which science curricula is connected to students' lives. The increased emphasis on teaching scientific practices provides a rationale for the diminishing importance of memorizing famous scientists' names or learning their decontextualized biographies. And the NGSS include more explicit and stronger language about climate change than previous standards. As important as these shifts are, they do not go far enough.

Soon after the NGSS were adopted in my state, I was working with a group of chemistry teachers to plan instruction around issues of environmental justice. Very quickly, our group became frustrated with the standards. Even though our learning activities were rich with sophisticated scientific practices and concepts, we were having a really hard time aligning these activities to the NGSS. Our frustration prompted us to take a closer look at the standards. We considered what others had written about the standards. Alberto Rodriguez points out that the process by which the standards were written made equity an add-on rather than a central tenet.[37] Several other authors analyzed how the ideologies undergirding the standards did not account for ideas about caring or valuing life, but instead positioned technical decisions as separate from moral, ethical, or political choices.[38] We agreed with these critiques, and they helped us to articulate our frustrations with the disciplinary core ideas. We found that the disciplinary core ideas described chemicals as useful products but disconnected this notion from the idea that they can also be contaminants or pollutants. We found that disciplinary core ideas simplified decisions about whether to extract materials from the Earth as an exercise in geologic and economic reasoning—without considering other ways of understanding the land or whose rights might be violated by its exploitation. This aspect of the NGSS illustrates, as environmental scientist Max Liboiron argues, that the enterprise of science has a colonial relationship with the land.[39] At one point, the standards even suggest that teachers engage students with figuring out best practices for exploiting tar sands or oil shale—so-called alternative fossil fuels that are even more environmentally destructive than the predominant ways of exploiting petroleum or coal.

In summary, the disciplinary core ideas of the NGSS follow the long tradition of science education as a promoter of the enterprise of science. By teaching to the NGSS performance expectations, students are consistently asked to consider how science may solve problems, but rarely are they asked to consider the limitations of science. And they are never asked to explicitly consider how the enterprise of science may have caused problems and could continue to make some problems worse. Furthermore, in promoting the enterprise of science, the NGSS do not ask students to consider that science has benefitted and harmed people and communities unequally across the social markers of race, class, and gender. Our analysis of the NGSS and the framework that informed the standards, led us to the conclusion that teachers should not be promoters of the enterprise of science. As an alternative, science teachers should encourage their students to appreciate the insights and innovations of science while also cultivating their ability to critique the oversights of scientific ways of knowing and the harms caused by the scientific enterprise. This more complex approach to disciplinary teaching can be scary in an era where anti-vaxxers and climate deniers undermine some of the most important contributions of the enterprise of science. But this chapter argues that science educators will be more effective at preventing the spread of conspiracy theories by engaging students with a more honest consideration of the enterprise of science.

The shifts in science teaching that this chapter advocates require that teachers take different stances toward their content areas, a process that is illustrated throughout chapters 4 and 5. One way to teach toward these alternate ends is the focus of chapter 3: to organize curriculum around SJSI rather than bounded and decontextualized phenomena. But the first shift required by teachers to teach for equity and justice is to change how they view their students, which is the focus of the next chapter.

CHAPTER 2

Teaching Transformative Intellectuals

Chapter 1 asked readers to reconsider *why* they teach science. This chapter asks teachers to reconsider how they view their students, in other words, to *whom* they teach science. Two contradictory clichés capture the problematic ways young people are viewed in our society. On one hand, we often hear that "youth are our future." On the other hand, we hear griping from adults about "gen Z" or "gen alpha" or whatever label is currently being applied to adolescents and young adults by the people who were similarly characterized just a generation or two earlier. Neither of these clichés do justice to the complex ways young people are thinking about or living in the world in the present. Nor do these clichés acknowledge the ways in which young people are also navigating the intersecting ways that their lives are shaped by racism, sexism, homophobia, dis/ability, and economic dispossession. In other words, some members of Gen Alpha have the resources and opportunities to position themselves as gifted exceptions to adults' generalizations about youth whereas others are dealing with extra layers of criminalization and dehumanization. Transformative teaching involves rejecting racist, criminalizing, and other discriminatory and limiting views of youth and consciously and actively considering the full humanity of each student.

One of the great joys of teaching is getting to know a whole new crew of beautiful and complicated young people every year. One of the great challenges of teaching is that our school system prioritizes conformity and assimilation by its very design. Some misguided curriculum developers consider the problem of developing meaningful curriculum to be a problem of 'scale.' They assume that designing curriculum for a small group of students would be simple and that the problem becomes more complex at scale because larger numbers introduce more diversity. But the problem encountered by those who design curriculum for mass distribution is not primarily a problem of scale, but a problem of normativity. Oftentimes curriculum developers begin (whether they admit it or not) with a 'typical' student in mind. In a society shaped by white supremacy, heteropatriarchy, and other forms of oppression, it is not hard to imagine what demographic characteristics position a student as 'typical,' versus what social labels position a student as outside of the norm. The typical student is implicitly constructed as a white, male, monolingual English speaker, who is middle class, heterosexual, and conforms to a normative view of 'ability' physically and neurologically.

A related (and also incorrect) assumption about diversity as it relates to curriculum is that culturally sustaining pedagogies are only possible in segregated or ethnically homogenous settings. Being responsive to who students are—and teaching to support their self-actualization—is not made more difficult by diversity. This kind of teaching is made difficult by the extent to which our rules and assessments value normativity and standardization. Teaching in responsive ways requires teachers to learn about and value students' whole selves. Then teachers have to figure out how to invite students to consider, try out, play around with, practice—and even reinvent or change—the ideas and skills valued in science content areas in additive and affirming ways.

TEACHERS' POSITIONALITY AND COMMUNITY MEMBERSHIP

This chapter focuses on how we think about who our students are and what they bring into the classroom. But first, it is important for teachers to think reflexively about themselves in this way. When I am teaching preservice teachers, one of the first assignments I give them is to consider their pathway to becoming a science teacher. Then, I ask them to carefully compare the resources, opportunities, and environments of their own K–12 education with those offered by the schools where they are learning to teach. For me, the elementary school I attended had a lot in common with the schools where I taught, but the high school I attended was very different. The public elementary school I attended, like those where I taught, served mostly students who were marginalized by racism and dispossessed by the economic system. In contrast, the elitist high school I attended, while also public and tuition-free, served mostly children of professionals. It was affiliated with the local university and was highly selective in its admissions. The student body was predominately white and almost exclusively white and Asian American. When I was a senior at this school, I was part of a group of classmates who challenged the recruitment and admission policies of the school for being racist.

Even though my elementary school was located about a half-mile away, in the same college town with a relatively robust tax base, it was under-resourced. When I was in second grade, there was talk of closing our elementary school because the building was falling apart. The way I remember things, a precipitating event in this saga involved a piece of decaying plaster falling from the ceiling and striking a fifth grader in the head. As a second grader, I tagged along with my parents and neighbors to circulate "Save Our School" petitions door-to-door in our neighborhood. Fortunately, the campaign was successful; the district reversed its initial plans to close the school and instead built a new wing to replace the crumbling section of the building. Like the medical waste incinerator story recounted in chapter 1, this story taught me about the barriers that exist to well-being and self-determination in communities of color *and* about the power of organized communities to make progressive change to those ends.

Many years later, I was honored by and excited for the opportunity to teach at a high school founded by a grassroots struggle waged by a Mexican community in Chicago. The school's story resonated with this story from my childhood. In both cases, I was cognizant of the white privilege I experienced compared with most of my neighbors in the majority Black neighborhood where I grew up and, later, compared with students in the predominately Mexican neighborhood where I taught. I have lived and worked in Mexican communities in US cities for much of my adult life, and in such places, my name, *Daniel Morales*-Doyle, often leads people to ask (or sometimes assume) whether my family has roots in Mexico. For a long time, this was a question I had myself. I had trouble reconciling that my Morales family was from Louisiana, without clear roots within the modern boundaries of Latin America, and yet fit into the ethnic category of 'Hispanic.'

This confusion was built into the creation of the 'Hispanic' category. It was first included on the census in 1970, as the result of a compromise between the federal government and grassroots organizations in diasporas that are quite different from each other: Mexican communities in the Southwest US, Cuban communities in Florida, and Puerto Rican and Dominican communities in the

Northeast US.[1] The goal of the compromise was to include enough people to demonstrate the existence of a nationwide demographic group that deserved federal attention. My grandfather Morales was raised as part of a group that fits under this large problematic umbrella, a small Spanish-speaking community called *Los Isleños de Louisiana*.[2] This community was started by settlers from Spain's first colony, the Canary Islands, making it part of the complex and cruel process of Spanish colonization around the world. The community maintained their unique Spanish dialect and cultural traditions for generations, and even centuries, after Louisiana was passed back to France and then to the US. In these ways, they resemble some other groups of *hispanos* in the US southwest and other descendants of Canary Islanders in Latin America.

Without a clear view of this context, I learned in school to check the "Hispanic" box for ethnicity and the "white" box for race. This seemed to fit as I moved through school in the 1980s and 90s. But these categorizations do not fit for most Latine people in the US, who are often racialized and othered in ways that defy the racial categories on the census. As an adult who has learned more about race and ethnicity and continues to learn more about my family's history, I struggle with whether to continue checking the Hispanic box on forms. I struggle even more with the question of whether to identify with terms like Latino and, more recently, Latinx or Latine. Unlike Hispanic, these terms have emerged from within communities naming themselves to assert their solidarities. They are not unproblematic terms. But whereas Hispanic is an intentionally Eurocentric framing, the terms Latino/Latinx/Latine tend to be linked with greater acknowledgement of the Indigenous and African ancestry of peoples throughout Latin American diasporas. Even still, 'Latin' highlights a European colonial frame, and anti-black racism and Indigenous erasure remain prevalent in Latin America and Latine communities in the US. Whenever it seems like an easy decision to check 'non-Hispanic,' I think of all the people who have anglicized their names and erased their family histories to assimilate. My life and work in Latine communities has been informed, motivated, and shaped by these considerations and related experiences. Within the problematic racial and ethnic categories of the United States, I aim to work in solidarity with Latine communities while mindful of my white privilege—a stance I view as an alternative to embracing whiteness and anglicization. My relationships with the land on which I live and the communities who have welcomed me are filled with love and commitment and fraught with discomfort and contradiction. I am prompted to sit with the contradictions and harms of the choices and commitments made by my ancestors from Ireland and the Canary Islands. Marginalized by processes of colonization on their home islands, they participated in the same imperial projects by settling on Indigenous lands in North America. In Chicago, these are the lands of the Council of Three Fires peoples, the Ojibwe, Potawatomie, and Odawa, as well as peoples like the Menominee, Ho-Chunk, Miami, Peoria, and Sac and Fox. In Louisiana, these are the ancestral lands of the Chitimacha and Choctaw peoples. I include extensive biographical information here to model the type of reflection that teachers might do. I know this writing risks coming across as self-indulgent, performative, or disconnected from science teaching. But it matters how teachers position themselves *vis-à-vis* larger sociopolitical projects and historical contexts. In fact, sitting with the discomforts of history and the contradictions of schooling are the foundation for transformative dispositions in the classroom.

Whether teachers consider themselves part of their students' communities informs how they teach. Even this notion of community membership is not simple for most people. Unlike many teachers in urban schools, I have generally lived in the communities where I have taught, or in similar neighboring communities. But I have generally not felt entitled to consider myself among my students' community elders, even as my own children have matriculated into educational settings that overlap with my work. The extent to which community membership is determined by geography, cultural affiliation, racial and ethnic identity, or other means is different across contexts and varies for individuals and for groups. Teachers who are considered by their students to be community elders can explicitly draw on their community's traditions and values to shape their curriculum and pedagogy in science class. In segregated settings, teachers who are more privileged outsiders in marginalized communities must adopt a humble stance as a teacher-learner about those traditions and values. They should encourage their students to learn from the wisdom of their elders and communities while encouraging them to consider the ways of knowing valued by scientific disciplines. This latter stance works well for teachers in culturally diverse settings also. In any context, teachers should invite students into scientific ways of knowing as one way of interacting with and understanding a complex world. Students should be encouraged to wonder about the world and engage in ways that feel right and fit with their cultural commitments. They should also be invited by their teachers into scientific ways of knowing as a set of pluralistic and additive possibilities, not as a replacement for their own ways of knowing nor as a universalist endeavor.[3]

REFRAMING RESISTANCE

Parents often come to understand that resistance from young people, especially during certain developmental stages (like age two or adolescence) is normal, unavoidable, and even healthy. This is especially true in a school system that relies on passivity and compliance from students. I was reminded of this fact during my first summer teaching at a school with explicit commitments to social justice. My colleague and I had been asked to teach two sections of environmental science over the summer to account for the fact that an emphasis on reading and math during the school's first year meant that science was squeezed out of the curriculum. After weeks of collaborative planning to develop science curriculum informed by local struggles for environmental justice, we were excited for students to be engaged. We hoped they would be enthralled. Our lessons communicated to students that one important reason they should learn science was to participate in efforts to protect their community from polluters. Local grassroots organizers had helped us identify the most meaningful issues in the neighborhood and then we connected these issues to the science we were charged with teaching. We had the full support of the principal of the school, who grew up in the neighborhood. He shared our dream that young scientists from our school would play a pivotal role in shutting down local polluters. This work was difficult. Sometimes the connections between science and community in the lessons felt like a stretch; other times the science seemed too superficial. But I had never been more excited to teach. In some ways, I felt like I was going to be teaching science the way I wanted to for the first time in my career. Then on the first day, mere minutes into teaching this curriculum, a tenth grader named Ramiro loudly objected, "I'm sick of all this social justice shit!"

Looking back on this moment years later, makes me crack a smile. Of course, I was frustrated in that moment—even devastated—and my negative feelings were normal. But so were Ramiro's feelings that he expressed so honestly. Resisting schooling, especially certain aspects of schooling, is part of how young people protect their dignity and make sense of their experiences in a deeply inequitable and often oppressive school system.[4] David Stovall and I have written elsewhere about Ramiro's stance and the complexities of responding to student resistance as teachers who view ourselves as upholding values of justice and equity.[5] An important consideration within these tensions is that communities are complex spaces where folks have different perspectives and priorities. What matters to some may not be as important to others. Young people have experiences and aspirations that are often different from their parents or neighbors. Culturally sustaining pedagogy emphasizes this dynamicity of culture as it relates to our teaching.[6] So, I learned to foreground youth experiences and found creative ways to prompt students to share their views of the issues we studied. For example, when I taught about issues of access and equity in public transit in environmental science class, I asked students to share frustrating stories with each other about riding public transit.

I also learned to regularly emphasize the broader goals and values of learning. For example, my syllabus included the following statement:

> The primary goal of this course is not individual success. It is collective success and community empowerment. This means that you are responsible for the success of your classmates and that you are expected to use the power you gain by knowing chemistry to serve your community. This could be by returning to your community after college to serve as a science teacher or a doctor or it could simply mean leading a laboratory experiment at a local elementary school this year.

These commitments are different from "learn-to-earn" or pursuing the STEM pipeline as some sort of 'escape' from the 'hood or *barrio*. We were explicit that learning does not have to be individualistic, competitive, nor in service of national economic or military prowess. Emphasizing these values regularly was meaningful to students. One student, Cristina, who was also quoted in the first chapter, had failed tenth grade chemistry because she became skeptical about the STEM pipeline and learn-to-earn rhetoric. While Cristina was attending a selective school with a STEM focus, her older sister had been pushed out of college because her undocumented status limited her access to financial aid. This caused Cristina to question her own opportunities in the STEM pipeline, which was featured as the primary goal of education at her previous school. She lost her motivation to study or engage with school science. In an interview for a research project, Cristina contrasted the messages she heard from teachers at her earlier school with the community-oriented purpose for learning at our school. She explained why she had more success even in more difficult courses after transferring to her neighborhood school: "I'm learning this for my community. It's not just for me. It's not just for me to get a good-paying job when I graduate. It's for me to help." This pushed Cristina to achieve an A in AP chemistry and a passing score on the AP exam, earning college credit. Nevertheless, not all students share Cristina's perspective. Ramiro's objection indicates that there will also be students who resist community or justice-oriented learning activities, which is OK too. When I reflect on Ramiro's response, I think about how reluctant I was to participate in my community's struggle to shut down the medical waste incinerators. Young people are still figuring out their commitments. A teacher's role is to support that process, not to determine it.

Contrary to the accusations of right-wing critics, teaching for justice is not indoctrination. In fact, that term better describes the conventional model of schooling with its heavy emphasis on standardization, patriotism, and the canon that prioritizes normativity and sameness. After attending a dual-language Catholic elementary school, my children attended our neighborhood public elementary school. Both schools are located in predominately Latine communities with mostly Latine students. My son came home one day during the first week of kindergarten and told me, "We do something in school that I don't think you would like." Concerned, I asked him what he meant. He responded in the adorable voice of a kindergartener: "Every day at the start of school, we pray to the flag of the United States of America." His 5-year-old interpretation of the pledge of allegiance made me chuckle; he was describing what indoctrination in schools really looks like. The pledge of allegiance and the overemphasis of the STEM pipeline are manifestations of schooling aimed at assimilationist and nationalist goals. In contrast, teaching science for justice prioritizes students engaging with sciences to make sense of disciplinary concepts and practices as they intersect with their lives, their communities, and broader political and historical contexts. Students are encouraged to express different viewpoints and embrace heterogeneous ways of knowing.

REFRAMING MOTIVATION

Still, regardless of our commitments to students doing things in their own way, teachers are responsible for maintaining some amount of order in a classroom with 30 or more different viewpoints and levels of interest or attention. This includes students who may feel like Ramiro or who may express their resistance in even less convenient ways. This can be frustrating for even the most experienced or patient educator. With my classes of new science teachers in graduate classes, I use the following exercise as a first step in dealing with these frustrations and I encourage readers to try it out themselves.

- First, spend a few minutes writing about your challenges with your most frustrating class. Your writing might begin with something like, "I dread seventh period every day because…"
  - It is important to express your feelings as honestly as possible in the first part of this exercise; nobody else will read it.
- Then, spend a few minutes examining your writing to look for any tendencies to blame students (or their families or their communities) for your frustrations.
  - It is common for teachers to blame students for their troubles.[7]
  - This is a feature of a school system that uses grades and test scores to sort students into categories where some are worthy of opportunities and others are not.
  - There is nothing to be gained by feeling bad about having these thoughts, but this is a feature of our profession that we must constantly resist.
- The next part of this exercise is to rewrite your frustrations in terms of the ways in which the structures of schooling—and not your students—have created your frustrations. If you are having trouble with this second part, consider the following chart from a research article about students' motivations to engage with science curricula (see Table 2.1).[8]
- Third, make a list of adjustments or strategies for dealing with your frustrations and thereby improving your effectiveness as an educator.

This exercise does not solve our problems immediately. A simple thought exercise cannot resolve the deep-seated contradictions of the school system. Instead, the goal of this exercise is for teachers to develop their ability to describe the problems they face as systemic and related to the goals of schooling. And it reminds teachers that they have agency within the constraints of the system. Teachers' energy is better directed towards changing the system (in ways big and small) than changing their students (who are beautiful, brilliant, and already working on themselves to self-actualize). In the day-to-day grind of teaching,

TABLE 2.1 Reframing the problem of motivation

Framing	What is the problem?	What are the components of the problem?	What is taken for granted?	What are the solutions?
Dominant	Students lack motivation to engage with science curriculum.	Students do not consider science to be important. Students lack confidence in their ability to do science.	The context and goals of the curriculum (and science itself) are assumed to be beneficial for students.	Provide more support for marginalized students.
Justice-centered	The curriculum is not worthwhile for students to engage.	The context of the curriculum is not relevant to students' lives. The goals of the curriculum are assimilationist and driven by labor force concerns.	Students are assumed to be autonomous and sophisticated thinkers.	Reconstruct the curriculum to reflect students' lives within the sociopolitical context (AND provide more support).

we can all benefit from reminders about the source of our frustrations and our limited-but-still-powerful ability to intervene.

Research on teacher education includes endless examples of teachers who view their teacher role as correcting deficits within students.[9] But some research also shows how teachers who initially blame students for their problems can develop the ability to see inequities as systemic problems.[10] In my research with colleagues, we have seen examples of teachers who come to see agency and complexity in their role. They have redirected their attention to collaborating with colleagues to construct learning environments that are welcoming, engaging, and meaningful to students. In one case, a student teacher named Isabella initially thought of her work as convincing her students to value science and education.[11] Both Isabella and most of her students were from Mexican immigrant families, yet she located the problem of educational inequity in her students' households. After several courses, workshops facilitated by community-based organizations, and working with an excellent mentor teacher (who is also Latine), Isabella began to see that the problem of educational inequity was systemic and historical. She realized that it was related to other forms of oppression her students were experiencing in and outside of school. She began to see her work differently. Rather than convincing students of the value of science and education, she began to ask questions of herself and her mentors about how she could bring critiques of racism into biology class and how to work with her colleagues to improve the school's discipline practices and policies. Isabella's shift did not provide her with solutions to the complex problems of teaching for equity, but with a different view of her work, she made different decisions about how to spend her time and how to interact with students.

FUNDS OF KNOWLEDGE FOR SCIENCE LEARNING

Educators have been trying to dislodge deficit-thinking about students for decades, but it persists—especially among white educators about their students of color.[12] More than thirty years ago, Norma González, Luis Moll, and colleagues at the University of Arizona worked to disrupt deficit thinking by engaging teachers in studying the rich knowledges in working class Latine households that were representative of many local students.[13] The term used for these assets were "funds of knowledge," a concept that was popularized in science education by Angela Calabrese Barton and Edna Tan.[14] A question for many science teachers is how to learn about students' funds of knowledge when we do not have the time or resources to learn the way González, Moll, and colleagues did. Furthermore, science teachers sometimes have trouble seeing the knowledges in students' households as directly relevant to their content areas in the way that social studies or language arts teachers might. A relatively simple assignment can address these questions and help science teachers make unexpected connections of their own.

The assignment that I call the "funds of knowledge narrative" began in my own family – both in terms of inspiration and in how I introduce the assignment to students. My grandfather Morales left economic hardship in his community in Louisiana to find work in a large meat packing plant on the south side of Chicago. As a laborer, he was not likely viewed by society (nor his children's teachers) as a person with a rich scientific knowledge. My grandfather's role in the meat packing plant was to treat excess fat from slaughtered animals with sodium hydroxide to make soap. My mother, the youngest of his eleven children, fondly remembers her father bringing bottles of glycerin home. He showed her how to combine this byproduct of the saponification reaction with dish soap to make bubbles, which brought her joy as a young girl. I explain to my students that these interactions represent my grandfather sharing knowledge of chemistry with my mother in ways that could have been integrated into her science education and sense of the family's funds of knowledge. This example serves as a model for students as they are assigned to find such a person in their own family or immediate social network. The assignment asks them to interview somebody who is not recognized or credentialed as a scientist in a formal sense, but who possesses sophisticated understandings of nature or scientific concepts. People often develop these understandings through their work, their hobbies, or knowledge that is passed down as familial wisdom. Depending on the age of students, the specific course, and the amount of time we have for this assignment, I have modified it to include more or less depth and formality. But most often, students write a short essay about where and how this person developed their scientific knowledge. Recently, students in my classes have produced evocative podcasts out of these 'funds of knowledge' stories and interviews.

Over the years, these essays have served to make several great connections to the curriculum and to affirm students' families as rich sources of knowledge. For example, a high school senior named Jade interviewed her mother who worked as an electrician for the local commuter rail system. Jade was proud of her mother, who is an African American woman, for challenging norms by taking up a trade dominated by white men in the US. She explained to her classmates how one of her mom's tasks at work was to refill large lead-acid train batteries with sulfuric acid. When our AP chemistry class learned about electrochemical cells, I was able to reference Jade's mom's work and ask students to explain why lead and sulfuric acid worked as components for a battery. I knew Jade's mom relatively well from our time together on the local school council, and I have kept in touch with her through the ten years since her youngest daughter graduated. Thinking back, I missed an opportunity to invite Jade's mother in on lab safety day to explain the reasons and procedures for working safely with acids and bases.

Reading these funds of knowledge essays and listening to students' sharing their family members' expertise has been important for *my* own ongoing learning of chemistry. Their stories have taught me about real-life applications of my content area that I did not learn while studying chemistry in college. Many years after Jade told me about her mother's work, I was leading a project with several teachers about heavy metal contamination and read about how, despite its known toxicity, more lead was being mined from the Earth than ever before.[15] Initially I was surprised by this fact given that lead had been banned from paint, gasoline, and water pipes decades ago. But I was able to understand it by referencing Jade's mom's work because vehicle batteries are one of the primary contributors to the present demand for lead.

In the same assignment, one of Jade's classmates, Marisol, shared a story about her father who worked in an industrial facility that brands itself, 'the largest bakery in the world.' This facility is located on the other side of a large park in my neighborhood. I frequently smell muffins and cookies baking while I am enjoying the park with my children. Marisol explained how one of her dad's tasks at work was spraying down sheets of cookies with an ammonia solution before they were baked. She expressed disgust at this practice and said that she no longer wanted to eat this popular cookie brand even though her dad explained that the ammonia was to kill microorganisms and that it all evaporated during the baking process. I referenced Marisol's dad's work when we learned about molecular geometry, intermolecular forces, and their connection to boiling point later that year. Then, years later, I was collaborating with a teacher at my neighborhood high school. As part of our collaboration, students used the EPA's toxic release inventory website to find the companies that reported the release of toxic chemicals into soil, water, and air in the neighborhood. The second facility on the list was the facility where Marisol's dad worked. They reported emitting large amounts of ammonia into our neighborhood air. Without the information provided by Marisol's dad, I never would have been able to explain to this new group of students why a bakery would emit such large amounts of ammonia into the air. These stories from my classes illustrate the power of inviting funds of knowledge from working-class students' families into science classrooms. Not only can this practice affirm students, but it often provides a view into how our disciplines operate in the real world. Science curricula tend to teach an idealized vision of scientific practitioners as well-paid PhDs working through their curiosities in a lab. But the realities of how science disciplines are utilized is more complicated and usually less glamorous. Chapter 4 focuses on how teachers can rethink our disciplines for justice and sustainability. Chapter 3 focuses on how to identify and define social justice science issues (SJSI) as a starting point for learning in those directions. The remainder of this chapter considers how students, with their different priorities, viewpoints, experiences, and goals respond to science curricula that deal with social justice.

STUDENTS AS CURRICULUM CRITICS

Each individual student is a complex human with interests, concerns, passions, identities, histories, present circumstances, and futures. A classroom full of students, then, contains a variety of human thoughts, emotions, and experiences that is hard to comprehend, let alone account for in lesson plans. In this light, student-centered curriculum seems almost impossible. Before lamenting, consider that the dichotomy between curriculum that is teacher-directed versus student-centered is an oversimplification.[16] Students interact with our curriculum in all sorts of ways, some intended and others not. Their interactions with curriculum could be overt resistance like Ramiro's objection to "all this social justice shit." They also include more subtle rejections, subversions, diversions, or co-optations of the teachers' goals. Natalie Davis, Shirin Vossoughi, and John Smith refer to these latter sort of interactions as "moves to an elsewhere."[17] Rather than bemoaning this variety of student responses, teachers can embrace the notion of students being curriculum critics and interpreters of their learning goals. Viewing student agency within the parameters of our curriculum as beautiful and normal allows us to encourage divergent and transformative thinking. In this section, I draw on research and experience in classrooms to describe some of the ways in which students have responded to justice-centered science teaching to support teachers in thinking about who their students are and who they may become.

STANDPOINTS TOWARDS SCIENCE CURRICULUM

Science curriculum organized around canonical ideas and in service of pipeline goals prioritizes the engagement of a narrow segment of students whose ways of thinking about the world and whose academic goals already align with school science.[18] Feminist scholars like Patricia Hill Collins, who emphasize intersectional approaches, may say that these students have a particular standpoint.[19] These standpoints are different from identities, but they are related in that they are shaped (but not determined) by how we are positioned as individuals in society. School science often teaches students the falsehood of the 'scientific method' as a universal way for producing knowledge and constructing truth. Not only is the idea of a singular 'scientific method' a myth, but philosophers of science like Sandra Harding recognize that how we construct knowledge depends, in certain ways, on our standpoints.[20] This is true for scientists and for students interacting with science curricula. Contrary to how critics characterize these views of knowledge as crude relativism, the importance of standpoint does not mean that all ways of understanding a phenomenon are equally good or useful. Another philosopher of science, Richard Levins, used two illustrative examples to explain this important nuance. Despite very different cultural, political, and linguistic traditions, many peoples around the world have named plants and animals at a level that roughly approximates the biological categories of species. Similarly, astronomical bodies of knowledge constructed from very different cultural standpoints have many commonalities because we all share a view of space as inhabitants of Earth. Still, within these overlaps, the example of Carl von Linné in chapter 1, shows how standpoint matters. Similar taxonomical categories can differ in important ways depending on their goals. Naming lifeforms to construct hierarchies that justify domination has different implications than naming lifeforms as a way of maintaining good relations with other inhabitants of Earth.[21] Likewise, the understandings we construct about outer space may overlap in recognizable ways while also being different depending on our goals. Is the goal of studying the night sky to aid the navigation of conquering ships and GPS-guided missiles or to understand our place in the universe? These two sets of goals will lead us to understandings that are similar in many ways and consequentially different in others. Our goals, context, and positionality matter for how and why we learn.[22]

Students challenge dominant conceptions of how and why we learn when they ask "Why are we learning this?" or "When am I ever going to use this in my life?" Teachers often view these questions as annoying distractions, responding with some version of the adultist cliché "Because I said so." But students are expressing genuine and reasonable dissent against the goals and priorities of school science. They are asking for the purposes of schooling to, at the very least, consider their goals and perspectives. If teachers' priorities are aligned with social justice and sustainability rather than standardization and normativity, they should welcome these challenges. Many students enter science classrooms with deep commitments to their communities and to issues of justice and sustainability. For students with these standpoints, constructing scientific knowledge in the context of an important issue in their community is often a good entry point and context for engaging with the sciences. One student, Curtis, referred to this standpoint as being like a *tourist in science* when he was reflecting on his experiences in my high school chemistry classes. For Curtis, and others who adopt similar standpoints towards school science, dabbling in the fields of biology, chemistry, or physics is worthwhile only insofar as it contributes to community and justice-oriented projects. From his tourist-in-science viewpoint, Curtis called out the curriculum in my AP chemistry class as challenging the canon only after the AP exam. Students who adopt standpoints like this are often characterized by teachers and researchers as unmotivated science students. But in fact, they are brilliant young people who have often figured out how to learn sciences through appropriation. Students can develop the metacognitive skills to ask themselves how the goals of the science curriculum align (or not) with their own goals and values.[23] When they figure out places of alignment, they appear engaged and motivated. When the curriculum is so irrelevant or dissonant that appropriation becomes impossible, they disengage and appear unmotivated. Still, other students, like Ramiro who was sick of the social justice themes in his classes, can view teachers' attempts at connecting the curriculum to the community differently. That is okay, but it should not prevent us from encouraging Ramiro to reconsider. It is important to remember that teachers *always* deal with different standpoints that students take with respect to their curriculum, even if their teaching aligns with mainstream goals. For too long, in too many science classrooms, the standpoint aligned with a narrow pipeline view has been the only one recognized as legitimate.

TEACHING TRANSFORMATIVE INTELLECTUALS

Teachers are often tired. They are overworked and undercompensated by school systems. They are disrespected by elected officials and media pundits. In this context, teachers can sometimes develop a calloused attitude towards their students—especially those who are most resistant. These teachers might consider that the same system that mistreats them causes their resistant students substantially more harm. It can be helpful for teachers to train themselves to view resistant students as suggesting or opening possibilities for a different kind of teaching and learning. With this consideration in mind, students' resistance can be inspiring instead of only frustrating. Some philosophers have given teachers who adopt this view the label of *transformative intellectuals*.[24] Other critical pedagogues have extended this concept to students themselves.[25] If teachers view their students as transformative intellectuals who are still developing their standpoints, they can take a different approach to the canon and the pipeline. Students who take standpoints like Curtis's tourist-in-science orientation are acting as transformative intellectuals by reimagining the relationships between science and community engagement. Marisol, whose father worked at the industrial bakery spraying cookies with ammonia solution, was another student who took on a tourist standpoint. In an interview with Marisol, who was attending an ivy-league university at the time, she was critical of mainstream diversity, equity, and inclusion efforts as she reflected on advertisements she saw on television:

> I feel like a lot of people now are pressured to go into the sciences not because of the value of how much of an impact the sciences can do for society, but because of the money, because they're in demand right now. Like just before I left to come [talk] with you, I was watching Univision with my grandma and there was this ad promoting Hispanics going into STEM fields. And I keep seeing more and more ads about this.

Marisol connected this narrow view of studying science solely for economic competitiveness with the curriculum itself:

> If you don't have social justice [in science curriculum], I feel like you're just sort of creating these people who are very science-focused, but yet they don't realize the implications or the power that they hold or the change that they can do with that sort of intelligence or skills or knowledge.

In addition to challenging the learn-to-earn ideology that pervades pipeline approaches to STEM education, Marisol suggests that a science curriculum that considers issues of social justice is important for students to consider how scientific knowledge is intertwined with power.

Teaching sciences is a much more exciting profession if we view our students as people who can potentially use sciences to transform the world while also transforming the scientific disciplines themselves. For some students, their engagement with justice-centered science curriculum inspires standpoints aligned with these views. Whereas students like Curtis and Marisol chose not to continue their formal study of sciences, there are students who view their participation in scientific communities as part of their efforts to work for social justice. For example, Cristina connected her interest in chemistry with her participation in the community soil project, discussed in chapter 1, with her work as a community organizer:

> So, I was like, I'm really liking chemistry and what I'm doing soil-sampling-wise, and it connected really well with what was going on in the school because I was fighting for the school, and I was doing the chemistry work too. So making

the connections of community and what you like to do or what you like to study is why I'm doing what I'm doing now. Usually when people ask me, without getting into the whole story of it, I say I realized that I liked chemistry and I liked working with my community, so I'm just putting them both together.

Cristina contrasted her community-driven approach to scientific engagement with the typical view of scientists as doing isolated, disinterested work like what has often been presented in science curricula:

Usually we think of scientists as they're just in the lab and just doing things internally and just blocked from the rest of the world... I don't want to do that at all. So I guess the traditional culture of science—I don't feel like I'm a part of it. But the way that it's changing or the way that it's becoming more involved with the outside world than just the lab—I do feel like I'm a part of that.

Cristina's comments here suggest that she views herself as part of changing scientific communities and institutions themselves. Reflecting on her views about the culture of science in an interview, Jade shared similar thoughts:

Yes, even though it's a heartless and inhumane culture. It's something that can be changed. But I feel like we need to incorporate new things to make it more helpful instead of just the old tradition with the old white man with a lab coat. Science was always my favorite subject as a kid, but we need to open it up.

In these comments, Jade, an African American woman, expresses a lifelong interest in science and a sense of agency for changing the exclusionary culture that has long defined communities of science and scientific institutions.

FROM DISINTERESTED TO CONCERNED SCIENTISTS

Teachers have often asked me about students, like Jade, who enter our classroom already loving the sciences. They worry that a justice-centered approach will marginalize the students whose standpoints *do* align with standardized school science—those students whose standpoints are typically centered. Over twenty years in science education, I have taught many students who have done very well in prior science classes and whose views align well with those expressed in science textbooks. De-centering the standpoints of these students may be even more important for them than it is for their peers who challenge the goals of school science. Rather than an experience of marginalization, learning towards different goals can be an experience of expansion and invigoration for these students.

Consider Jackson, a successful student who identifies as a Latino man and went on to choose physics as his major in college. Jackson explained to me in an interview that he dealt with contextualized science curricula by ignoring the context to focus on learning the abstracted science concepts. Reflecting on my chemistry curriculum in an interview, Jackson said:

> Even though on some of the problems you introduced the problem in kind of a real-world situation... I can see why it's helpful, but even though you might mention the real-world connection there, on the problem set sometimes it's kind of like ok I'm just going to ignore this and focus on the facts and work the problem out.

Here, Jackson aligns his standpoint with the type of abstract and reductionist thinking that is valued in most science disciplines. The ideal standpoint from a dominant science perspective is disinterested and detached. In other words, scientists are supposed to be neutral about the outcomes of their work. This kind of problem solving as an isolated technical undertaking has been prioritized by school science for a long time, and Jackson is good at it. He may have seen the context as a potential distraction, but after several years of learning science in justice-oriented classrooms, Jackson did not feel like his standpoint was marginalized. Instead, he reflected on how he came to see more connections between his favorite subject—astrophysics—and his community and society:

> Physics is kind of more one of those sciences where it's far away from society in terms of what it does or what it's focusing on. But it was able to show me that even though I'm going to be studying stuff that's light years away... I can still impact my community and my society whether that be just from making some sort of astronomical breakthrough that tells us more about either what's out there or where we came from... I mean... for as far away as physics seems from society, you can still make those breakthroughs where you can directly impact society.... I guess that's my long version of saying that AP chem taught me how to... how to... maybe that's why I was putting it the long way because I can't put it the short way. It was showing me that all sciences can have their impact on humanity.

When I started to ask a question to follow up on this profound statement, Jackson interjected to elaborate how sciences (like astrophysics) can "have their impact on humanity." He said, "In terms of just ourselves as biological beings—where the earth came from, where life came from, where all the matter in the universe came from." Jackson flashed a smile as he finished this statement,

"I mean for as much progress as we've made in terms of early universe stuff, we still don't know a lot about the early universe."

Education researcher Juan Garibay documents that STEM majors tend to view their career goals as disconnected from working for social change. In many ways, Jackson was aligned with that trend, telling me in an interview, "My main focus isn't exactly social justice, but...scientific advancement is what my goal for my career is." Jackson frequently expressed the standpoint that school science curricula tend to demand from students a willingness to engage in learning science concepts in abstracted isolation for their own sake. At the same time, his statements about connections between astrophysics and humanity suggest that engagement with justice-centered science curricula may have influenced Jackson in important ways. Jackson may have been deterred from becoming what Marisol described as "people who are very science-focused, but yet they don't realize the implications or the power that they hold or the change that they can do with that sort of intelligence or skills or knowledge." It is important to note that as Jackson expressed an increased awareness of connections between science and society, he referenced a fascination with the early universe and astrophysics. These are topics that teachers might not think of as being closely connected with students' lives. Perhaps more importantly, these topics sit well outside of the canon of high school physics, which typically focuses on basic kinematics and limited explorations of energy, optics, or electricity and magnetism. In this way, Jackson's reflections underscore the need to abandon the canon of school science, even for those students for whose standpoints are well-aligned with its form and content. They too deserve a more expansive, imaginative, and socially relevant science curriculum. Borrowing from the name of the organization, the Union of Concerned Scientists, we need to educate more scientists who are concerned about the social and environmental impact of their work and abolish the idea of scientists as disinterested observers of the universe.

THE NEED FOR TRANSFORMATIVE INTELLECTUALS IN THE SCIENCES

In 2020, the COVID-19 pandemic co-occurred with massive protests against anti-Black racism in the wake of George Floyd's murder by a Minneapolis police officer. This co-occurrence alongside the rise of right-wing nationalism in many parts of the world sparked an ideological reckoning for segments of society that had previously claimed neutrality with respect to issues of white supremacy.

In this context, there was a one-day strike carried out by many workers in the STEM enterprise who organized to #ShutDownSTEM as a wake-up call about the prevalence of anti-Blackness in technical fields. Movements for racial justice amplified the news that the pandemic itself had devastatingly disparate impacts across racial lines. There were many reasons for this disparate impact including the ways in which racial capitalism organizes the types of labor that people do and the ways in which environmental racism and unequal access to health care create persistently inequitable health conditions. Among these myriad reasons that COVID-19 disproportionately harmed Black, Latine, and Indigenous communities in the US were several that should prompt science educators to take a hard look at the mainstream curriculum.

Take, for example, the documented racial bias in an extremely common medical device used to measure blood-oxygen levels, an important factor for physicians in determining the appropriate course of treatment for patients with COVID-19.[26] Pulse oximeters are small medical devices typically placed on a patient's finger or earlobe. These devices transmit light of specific wavelengths through the skin. By detecting the amount of light transmitted or absorbed as it passes through the patient's finger or earlobe, the device can measure the oxygen saturation of the blood. This works because oxygenated hemoglobin and deoxygenated hemoglobin absorb or transmit the wavelengths emitted by the device in predictably different amounts. Of course, as a common cliché about racial difference reminds us, regardless of our skin color, red blood courses through our veins. Operating under this assumption, pulse oximeters should work equally well for people of different racial identities. Unfortunately, this cliché, which is often deployed in race-evasive ways, does not account for the fact that skin pigmentation also absorbs the light emitted by the pulse oximeter. In a medical system beset with white supremacy, pulse oximeters have been designed, tested, and calibrated mostly by medical scientists who share lighter complexions with their patients. The result is that the devices tend to overestimate the oxygen saturation of the blood in people with darker complexions. In the context of treating COVID-19 or other respiratory problems, this can result in a failure to give supplemental oxygen to a patient who needs it because the measurements of the device are erroneously high.

It stands to reason that a designer of medical technologies who had darker skin themselves would be much less likely to overlook patients with complexions like their own. Black and brown doctors are also more likely to be sensitive to the biases built into our medical system because of their own experiences with racism. This underscores that representation in STEM fields unequivocally matters. There is no question of the need for more Black scientists, engineers, and doctors as a condition for equity. But we also cannot let white engineers, scientists, and doctors off the hook. The designers and calibrators of pulse oximeters built in a bias against people with darker skin not because of their own lighter skin, but because of their ideological standpoints. If white supremacy were not a dominant ideology, it would have been commonsense for designers—even those with lighter complexions themselves—to account for the obvious range in skin colors among humans. Just as doctors account for different blood types or a range in what constitutes "healthy" in any medical measurement, they should see variation in skin color as normal and expect manifestations of human diversity. But we do not live in such a world. There is a long and troubling history of Western medicine embracing racist ideologies that makes this issue much more complex.[27]

Teaching about these issues is therefore also complex. Pulse oximeters fail to account for a very clear and discrete interaction between skin pigmentation and light. Conversely, other common medical devices and measurements have dubious "racial corrections" built-in that are predicated on white supremacy rather than biophysics. These devices and measurements rely on the false notion that darker skin color is associated with a range of pathologies and inferiorities in unrelated characteristics from lung function, kidney health, and intelligence. For example, the spirometer, a device to measure lung function, was designed and calibrated by white supremacist doctors in the mid-nineteenth century who assumed that Black people had inferior lung capacity.[28] Despite this racist assumption being long debunked, a racial correction persists in modern spirometry devices. Similarly, doctors apply another so-called racial correction to a measurement of kidney function called *estimated glomerular filtration rate* or eGFR for patients who identify as Black.[29] Bogus racial medical corrections made news recently when the National Football League (NFL) attempted to withhold lawsuit settlement payments from former players who suffered brain damage playing football. The NFL doctors and lawyers used racial corrections that assumed the baseline intelligence for Black players was systemically lower than for white players, thus arguing that the brain damage suffered by several

Black players did not fall within the threshold of the settlement. They were eventually pressured by lawsuits, advocacy by the players themselves, and negative media coverage to use a consistent (but still questionable) measure across players, regardless of race.

Comparing the racial bias of pulse oximeters with the racist corrections of the spirometer, eGFR, or IQ tests, we can see that there are fundamental understandings of human biology and the social construction of race that have simply escaped the grasp of too many STEM professionals.[30] While I have been a critic of learning standards, I would argue that every person who takes high school biology should understand that there is a beautiful range of human skin colors determined in some relatively complex ways by our genes that adapted to the intensity of ultraviolet light in the environments where our ancestors lived. Every person who takes high school biology should also understand that the categories we call race are not determined in the same biological way, but are social categories constructed to rationalize the oppression of slavery and settler colonialism.[31] They should understand that these categories have been continuously reinvented and refined to continue the justification of unjust sociopolitical hierarchies across centuries.[32] Understanding these concepts would prevent designers of technologies like pulse oximeters from normalizing whiteness and ignoring the role that skin pigmentation plays in how human bodies interact with light. Science educators should claim their role in preparing a generation of STEM and medical professionals who view the relationships between ancestry, health, and society with appropriate complexity and historical context. Science education that prioritizes justice can serve to develop a generation of transformative intellectuals—in and out of the sciences—who use their understanding to transform the sciences, medicine, and engineering and guide these impactful disciplines away from their racist legacies.

Supporting students to grow into their roles as transformative intellectuals requires a careful disruption of the canon and thoughtful expansion of the curriculum of secondary school science. I frequently hear physics teachers, in particular, take a standpoint similar to Jackson's by arguing that their discipline is removed from social phenomena. But the principles of light absorption and transmission used by the pulse oximeter are unequivocally disciplinary core ideas of physics. The same could be said for the spirometer and most medical and scientific instruments, which most often rely on physical measurements that are extrapolated to make determinations about biological or chemical systems. Therefore, there is an opportunity across all science classes to engage students with the complexities of how these different phenomena and concepts are entangled with broader themes. In my research and practice, I call these themes social justice science issues or SJSI. Designing curricula and teaching about SJSI is the topic of chapter 3.

CHAPTER 3

Social Justice Science Issues

In the last decade or so, there has been a major push for science teachers to shift from curricula organized around concepts to curricula driven by students making sense of phenomena. To the extent that science teachers have embraced this shift, it represents a major step forward for our field by opening alternatives to the pipeline critiqued in the Introduction and the canon discussed in chapter 1. Putting phenomena in the center of the curriculum can shift teachers away from laundry lists of abstract canonical concepts. They may give teachers a way to respond to the themes of chapter 2 and the frequently related student question: "Why are we doing this?" Beginning from phenomena *may* dislodge the tendency of science curricula to narrate a decontextualized Eurocentric story of science if we focus on students' reasoning about the world rather than the historical development of canonical concepts. Moreover, a focus on students' sense-making can push teachers away from spending much of their time goading students into regurgitating standard explanations or coaching them to faithfully follow algorithmic problem-solving techniques.

At the same time, if we are not careful, the shift towards making sense of phenomena in science class can still easily lead us back to tired and outdated approaches to science teaching. For example, decontextualized mundane phenomena may not be much better at inspiring students' interest than seemingly random abstract concepts from the canon. Spending weeks discussing phenomena like an ice cube melting or a nail rusting can quickly feel like watching paint dry or grass grow. One teacher with whom I collaborate described some popular phenomena-driven curriculum as "lacking a soul," a sentiment documented in research by Alexis Riley and Felicia Moore Mensah.[1] But this is not to say that these phenomena cannot be fascinating nor am I arguing that there are not good reasons to understand them – and that includes paint drying and grass growing! But we must find ways for phenomena to reflect our students' lives and to give them opportunities to project the future they want to create.

For example, understanding the process of ice melting may be much more compelling if it is set within the context of local changes related to climate change. On the other hand, teaching about climate change as a scientific phenomenon without political context may be more likely to inspire misconceptions, false solutions, or hopelessness than it is to inspire young leaders for climate justice. This means that science teachers must make important decisions about what to do when encountering disciplinary boundaries, like those between chemistry and environmental science, between physics and political science, or between biology and public health. Beyond contextualization, it is important to recognize, support, and prioritize students' sophisticated thinking.

Teaching through phenomena does little good if the end goal remains for students to repeat the same canned explanations that the previous generation of students read in textbooks. This implies engaging students in asking questions, constructing explanations, and grappling with issues to which there are no canonical answers. For this reason, this book advocates organizing curricula around social justice science issues (SJSI) with phenomena embedded therein. I describe SJSI as themes rather than phenomena because they do not have clear boundaries the way anchoring phenomena do.[2] They do not have a clear beginning and ending. They defy the "gapless explanations" that some science teaching models advocate because they cannot be fully understood using scientific ideas.[3] SJSI are not scientific themes. They are more like what Paulo Freire called *generative themes* because, as explained below, they emerge from listening to students, their families, and their communities.[4]

Organizing curricula around SJSI provides teachers with opportunities to inspire their students' engagement with transformative ideas, with their communities, and with the larger world. A few examples of SJSI curricula have been scattered in the previous chapters. The goal of this chapter is to outline a process by which teachers can identify SJSI that are responsive to their students' contexts, build their own understandings of the SJSI within the broader historical and sociopolitical contexts, and then work with students to (re)define those SJSI as a context for science learning. This includes how science teachers can navigate disciplinary boundaries and implicit ideological lessons, which are also known as the hidden curriculum.[5]

In its simplest form, identifying SJSI involves teachers listening to students and engaging with parents, families, and local community organizations. This process can be done in a more formal, participatory way with enough time and resources, but it can also be something that teachers do informally and gradually. Identifying SJSI requires teachers to study science, technology, and society because most science teachers did not learn their content areas in contextualized ways and therefore often have trouble making connections between the curriculum and the world. This studying can be individual work, and this chapter includes some suggestions for that approach. But teacher learning is more effective in a collective group, a topic which is addressed near the end of the final chapter.

Even though addressing SJSI in classes is exciting, it can also be intimidating for teachers because it inspires unanswerable questions and difficult conversations. Therefore, this chapter provides advice about avoiding some of the pitfalls and misconceptions that arise while teaching about complex and controversial issues. After identifying a potentially generative SJSI, teachers work with their classes to redefine that SJSI in ways that are meaningful to students. Together teachers and students should define SJSI in ways that (1) imagine justice rather than gaze at suffering, (2) explicitly counter problematic dominant ideologies, and (3) interrogate systems rather than individual behaviors. The latter half of the chapter illustrates these three principles with several common examples found in science curricula.

IDENTIFYING SJSI

The first criterion for identifying SJSI is that they should be meaningful to students. This can also feel like the most difficult criterion to meet. Youth popular culture changes quickly. Classrooms, including those that appear homogenous in terms of students' race and ethnicity, are full of divergent perspectives and interests. Students have a lot on their minds that has very little to do with school science. Indeed, identifying issues that find overlap between students' interests, concerns, or aspirations and the science curriculum requires lots of creativity, content knowledge, and time. Most importantly, it requires *listening* to students and *building relationships* with their communities and families. An important caveat is that we should not limit our science teaching to issues raised by students or concerns that are already familiar to them. As science educator Mindy Chappell has argued, the canonical and assimilative character of schools means that there are many fascinating, important, and relevant topics that may be outside of students' views. It is our responsibility to introduce them.[6] The key is finding ways to connect what your students care about, what matters in your discipline, and what matters in the world. This section describes three related ways for teachers to identify SJSI that invite students to consider the value of scientific ways of knowing and the complexities of the scientific enterprise. The section closes by synthesizing these three strands in a more formal, participatory process.

Listening to Students

The great joy of teaching is the daily opportunity to interact with energetic, creative, and brilliant young people. But sometimes the demands of the job, the structures of schooling, or problematic deficit views cause teachers to lose sight of this joy. Likewise, sometimes the hardships of life, structures of schooling, or other social pressures cause young people to present themselves in classrooms as less vibrant or curious than they really may be. Reconnecting with the joys of teaching and learning often starts by suspending judgement. As discussed in the previous chapter, for teachers, this means viewing student resistance as normal—and even beneficial. It also means having an open mind about those themes, topics, and activities that matter in students' lives outside of the classroom.[7] Identifying SJSI that can ultimately be defined in meaningful ways starts by listening to students and asking reflective questions about these conversations or observations. Here are some of these questions.

- When students become animated in excited conversations or heated debates with each other, what are they talking about?
- When students have unstructured time or a little bit of cash, what do they do with it?
- When students open a search engine in a computer lab or on a tablet in the classroom and have a few moments of free time, what keywords do they search?

- What patterns do I recognize in the stories students have shared with me about their lives outside of school?
- What non-academic questions have students asked me frequently?

At first, the answers to these questions might not seem to have anything to do with science curriculum. But over time they can lead toward engaging curricula, if science teachers take students' ideas seriously, continue to ask themselves what is useful or fascinating about their content area, and exercise some creativity. This requires an explicitly non-judgmental stance toward youth popular culture and a humble and open-minded view of other ways of understanding the world. You may have legitimate critiques about some of the ideologies reflected in popular culture that your students consume. In this listening stage, foreground what your students find compelling and figure out later what aspects are appropriate to raise in the classroom or how you might encourage them to take a closer look at how some aspects may be problematic.

The following examples illustrate how identifying SJSI is not as simple as asking students what they want to learn about, nor is it a process that teachers can do without student voice. Identifying SJSI is a process that recognizes that teaching and learning is always a reciprocal process with direction from the teacher and agency by the students.[8] Listening to students, valuing their ways of knowing, and defining SJSI together with them does not imply teachers abdicating their responsibility to carefully plan the curriculum, nor does it imply giving students free reign to choose the topics of study. Identifying SJSI is about looking for shared themes between our content areas, students' lives and communities, and the broader sociopolitical contexts.

To begin from an illustrative example, high school teachers have likely noticed that lots, but not all, of their students think or talk about romantic relationships. Teaching in the early 2000s, I noticed that some students were also fascinated by (or critical of) ostentatious jewelry worn by celebrities. These two observations do not seem to have anything to do with each other or with science curriculum. But then, in 2005, I was teaching with an edition of the *Chemistry of the Community* textbook, in which there were photos and accompanying diagrams of three allotropes of carbon (graphite, "bucky balls," and diamonds) that caught students' attention.[9] In a class conversation about this page of the textbook, students mentioned a recently released music video. The video showed imagery alluding to forced child labor in diamond mines with a haunting sample singing De Beers company's slogan for diamond engagement rings: "A Diamond is Forever." Over several years, I turned these observations into a unit in my chemistry class that taught the basics of atomic and molecular structure and their relationship with physical and chemical properties. The SJSI of this unit was the diamond cartel operated by the Oppenheimer family and their De Beers corporation.[10] The curriculum asked students to consider the value of diamonds—and whether they were an appropriate symbol of romantic love and commitment—by constructing understandings of their chemistry and their role in European colonialism and apartheid in Africa. Below, I explain how this curriculum evolved over time, and I describe some of the limitations, opportunities, and pitfalls that came with organizing curriculum around this SJSI.

With this kind of attention to what students find fascinating, I experienced less resistance than some of my colleagues who faithfully followed the curriculum as published. But this does not mean that my classroom was devoid of student resistance. A few years later, I was teaching physics when a student complained that my class was not relevant to their aspirations to have a career as a video game designer. Hearing this complaint made me realize that I was not making some connections to student interests that were right in front of me. Modeling the movement of the physical world is an essential part of the physics curriculum and an ever-evolving component of video game design, which is a topic of interest to many young people. Not being a serious gamer myself, I talked about this idea with a group of teachers, coaches, and community members. A colleague explained to me that many of the most popular video games communicated nationalistic and militaristic ideologies. He described one recently released game in which the objective was to guide the main character, a US soldier, on a mission to assassinate a communist leader of a Latin American country. Once again, I saw the connection between the field of physics and ideologies of militarism and imperialism. My colleague's critique of this game led me to wonder how physics teachers might use the SJSI of video game design to engage students with critical considerations of how we model reality and imagine alternate possibilities. I never had the opportunity to design such a unit myself, but research by Sepehr Vakil describes an excellent youth-generated example. In the context of a high school computer science class, two young women of color designed "a video game to help girls of color resist negative stereotyping in STEM environments."[11]

Connections between how the physical world is modeled in physics classes and in video gaming is a potentially generative way to think about SJSI for physics. In the next chapter, I describe one way that I engaged with a consideration of video game consoles as an SJSI in chemistry class.

The previous examples emerged from students' direct responses to the curriculum, but more often, listening to students implies hearing the stories they tell and thinking about the questions they ask outside of class. These narratives and questions often take more time, reflection, and creativity to bring back into the curriculum. For example, over a period of several years of listening to students, I figured out an unexpected link between some of the experiences they recounted, a common question they asked me, and the chemistry curriculum. Unfortunately, I frequently heard firsthand accounts of police harassment and brutality from Black and Latine students. One unethical practice of the Chicago Police Department that students shared is that officers would pick up young people from one neighborhood and drop them off on a street corner in another section where they were likely to face hostilities for being outsiders in that community. The police were stoking the tensions created by economic dispossession, social marginalization, and racial segregation; they were inciting rather than preventing violence. Even as hearing about this practice outraged me, for a long time I did not see any way to address police harassment or brutality in chemistry class.

As a science teacher, another type of question I was frequently asked was about drug prescriptions. Medical settings like hospitals, clinics, or pharmacies can be intimidating and students sometimes see their science teacher as a more approachable science expert. This can especially be true in multilingual families where young people often accompany older family members to the doctors' office or the pharmacy to serve as translators because they are more comfortable speaking English than their elders are.[12] Of course, I would respond to these questions by telling students that I am not a medical professional and that they needed to direct their questions back to somebody who was. But I also began to recognize that it was my responsibility as a science teacher to provide students with opportunities to build confidence and competence that would make asking questions of doctors and pharmacists more comfortable and productive. I felt a responsibility to them just as they felt a responsibility to their family.

Eventually, I began to realize that there was a chemistry connection between my students' stories about police harassment and their questions about prescription drugs. Both issues were related to the ways in which the chemicals that we call drugs are developed, regulated, and policed. The over-policing, surveillance, and police harassment and brutality that is common in Black and Latine neighborhoods are related to the so-called war on drugs. Indeed, the stories of harassment that my students told me often included police accusing them of being involved in the illicit drug trade or frisking them in search of marijuana or other prohibited substances. While police target working class Black and Latine communities in their enforcement of drug prohibitions, research shows that drug use is consistently equivalent across the lines of socioeconomic status and race and ethnicity.[13] This unit asked students to reconsider public discussions about drugs with a deeper understanding about their chemical composition. This kind of science learning led to students understanding the chemical equivalence of generic and brand name drugs. Some students have remarked that it helped them to feel more confident at the pharmacy or less vulnerable to frequent suggestions by advertisements to ask their doctor about this drug or that one. These examples are described in more detail in chapter 5.

Engaging with Parents, Families, and Community Organizations

As discussed in chapter 2, students' families are rich sources of knowledge. Parents, guardians, and other family members influence our students more than we ever will as teachers, and that is a good thing. Unfortunately, separating young people from their families has been a hallmark tactic of schooling as a weapon of colonialism.[14] This ranges from the most egregious example of Native American boarding schools to more subtle ways that schools teach students of color to reject the values and wisdom of their families and elders.[15] Teachers who espouse values of equity and justice should always seek to uphold and celebrate local practices and examples of what this means. One year, days before school started, regional district administrators fired our principal without cause. Students immediately mobilized to protest this destabilization of the school. In the ensuing struggle, they brought together their parents, teachers, and local organizers to eventually force the district to reinstate the principal. Reflecting on these efforts as part of a research project, members of each of these constituency groups—students, parents, and organizers—explained the power and beauty of their campaign: it allowed community members to recognize each other's insights, wisdom, and commitments across generational lines that can often be divisive.[16] While identifying SJSI, science teachers should seek out wisdom from students' families in respectful ways. One approach is the funds of knowledge activity described in chapter 2. Indeed, learning from Jade about her mom's work with lead-acid batteries as a train electrician or from Marisol about her dad's work with ammonia in the bakery continues to inform how I understand the science of local industries to this day. These parents have been part of my science education just as I have been part of their children's. Teachers can also build relationships with parents by calling home to share an example of their children's brilliance, by engaging in meaningful ways during parent–teacher conferences and by showing up to students' extracurricular activities to support the school's athletic teams and arts programs. After my own children were born, I struggled to balance the demands of parenthood with the demands of being an engaged teacher. But I learned to seek coherence, rather than balance, through simple acts like bringing my children to school-sponsored performances or sporting events. These simple forms of participation can build the relationships and inspire the learning that help teachers identify SJSI for science curricula.

Like classrooms or families, communities are complex places with many different viewpoints, priorities, and ideologies. Oftentimes politicians, initiatives, or policies that claim to do the will of the community simplify this complexity. At the same time, there are often people and organizations who have intimate knowledge about what issues matter locally. Grassroots organizations conduct community needs assessments, asset-mapping, or other similar activities to identify community challenges, strengths, concerns, and aspirations. Even when organizations do not formalize these processes, their staff and volunteers tend to have deep knowledge about what matters in the community. Of course, living and teaching in the same community is the best way for teachers to have a sense of what matters locally. Unfortunately, racist education and housing policies mean that students of color are less likely to be taught by their neighbors or community elders than white students are. Even for teachers who are members of the community where they teach, there is much to learn from folks whose work involves constant attention to community concerns outside of the school. For this reason, building relationships with local grassroots organizations can be an excellent way for teachers to identify SJSI. The coal power plant example that I described in chapter 1 provides one clear example of how teachers can learn from community organizations. I include more examples below that illustrate how interactions with community organizers can help young people see SJSI and their ability to do something in more complex and hopeful ways.

Engaging with community organizations in a principled way requires teachers, especially those who may not be familiar with the work of organizing, to proceed with care. As under-resourced and overworked as educators tend to be, community organizers often work in even more tenuous conditions. As with parents or other community members, teachers should be mindful of how they ask for organizers' time, energy, and wisdom. Teachers should seek to form reciprocal relationships to make them sustainable over time by finding ways to volunteer or contribute to the organization's goals in and outside of the classroom. Oftentimes, it can be helpful to organizations if teachers are willing to distribute educational materials developed by the organization or to promote their volunteer or internship opportunities with students. But there may be other ways for teachers to show up for an organization's event or even donate financially to a cause. Again, this involves teachers weaving together their lives and their profession by participating in the communities where they teach.

Teachers should also consider potential power and resource differentials between the school and the organization as community institutions.[17] Again, while public schools are typically under-resourced, they nonetheless receive state funding and recognition in ways that are not available to most community-based organizations. It is also the case that not all non-profit organizations are created equal. There are grassroots organizations that are representative of the community and draw their power and much of their funding from their constituents or from funders or government sources that respect community self-determination. There are others that would be better characterized as 'artificial turf' organizations. These metaphorically synthetic organizations are often created or funded by wealthy outsiders who have agendas that did not emerge from the community. They tend to have a more corporate structure and position their work as charity, casting the community as a place of deficits. They practice false generosity; wealthy donors position themselves as benefactors, even as their involvement enhances their power and influence to benefit their image and the status-quo over the community or social change.[18] Sometimes artificial turf organizations have a structure that represents a fast-food chain in which offices of a larger organization pop up in different neighborhoods. Other times, they are a stand-alone group with a single wealthy benefactor seeking name recognition, influence, or a particular political goal. Teachers should be discerning about what kinds of organizations they approach to form relationships because there are examples of grassroots groups that succumb to what some organizers call 'the non-profit-industrial complex.' These transition from a true community-based organization to a more corporate structure. At the same time, there are national alliances of truly grassroots groups or local chapters of organizations that are deeply rooted in communities. Approaching organizations with humility and discernment means being respectful of organizers time and knowledge while also looking into an organization's funders, political stances, and whether its staff, volunteers, and leadership reflect the community they serve.

Studying Reality for Generative Themes

When famed critical educator Paulo Freire was briefly the Secretary of Education for the largest city in Brazil, essentially the superintendent of São Paulo schools, he led an interdisciplinary project aimed at supporting the development of curricula from themes that resonated with the local community.[19] This process had three phases, translated from Portuguese as (1) the study of reality, (2) the organization of knowledge, and (3) the application of knowledge. In this project, the study of reality involved teachers working together with community members on a participatory research project to identify *generative themes*, which were concepts that mattered to people in their local, everyday contexts. As mentioned above, SJSI are a type of generative theme. Whenever possible, my recommendation for teachers is to identify SJSI using a thoughtful, systematic, and participatory process like Freire's study of reality. For example, during school breaks, teams of parents, students, community members, teachers, and disciplinary experts could work together on participatory research projects to identify generative themes. Alejandra Frausto Aceves and colleagues led such a process over a couple of summers at the *Instituto Justice and Leadership Academy* in Chicago.[20] Unfortunately, because our education system is not organized to be responsive to community concerns, rarely are resources or infrastructure available to take this approach. As discussed in previous chapters, our school system prioritizes other end goals (like workforce preparation and assimilation into mainstream culture). But even still, the recommendations above for listening to students and engaging with parents, families, and community organizations can serve as an informal and very doable way to identify SJSI that meet the criteria of being meaningful to students and locally relevant.

UNDERSTANDING SJSI BY STUDYING SCIENCE-TECHNOLOGY-SOCIETY

In the São Paulo interdisciplinary project, after the study of reality identified generative themes, educators engaged in the second phase, "the organization of knowledge." In this phase, teachers made sense of the generative theme in terms of their content areas. In other words, the organization of knowledge is part of the curriculum planning process for educators to connect what matters in the community with what they are responsible to teach. This can be difficult because most science teachers did not learn our disciplines in deeply contextualized and community-connected ways. We learned our disciplines in isolated abstraction, or what mathematics educator Ole Skovsmose calls "purified significance."[21] We were told that the STEM disciplines were important for our own career opportunities or for the world. But in terms of our day-to-day learning, the significance of the content was glossed over or not even addressed. Even in STEM careers, complex problems are divided into smaller technical and repetitive tasks in much the same way that physics or chemistry textbooks provide repetitive problems to practice an isolated skill. Skovsmose argues that this process makes it easier for engineers or scientists to work on politically or morally objectionable projects (like designing weapons of mass destruction) without fully considering the implications of their work.

For science teachers, our experience with this kind of abstracted education means we have a lot to learn about how our disciplines function and matter in the world. We need to study above and beyond the science assessed by content exams for state licensure or the topics covered in our degree programs. We need to study to understand how SJSI are woven into the fabric of society and sometimes connect to nuances or subfields of our content areas that we did not learn in college. This kind of study is best done in groups, but teachers should also study individually. Individual study can take the form of regular but unstructured engagement like leisure reading or watching documentary films. Or teachers can study in more targeted ways while planning lessons around specific SJSI. The realm of study that is most helpful is a field unto itself (and also an approach to science education) known as Science-Technology-Society, or the alternative

Science and Technology Studies, both of which are abbreviated STS and are more-or-less synonymous for our purposes here.[22]

Above I described how I came to understand the topic of drug development as an SJSI that was meaningful to my students. While studying chemistry in college, I synthesized acetylsalicylic acid (or aspirin) in an organic chemistry laboratory course. But it was my leisure reading in the realm of STS that helped me make connections between that laboratory experience and the SJSI. Recently, the chemical similarities between illicit drugs and prescription drugs have been a topic of more public discussions. Synthetic opioid painkillers have garnered lots of media attention for the addiction and overdose problems they cause—whether users obtained them via prescription or on the street. I was able to make this connection many years ago, in part, by reading a popular book about the shared chemistry and history of the most taken pill in the world, aspirin, and the drug that causes the most overdose deaths in the world, heroin.[23] These two drugs were developed by the same corporation, Bayer, using the same chemical process, acetylation—to very different results. By reading critical histories of science, I learned that both these drugs (and many others) were examples of the co-optation of Indigenous peoples' knowledge of medicinal plants by European chemists.[24] Notably, I had rarely learned about the historical or political context of my content area while earning my degree in chemistry. Instead, I became fascinated about these contexts as a teacher in search of curricular connections. Over time, the combination of listening to students and engaging with families and community organizations, while also learning about the historical and political contexts of our disciplines, lead teachers to identify or clarify SJSI. There are insightful academic articles and engaging popular books in the realm of STS that can help teachers with this process. Sometimes, teachers might seek out a particular topic to learn more about the context. In those cases, there are textbooks and other large volumes that can serve as references. Just a short list of examples might include Clifford Connor's *People's History of Science* and the online collection edited and published by the History of Science Society entitled *An Introduction to the History of Science in Non-Western Traditions*.[25] But there is an ever-increasing collection of wonderful popular STS books like Ruha Benjamin's *Race After Technology* or *Viral Justice,* Robin Kimmerer's *Braiding Sweetgrass,* and Ainissa Ramirez's *The Alchemy of Us,* just to name a few.[26] For those interested in issues of social justice and video games, the work of Kishonna Gray provides excellent insight.[27]

Reading STS books, as we stay committed to our own learning about how science content areas show up in the world, can lead teachers to unexpected, organic, and slow-developing connections. Many of the endnotes in this book reference STS books and articles that have been extremely influential in my teaching. Sometimes, teachers will find the politics of these books well aligned with their own. Other times, there will be serious disagreements with the authors' interpretations. But in both cases, consistent engagement with STS makes for a more responsive, creative, and critical science teacher.

DEFINING SJSI: HOW TO POSE THE PROBLEM

As earlier chapters have suggested, even with pressures of high stakes testing and prescriptive curricula, science teachers have the power to communicate with students about why they should learn science—or even what counts as learning science. Some researchers refer to this as the teachers' *framing of activity* and note that recent reforms and trends favor frames about explaining real-world phenomena (rather than frames about learning science concepts for their own sake).[28] While justice-centered science teaching has much in common with phenomena-based instruction and what has long been called problem-based learning, there is an important distinction between how these approaches treat the relationships between worthwhile phenomena, important scientific ideas, students' lives, and broader contexts. Phenomenon-driven teaching begins from anchoring phenomena identified by teachers or curriculum designers as suitable for communicating the big ideas of science. Then learning activities are organized around a 'gapless' storyline designed to lead students toward canonical explanations.[29] This common approach prioritizes students' arrival at simplified versions of long-settled scientific consensus. The priority is the internalization of the ideas deemed most important by curriculum publishers and the standards. Implicitly, students learn that science has the power to explain natural phenomena.

In contrast, justice-centered teaching *embraces the gaps* in our ability to explain the world with scientific ideas. This approach prioritizes students' engagement with their communities and the broader world. They explicitly learn that scientific ideas are extremely helpful and also very limited in terms of solving problems or understanding phenomena that matter to us. Students have opportunities to use important scientific ideas to make sense of SJSI. Indeed, they often are able to explain components or facets of the SJSI in canonical terms, as illustrated through the concept of solubility in chapter 1. These components or facets are often scientific phenomena themselves, so an SJSI approach is not mutually exclusive from a phenomena-based approach.

In an SJSI approach, students also have opportunities to grapple with questions to which teachers do not have the answer and problems that imply crisscrossing disciplinary boundaries and engaging ways of knowing beyond biology, chemistry, and physics. Justice-centered science pedagogy aligns better with what Freire called *problem-posing* education. The first part of the chapter explained how teachers might identify meaningful SJSI by listening to students (and their families), working with community organizations and engaging with the STS literature. Once teachers have identified a potentially generative SJSI, they should work with their classes to *define the SJSI* in ways that are meaningful to students. The remainder of this chapter illustrates some *dos* and *don'ts* with respect to defining the SJSI by applying three principles to several common examples. These principles are to define the SJSI in ways that turn students' attention toward (1) imagining justice, (2) challenging dominant ideologies, and (3) interrogating systems. Working together to define SJSI according to these principles then leads to teachers inviting students to *apply a scientific lens*, which is the phase where a justice-centered curriculum most resembles a phenomenon-driven curriculum. This phase is similar to the third phase of the São Paulo interdisciplinary project, the application of knowledge.[30]

Define SJSI with Students to Imagine Justice, not Gaze at Suffering

With the increasing frequency of catastrophic weather events caused by climate change, it is common for images of destruction caused by these disasters to appear in social media feeds, newspapers, and television news coverage. When I was a young teacher, telecast images of New Orleanians standing on their roofs in the aftermath of Hurricane Katrina were burned into my memory and there have been countless examples since. In most of these disasters, people marginalized by racism, colonialism, and economic dispossession are disproportionately harmed. In teaching about this disproportionate impact, it can be tempting to foreground these sensational images depicting suffering to emphasize for students the importance of learning about the ecological causes and effects. But in referring to Hurricane Katrina as an "unnatural disaster," Manning Marable argued that "the public spectacle of Black anguish is a 'civic ritual' that reconfirms the racial hierarchy of the United States."[31] Similarly, Indigenous educator Eve Tuck criticizes damage-centered approaches that emphasize the suffering of marginalized communities. In a diverse classroom, a damage-centered approach risks leveraging some of the students' suffering into a spectacle for the educational benefit of others. *Rather than encouraging students to gaze at suffering, work with them to define SJSI in ways that dream toward justice.*

To illustrate this principle, I return to the unit that I developed about the chemical composition and properties of diamonds. Not too long after I started teaching that unit, a Hollywood feature film was released about the topic of diamond cartels fueling brutal civil wars in West Africa. The next year, there was a documentary film that followed three hip-hop artists known for their gaudy diamond jewelry as they traveled to Sierra Leone to see the devastating impact caused by those wars. Soon thereafter, students began asking me to show these films in class. It seemed like these were compelling ways to pull students deeper into the themes of the unit and to connect popular culture with the curriculum. And for a while, I showed clips of these films in class. But every time I did, I felt discomfort with the ways our class was gazing at the suffering depicted in the films. The films seemed to inspire as much pity and horror as they did critical thinking.

As I had learned more about the diamond cartels, I came across another documentary that was much older, less spectacular, and not as glossy. This documentary turned its gaze the other way—at Cecil Rhodes, the Oppenheimer family, and other European colonizers in Africa who built huge fortunes by creating an extractive diamond cartel. In my lesson plans, I scrapped the Hollywood depictions of conflict diamonds in favor of this PBS *Frontline* series on the diamond cartel. Students remained captivated, even if they complained about the standard definition video quality. Instead of gazing at suffering, we were able to more cogently critique those who benefitted from exploitation. Even more importantly, critiquing unjust social relations from this angle felt more likely to avert despair and instead inspire students to imagine economic and social relations that were more just and less extractive. We could see that there was enough wealth to support a different standard of living for everybody, but that it was being unjustly concentrated in the hands of a few.

In chemistry class, a key part of this process was for us to learn to see diamonds as crystals of carbon atoms with special molecular structures that led to special physical and chemical properties. This chemical view of diamonds demystified them and allowed us to also see them as small pieces of the Earth whose economic value had been artificially inflated and extracted by greedy white supremacist colonizers using various forms of political and economic manipulation. I worked with colleagues to design problem sets where students compared the physical and chemical properties and monetary value of natural diamonds, C(*s*), and similar materials like synthetic diamonds, also C(*s*), cubic zirconia (ZrO_2, *s*), and moissanite (SiC, *s*). Students were able to compare molecular structure and chemical composition with properties like hardness, refractive index, and melting point—and with the cost per gram of each crystal. By critically analyzing the relationship between chemical composition and economic value, students were able to consider how diamond's tetrahedral geometry and covalent bonds undergird a series of special properties that are fascinating and potentially useful beyond being symbols of wealth or twisted notions of romantic love.

Define SJSI with Students to Explicitly Counter Problematic Dominant Ideologies

History educator Howard Zinn titled his memoir with a metaphor that is familiar to physics teachers: *You Can't Be Neutral on a Moving Train*. For physics teachers, the moving train conjures problem sets related to frame of reference. Many physics curricula ask students to add or subtract velocities of balls being tossed between two passengers or thrown off the train to a stationary target. Zinn's point was that all ideas or perspectives are not given equal consideration in a society that is dominated by a particular ideological and cultural framework or where the power and money of a few often drown out other voices. For science teachers, the impossibility of neutrality means that it is actually misleading to teach what is sometimes described as 'both sides' of issues like climate change or evolution. It is likely clear to most readers that science teachers must take a clear stance against the ways that right-wing pundits and politicians have attempted to obscure the clear science of these topics. But there are also more subtle ways that science teaching may reinforce widespread false beliefs. Zinn's point about neutrality is therefore very important for science teachers to keep in mind as they work with students to define SJSI to openly counter problematic dominant ideologies. In fact, explicitly taking up ideological, political, historical, or sociocultural considerations distinguishes an anchoring phenomenon in mainstream science curricula from SJSI.

The SJSI of racial health disparities provides a set of important examples for understanding the ways that well-intentioned lessons can inadvertently reinforce problematic dominant ideologies. There are high school science teachers that use sickle cell anemia as an anchoring phenomenon to teach about genetics, a middle grades curriculum that uses high skin cancer rates in Australia as an anchoring phenomenon to teach about the electromagnetic spectrum, and many teachers who include racialized disparities in diabetes, cancer rates, or asthma in their biology curricula. These phenomena can be transformative SJSI, but they also represent a risk for reinforcing problematic false beliefs about race. How teachers work with their students to define the SJSI largely determines which direction these lessons go. Of utmost importance here is how teachers deal with disciplinary boundaries and sociohistorical context.

Countering ideologies of racism As discussed in chapter 1 and revisited at the end of chapter 2, the fields of biology and medicine have contributed a great deal to the ideology of white supremacy by trying to categorize people into subgroups based on superficial phenotypic differences like skin color and hair texture. This practice has been especially pernicious because biologists have maliciously and erroneously formulated human taxonomy as a hierarchy linked with traits like intelligence, temperament, or athleticism. The term for this longstanding and persistent problem is *scientific racism* and it has been around at least since Linnaeus's infamous 18th century text *Systema Naturae*. It is important to note that for as long as scientific racism has existed, there have been critics and dissidents who worked tirelessly to debunk and discredit this dehumanizing work. Some of the earliest people to do this important work were African American scientists working in grassroots and subversive ways—even while chattel slavery was still legal in the US South.[32] But despite repeated debunking, scientific racism has been reinvented within each subsequent paradigm or era in the field of human biology.[33] Even now, as there is consensus within the field of biology that genetics vary as much *within* as they do *across* so-called racial groups, there are 21st century versions of scientific racism. For example, social genomics research, commercial DNA testing, and race-based medicine continue to reinvent debunked ideas about human genetic variation as they pursue dubious connections between genes and social outcomes.[34] Given its persistence in research, it is not surprising that a sizeable fraction of the public still believes the falsehood that racial difference is a sound biological concept and that racial groups are fundamentally different from each other.[35] And there is evidence that bringing up the topic of race in biology class in acritical ways can reinforce these false, but common, beliefs.[36]

Of course, racial difference was constructed as a sociopolitical tool to justify slavery, colonization, and other forms of oppression and exploitation. While its persistence is a source of pain, its social construction implies that humans can also deconstruct race. This does not make racism any less real. Instead, it presents a challenge and an opportunity to biology teachers who believe that it is important to teach about the consequences of racism. Without careful attention to context, teachers may end up accidentally reinforcing false beliefs. This is *not* a suggestion for science teachers to avoid the topic of racism in general or racial health disparities in particular. In fact, as chapter 2 noted, avoidance is often part of the problem.

A quick consideration of the impacts of these false beliefs may inspire teachers to take this challenge head-on. For example, medical technologies like those discussed at the end of chapter 2 suggest that we need to rethink what students learn in biology class. Perhaps even more troubling, research indicates that a shocking proportion of white medical students have false beliefs about the biology of Black people that are rooted in scientific racism and likely influence disparities in treatment for pain and other ailments.[37] Given that it is not possible to be admitted to medical school without exceptional grades in science courses, this is an indictment of the status quo of biology education and a call for taking up anti-racist science pedagogies. So how can science teachers take up the topics of race and racism in a way that avoids reinforcing the ideologies underlying white supremacy? It requires explicitly countering racist ideologies through their teaching.[38]

Teaching that effectively counters false beliefs about racial difference requires science teachers to step outside the boundaries of their disciplines. For example, students should learn how race has been constructed historically as a tool of oppression. If this feels too much like teaching history instead of science, consider dusting off that old lesson about Carolus Linnaeus and teaching about his contributions more honestly. Or consider collaborating with a social studies teacher to link your unit on genetics with a unit they teach about oppression as a way to carefully debunk the common false belief that race is a biological concept. Remember that these units should direct students' gaze toward critiquing those who are responsible for constructing race and then toward justice in the form of imagining critical deconstructions.

Do not be afraid to venture into the realm of public health either. Units on health disparities should foreground the ways systemic racism impacts exposure to pollution or access to healthy food and quality health care. If you teach about gene-linked diseases like sickle-cell anemia, it may be better to frame the issue around inequitable research funding for this disease compared with others. Furthermore, it is important to teach that the sickle cell trait is found in many people who are not racialized as Black (e.g., descendants of certain Mediterranean groups who are racialized as white) and that it is *not* found in the vast majority of people who are racialized as Black. This emphasizes that the ways people are racialized do not neatly correspond with their genotype (or even with their phenotype, oftentimes).[39]

In one popular middle school science curriculum, a unit on electromagnetic radiation uses the prevalence of skin cancer in Australia as an anchoring phenomenon. The unit has a short introduction on melanin, but conveniently avoids the history of settler colonialism and the attempted genocide of Australia's Indigenous peoples. It was that inhumane process that led to so many contextually melanin-deficient peoples populating a region of the world with intense ultraviolet radiation. For students to truly make sense of this phenomenon, teachers need to push past disciplinary boundaries and deal with settler colonialism. Even with the prevalence of skin cancer among people of lighter complexions, people of color who get skin cancer have lower chances of survival, in part, because medical professionals are not taught to diagnose this condition as it appears on darker skin.[40] Given the present discussion, teachers are also likely to notice that there is a risk that this phenomenon could reinforce notions of race as biological without explicit and careful teaching otherwise. There is also a risk of shifting the unit toward gazing at suffering.

The social construction of race is a popular term for a relatively abstract and complex process. The social construction of race has happened in dynamic ways over several hundred years and across multiple contexts. Therefore, teaching this concept requires a great deal of care and planning, just like teaching complex scientific concepts. Just telling students that race is socially constructed will not be any more effective than simply telling them that the laws of classical physics do not apply at the submicroscopic scale in hopes that they will understand quantum mechanics. In the present context, teaching about the social construction of race is also likely to attract the attention of right-wing reactionaries, which underscores the importance of doing this work in collectives.

Fortunately, there are an increasing number of useful resources and examples to support biology teachers in these sorts of lessons. The first episode of the classic PBS documentary, *Race: The Power of Illusion*, is an excellent starting point and is available to check out in many libraries. Marcela Bernal-Munera has replicated and expanded some of the lessons from that documentary in her community college classes for future health professionals.[41] Two of the experts featured in the documentary, Joseph Graves and Alan Goodman, recently published a book that biology teacher David Upegui recommends for science teachers.[42] Upegui and several other visionary high school teachers around the country make deconstructing race a central theme in their curriculum.[43] The Howard Hughes Medical Institute has produced some helpful videos about the genetic basis of skin color variation, which explain how racism has hindered the scientific community's understanding of this phenomenon for generations. Perhaps the best starting place is the STEM Teaching Tools website, which provides excellent science teaching briefs in general, and they have a particularly good one on anti-racist science pedagogy.[44]

Countering ideologies of heteronormativity and ableism   Scientific racism is not the only problematic ideology that we risk reinforcing through otherwise engaging science instruction. Kristen Gunckel describes an engaging elementary school lesson that involves students studying live crayfish. But she also explains how this common type of lesson teaches students the dominant ideology of heterogendered normativity, thus marginalizing people with non-binary gender expressions.[45] Indeed, the way the high school biology curriculum has traditionally dealt with notions of gender and sexuality has been problematic. Similar to notions of race, biology students should learn that gender is a social construction, and that biological sex is not a simple binary either.[46] In fact, biologists understand that there is a great deal of complexity and diversity with respect to the notion of sex at every level of expression from chromosomes to genitals.[47] Fortunately for science teachers, this is another area in which the number of resources available is growing. For example, the website www.genderinclusivebiology.com contains an excellent set of resources put together by three science teachers: Sam Long, Lewis Steller, and River Suh.

When she was earning her professional educator license, high school science teacher Mariel Rancel showed me how biology curricula also reinforce problematic medical definitions of dis/ability. She argued that biology curricula needed to be redesigned with a disability studies perspective, which acknowledges that ability is socially constructed similarly to how categories of race and gender have been created. Indeed, education researchers argue that teachers need to understand how forms of oppression intersect for students who are marginalized by their position in more than one of these social categories.[48] In his research, Phillip Boda argues that disability studies is helpful specifically for science teachers to understand and question how their students are categorized and labeled.[49] Problematic ways of viewing ability are also tied into ideologies of meritocracy and individualism, which are discussed below.

Countering ideologies of capitalism With the NGSS inclusion of engineering practices into science learning standards, design activities have become increasingly popular in science classrooms. In many of these design activities, the scenario positions students as capitalists, the owners of the means of production. They have some product to design, and their central considerations are how it works, what it costs to produce, and what its price will be. The students' goal is profitability. While these activities may sometimes beget high levels of student engagement with the principles of engineering, the hidden curriculum in these lessons is the inculcation of capitalist values. Teachers can take advantage of the engaging aspects of these activities while making some relatively easy shifts in the definition of the problem. In other words, we can invite students to take up engineering in ways that do not prioritize the values of capitalism. For example, in one of my chemistry teaching methods courses, a student teacher designed a clever activity about the separation of mixtures. The premise of this design challenge positioned students as business owners working to recover a profitable material from a mixture with less valuable components (the teacher notes had instructions for a mixture of sand, salt, and iron filings). With a little coaching, the student teacher was able to redefine the problem to achieve the same chemistry learning goals while it communicated different ideological commitments. By posing the hypothetical problem of cleaning up a local park that had been damaged in a storm, this teacher restructured the activity to encourage cooperation, community service, and sustainability instead of maximizing profit through extraction—all without changing much of the laboratory set up. The focus of chapter 4 is illustrating how teachers can make similar moves to modify, appropriate, or extend already existing curricula toward alternate goals. As the NGSS encourage science teachers to incorporate engineering concepts and practices into their curricula, teachers need to consider the values and ideologies they are communicating and how engineering education might include a "dimension of care."[50]

In another popular science activity that can be found in several websites and textbooks, students metaphorically mine for chocolate chips by tearing apart cookies with simple tools, like toothpicks. The lesson is often connected with the NGSS elementary or middle school performance expectations associated with Disciplinary Core Ideas ESS3A: Natural Resources and ESS3C Human Impacts on Earth Systems. The ideological lessons taught by this activity hinge on the ways students are asked to make sense of their role and their relationship to the Earth. Are they asked to maximize the profitability of their mining enterprise? Are they asked to view the Earth as a repository for human consumption? Or are they prompted to ask more critical questions about the extractive economy and the inequitable impact that mining has on some human communities and ecosystems compared with others? In the excellent resource *A People's Curriculum for the Earth*, Bill Bigelow describes a thoughtful approach to engaging high school students directly with a version of this cookie mining activity that was designed by a coal industry organization.[51] In Bigelow's example, students are asked to openly consider the ideological lessons of this activity. Indeed, the ideologies of capitalism and settler colonialism prompt us to view land as a fungible resource that can be traded for money. The mainstream scientific fields of geology and chemistry often align themselves with this unsustainable and harmful view of land that has dispossessed Indigenous people and caused immeasurable ecological harm. The cookie mining activity—and others like it—can be taught in ways that problematize mining practices superficially, while still reinforcing these ideologies. Or students can be explicitly challenged to consider these dominant views of the earth. The Learning-in-Places project (www.learninginplaces.org) provides excellent frameworks and resources for engaging in transformative and anti-colonial science education with elementary school students that are thought-provoking and inspiring for teachers of older students too.[52]

Countering the nature-culture divide When my children were participating in online classes during the COVID-19 pandemic, I overheard an elementary language arts lesson on pronouns. One of my children, who has consistently challenged gender norms at the school and in our household, was questioning the teacher. What I expected to be a conversation about gendered pronouns took a different turn as my child questioned the teacher's insistence that 'it' is the appropriate pronoun for animals. They insisted, "But humans are animals! And we use he, she, and they for humans." Indeed, children learn in science class that humans are part of the animal 'kingdom.' But in dominant Western ideologies, humans are generally treated as separate from nature.[53] For scientists, this means treating nature as the object of their study. For engineers, this means nature is something for humans to exploit, dominate, or control. Megan Bang, a science educator who co-leads the Learning-in-Places project mentioned above, has identified the nature–culture divide as a problematic ideological component of dominant Western science that shows up frequently in science classrooms.[54] When it does, it often positions students' ways of understanding the world (especially those from non-Western cultural traditions) as incorrect, when, in fact, they often reflect more sustainable worldviews.

In phenomenon-based instruction, the framing of natural phenomena can reinforce this problematic ideology. This is important to keep in mind when organizing lessons around SJSI. To return to the Hurricane Katrina example, in Earth or environmental science courses, so-called natural disasters are often a fascinating and relevant topic for students. It is usually straightforward to align these lessons with standards. But in the twenty-first century, we cannot understand earthquakes, hurricanes, or tsunamis as occurring separately from human society. Students should be asked to consider how human activity is increasing the severity, frequency, or scope of these events. Indeed, this consideration is included in the NGSS disciplinary core idea of Earth systems and human activity. Even beyond the causes of natural disasters, students should also consider how humans influence their effects. When an earthquake or tsunami damages a nuclear power plant, it can cause radioactive contamination, as was the case in Fukushima, Japan in 2011. When a hurricane scatters debris from a toxic waste dump, it exacerbates the harms of environmental racism because of where these sites tend to be located. This was the case in New Orleans during Hurricane Katrina in 2005 and Hurricane Betsy more than 40 years prior. The well-being of humans is ultimately (and intimately) wrapped up with and dependent upon the well-being of Earth and more-than-human inhabitants.

Define SJSI with Students to Interrogate Systems

Perhaps the most prevalent problematic ideologies in STEM education are individualism and meritocracy.[55] This set of beliefs, explaining how the characteristics and behaviors of individual people are solely responsible for their life outcomes, is false. Moreover, there is some evidence that students who espouse these beliefs misinterpret their own successes and failures, often to their own detriment.[56] There is also a tendency for students who study STEM in college to feel less social agency.[57] Therefore, it is important for science teachers to define SJSI with their students in ways that interrogate systems, rather than assigning individual responsibility for social problems. In fact, teaching students to think systematically about SJSI is well aligned with the call for students to apply systems thinking to technical problems.[58] This is the only way for teaching about SJSI to promote realistic collective interventions for our most vexing problems.

The area of nutrition and the practice of healthy eating are common bases for phenomena in recent biology curricula. There are myriad ways to frame healthy eating that recognize injustices in food systems, but not all these framings are equally likely to engage students with critically thinking about the intersections of social and ecological justice, food, and sciences. For example, consider a teacher who, in paying attention to how students spend their time, notices that many students frequently eat at a nearby corporate fast-food chain or tend to eat a bag of spicy-hot chips for breakfast on their way into first period. In one approach, the teacher might view these as a bad habits that students have developed because they do not understand the biological concepts underlying nutrition. They assume that students simply need to understand how different foods provide human bodies with different ratios of vitamins, minerals, fiber, and energy. The teacher may also assume that students are unaware of healthier options, but that education may be able to guide them in the right direction. In this common line of thinking, making healthier food choices becomes the framing for teaching students, in NGSS terminology, to "use a model to illustrate that cellular respiration is a chemical process whereby the bonds of food molecules and oxygen molecules are broken and the bonds in new compounds are formed resulting in a net transfer of energy."[59] But this hypothetical framing of the reasons for learning biology conveys several problematic assumptions that compromise teachers' ability to challenge the roots of social injustice and to provide students with opportunities to construct their own visions of alternative futures.

Assuming students have unhealthy eating habits that are rooted in their ignorance is a deficit perspective similar to those views of students critiqued in the previous chapter. A deficit framing of the phenomenon of nutrition perpetuates a tendency for science education to adopt paternalistic goals for minoritized students. Katie Kirchgasler explains how science education for racially minoritized students has historically focused on practical issues of health and hygiene rather than academic topics found in the curriculum in schools that serve wealthier and whiter students.[60] This approach makes false, racist assumptions about the ability of youth and their parents to care for themselves and each other. It also systematically denies students opportunities in science classes to demonstrate their sophisticated forms of sense-making. Furthermore, framing the problem of healthy eating in terms of individual choices obscures broader problems of an unjust and unsustainable food system. Jomo Mutegi makes this point in his analysis of a well-intentioned middle grades food curriculum that does not engage students in considering how the food system is entangled in the ongoing oppression of the African diaspora.[61]

For these reasons, many justice-oriented teachers eschew an individualized framing of this problem and instead focus on the SJSI of food deserts, or neighborhoods where healthy food (like fresh produce) is hard to access. Food deserts are caused by systemic racism in urban planning, housing, and the political economies of food. For that reason, activists like Karen Washington use the term *food apartheid* to highlight the systemic and political character of this problem.[62] This shift illustrates a key principle that teachers should keep in mind when it comes to defining SJSI: *locate the problem in systems rather than in students or their communities.*

Even defining food deserts as an SJSI can become a deficit framing where students locate the problem in their communities rather than in broader systems. Science lessons about nutrition that do not locate the problem in systems may inadvertently send marginalized students the message that they should replace familiar and comfortable foods with those that are currently trendy among upper middle class white people for their purported health benefits. Furthermore, food desert framings can obscure the interconnections of the larger food system with a narrow focus on the consumption of food while ignoring its production and transport. The bigger picture of the global capitalist food system is that it is set up to maximize profits by exploiting and dispossessing people, other animals, and the Earth at every turn. For these reasons, framing the SJSI as food justice or food sovereignty is more likely to engage students with both the role of the enterprise of science (intertwined with big agribusiness) in contributing to injustices. It is also a better framing for considering the potential for scientific practices and concepts (along with other ways of knowing) to address nutrition in sustainable ways.

While the example of food illustrates the complexity of SJSI teaching, a story from an afterschool meeting of youth activists illustrates a straightforward way to deal with the complexity. This example also shows how working with community organizations can help science teachers to engage their classes in the interrogation of systems while affirming students' ways of being. Several years ago, I attended a meeting where educators and organizers were working with high school students to plan a city-wide youth-led forum on social justice projects in school settings. At the time, there was a national boycott against corporate fast-food chains to protest their manipulation of the price of tomatoes. Their demand for low prices relied on pressuring growers to further exploit farmworkers, most of whom were immigrants to the US from Central America or the Caribbean. The group of students, composed mostly of Latine and Black youth, was discussing this boycott when one student activist complained in a lighthearted way about not being able to participate. He argued that the food was too tasty and too cheap to give up, which prompted laughter and nods of agreement from several of his peers. Besides, he continued, there were no affordable or convenient alternatives in the neighborhood. He challenged the group to consider that fast-food chains were the only way to stave off hunger with only a few dollars in his pocket and only a few minutes between the end of school and various meetings, events, and family commitments. One of the adult organizers in the room responded with a gentle challenge. He pointed out that in most neighborhoods in the city, even those harmed by food apartheid, it is possible to construct a healthy and affordable sandwich from familiar ingredients. He gave a couple of examples: a loaf of whole wheat bread and a jar of peanut butter could go a long way or a *bolillo con aguacate* (a roll with avocado) makes a delicious and healthy snack. Not all the young people in the room were persuaded that these ingredients were affordable, tasty, or readily available. Others were skeptical that they would replace their fast-food favorites permanently. But nonetheless, the group reached a consensus to participate in the boycott and try out alternative snacks.

There are several lessons that science teachers can take from this story; indeed this small moment still has a lasting impact on me years later. While the organizer acknowledged the existence of disparities in access to healthy food, his suggestion to a group of youth that they could replace corporate fast food with familiar ingredients highlights that healthy eating should be culturally sustaining. All cultures have healthy food traditions appropriate for daily sustenance and some that are more indulgent for special occasions. A science lesson should not teach students that family traditions are making them unhealthy. This meeting occurred long before the craze of avocado toast swept across high-priced coffee shops in gentrifying neighborhoods, even finding its way onto the menus of some corporate fast-food chains. In fact, at the time, the mainstream view of avocadoes (which have been a healthy part of Central American diets for millennia) was that their high fat content made them unhealthy. This example shows us that rather than marginalized communities needing to learn about nutrition, health food fads often involve privileged white people co-opting the traditional foods of communities of color.

The context of the organizer's suggestion is also important. It was not a conversation about changing individual eating habits for improving personal health. It was a conversation about participating in a collective organized effort to protest and improve the exploitative, unhealthy, and unsustainable food system that is controlled by fast-food corporations and giant agribusiness. Students should not be led to believe that their individual choices will change these systems. Instead, they should consider how meaningful change comes from collectively organized efforts that they can participate in or even initiate themselves. Within this context, people often decide to improve personal habits as a beneficial side effect of the ethical and political commitments they are developing—not with the illusion that better individual choices are the solution to a systemic problem. For example, being present in that meeting deepened my own commitments. My initial participation in the boycott led me to avoid eating at those fast-food chains ever since.

This example ultimately illustrates why science teachers should consider working with students to define SJSI related to nutrition in terms of food sovereignty or food justice. These terms locate the problem in systems not students or their communities. They also imply that addressing these problems requires collective action rather than changing individual habits. To define the SJSI with students, teachers should consider how to foreground students' knowledge and the assets of their families and communities. One possibility may be to ask students to have a discussion at home about a healthy dish that has been popular among their immediate or extended family. If students bring recipes or descriptions of these dishes to share with each other, it could begin a conversation about what makes food healthy and about the sourcing and cost of the ingredients. From that point, documentary films or short readings could introduce the concepts of food justice or food sovereignty. Even cookbooks could be a source of inspiration here, as there have been a series of recent books that weave together short, readable passages on these concepts with recipes that draw on heritage cooking in the traditions of Mexican, African American, and Indigenous communities. Books like *Decolonize Your Diet* by Luz Calvo and Catriona Rueda Esquibel, *Vegan Soul Kitchen* by Bryant Terry, and *The Sioux Chef's Indigenous Kitchen* by Sean Sherman and Beth Dooley may be good resources for teachers.[63] There are also several well-written books that weave together concepts of biochemistry with recipes to help teachers make connections between food and their content, with appropriate scientific depth for high school courses. Once students and teachers have a shared understanding of the SJSI, then it is the teacher's responsibility to provide students with opportunities and scaffolding to make sense of scientific phenomena embedded in these SJSI in ways that afford them intellectual respect.

Defining SJSI is a process that is done collaboratively between teachers and students in class. This process is neither teacher-centered nor student-centered, but instead recognizes that teaching and learning are always co-constructed activities where both teachers and students have important contributions.[64]

Processes where students are asked to identify or define problems without much direction from the teacher are often romanticized as true inquiry or the student-centered ideal. But allowing students to define problems without guidance or direction often reproduces inequities because students are also influenced by dominant ideologies and therefore may come up with deficit framings of the problem themselves. Specifically in the context of science classrooms, open-ended approaches sometimes fail to account for the responsibility of teachers to provide students with access to disciplinary ways of understanding problems. This oversight can have serious implications for students' academic success. Students working on their own are less likely to frame a problem in a way that facilitates meaningful engagement with science and engineering practices nor the disciplinary core ideas of the sciences (biology in the nutrition example). Table 3.1 summarizes some of the principles and examples described in the latter half of this chapter to encourage science teachers to work with students to refine the ways they define SJSI in their classes.

TABLE 3.1 Shifting from phenomenon-driven to problem-posing science education

Example categories of commonly decontextualized phenomena		*Examples of large contextualized problems*		*(Re)define SJSI with students to…*
Diseases and their causes (e.g., cancers, diabetes; genetics, diet)		health disparities food apartheid medical apartheid		Debunk race as a biological concept and adopt an anti-racist stance.
Material lifecycles (e.g., mining, disposal, recycling)	Interrogate systems →	environmental racism weapons & war	Challenge problematic ideologies & imagine justice →	Support movements for climate justice, food sovereignty, and peace.
Generating energy (e.g., renewable versus non-renewable sources)		land & water rights climate change		Imagine a just transition away from an extractive economy.

ADDRESSING SJSI: PEDAGOGIES OF HOPE

Some teachers avoid dealing with controversial issues in their classroom for fear of inciting despair as students grapple with the weight of oppression. This is a valid concern; classrooms should be places where students experience joy, curiosity, and wonder. Their feelings, more than any equation or concept, will likely be what students remember about school learning experiences. But deep, meaningful emotions like joy and wonder are not inspired by superficial lessons nor boring phenomena that gloss over the complexities of the beautiful yet profoundly unjust and unsustainable world in which we live. For this reason, critical educator Jeff Duncan-Andrade draws on Cornell West to distinguish between education that peddles hokey hope versus teaching that inspires critical hope.[65]

For science teachers, cultivating critical hope involves sitting with a series of tensions in our work, which is the focus of chapter 5. Critical hope requires equitable academic expectations so that students have access to real opportunities that currently exist within the problematic structures of schooling and the STEM pipeline. At the same time, students should understand these opportunities as openings to create something new. It is difficult work for teachers to provide students with access to canonical, sanctioned forms of knowledge and skills while also supporting them to deviate from (and critique) these sanctioned forms of knowledge production. It requires courage to position students as experts and support the type of imaginative creativity that school often stifles.

Critical hope in science education implies encouraging engagement in and beyond the sciences. This requires humility about the role of the sciences in shaping just and sustainable futures. Research that has emerged from the collective of teachers, scientists, and organizers with whom I work has shown us the importance of teaching about environmental justice victories.[66] We have grappled with the very limited role of science in these victories, and we have also heard from organizers that understanding the science was important for them. By connecting with community organizations, science teachers can provide their students with opportunities for real engagement in issues that matter. This kind of connection between school and community can also help students, especially those from marginalized social groups, to see themselves as part of centuries-long traditions against colonialism and oppression.

In teaching students that race is socially constructed or that climate change is caused by an extractive economy, we are also teaching them that social movements can change these conditions. Furthermore, we are teaching them that the role of science, technology, and engineering in these efforts is fraught. Problem-based approaches to STEM teaching often imply to students that science or engineering are the solutions to our problems. Teachers who see themselves as promoters of the scientific enterprise frame science as inherently benevolent and beneficial. Promoting STEM as the solution to our problems is peddling hokey hope. The examples above illustrate how, in reality, the scientific enterprise has played an important role in causing our most pressing problems. Likewise, they show that there are not simple technical solutions. In defining SJSI with students, it is important for teachers to leave the role of scientific knowledge or engineering practices as an object of inquiry. Rather than asking students to engineer a solution to a complex problem, we might ask them to consider how scientific knowledge or engineering practices might be useful in addressing the SJSI *and* how they might have contributed to an SJSI in the first place. In transition from defining a SJSI with students to diving deep into some of the relevant scientific ideas and practices, it may be useful to encourage students to think of this process as applying a scientific lens. The focus of the next chapter is planning learning activities and assessments that scaffold students applying scientific lenses to SJSI—without requiring a teacher to design an entire curriculum from scratch.

CHAPTER 4

From SJSI to Curriculum and Assessment

The goal of chapter 3 was to inspire exciting ideas about potential SJSI curriculum and to inform processes for engaging students and the school community to define SJSIs in local contexts. My proudest work as a high school teacher emerged from such a process, culminating in the soil project described in chapter 1. In that project, students presented results from their authentic scientific studies of contamination in the local environment to their neighbors, parents, and other community members at a family science night. That project began several years earlier with a dialogue between community organizers and science teachers to inform curriculum that was connected to campaigns for environmental justice. The students' presentation focused on analysis of data they collected about the local environmental impact of coal power plants recently shuttered by grassroots community efforts. It took me many years to be able to lead a project like this in chemistry class. Along the way, I had to learn new science, immerse myself in local politics, and develop teaching practices and curriculum over time. One of the most important things I learned was that rather than curriculum contributing to the campaign to shut down the coal power plants (as I originally hoped), the grassroots campaign enabled and enhanced the curriculum. More than anything, this kind of teaching required building relationships with community members, organizers, and colleagues across multiple institutions.

This chapter focuses on examples that may be more approachable as starting points for teachers. Even though they do not have as many moving parts as a full-fledged youth participatory science project, the examples in this chapter nonetheless position students to use disciplinary practices and concepts to address meaningful issues. The examples in this chapter can be done by individual teachers or through the collaboration of small groups of teachers within the same building. Rather than presenting a series of disconnected activities, the chapter embeds these examples within a structure for planning to teach science toward alternative futures over the course of an entire school year—and even in ways that are vertically aligned across students' entire high school experience.

In other words, this chapter focuses on how to bring exciting ideas for SJSI projects to life—even within the challenges and limitations that science teachers face in schools. Specifically, this chapter describes strategies for (1) developing assessments, (2) working with content area standards, and (3) modifying published curricula to meet goals oriented toward justice and sustainability. For teachers who already take up SJSI in their classrooms or who feel ready to dive into the approaches advocated by this book, I hope this chapter helps prepare you for difficult conversations with skeptical colleagues or administrators. For teachers who feel skeptical, worried, or overwhelmed about the ideas in this book, I hope this chapter makes teaching about SJSI feel within your reach.

AUTHENTIC ASSESSMENTS, STANDARDS, AND BACKWARD PLANNING

Most teachers are required to align their curriculum to learning standards that, despite recent improvements, are still representative of the canon critiqued in chapter 1. Furthermore, students' opportunities and school accountability measures are usually tied to assessments imposed from outside of the classroom. Planning curriculum that addresses SJSI does *not* imply neglecting these realities. Instead, teachers can negotiate the tensions between standardization and responsiveness by thinking about standards and assessment strategically.

Standards are most problematic when they reinscribe narrow notions of what counts as science learning. This often becomes the case when curricula treat standards as the vision that guides teaching and learning. In contrast, within curricula organized around SJSI, teachers can use standards to make smaller decisions about how to approach complex and multifaceted issues. Similarly, assessments are most harmful when they are high-stakes or are used to compare students' performance against others. But assessments that consider how students' learning might be meaningful in their lives outside of school are important opportunities for teachers and students to evaluate and reflect on their work together. The former approach to assessment is normative and punitive, while the latter can be informative and generative.

Authentic assessments have been defined in many ways, but in this book, the term encompasses two basic criteria. First, an authentic assessment prompts students to do something or produce an artifact that matters outside of their science classroom. Secondly, an authentic assessment provides teachers with information about how students are taking up scientific practices and ideas, which includes those valued by the standards. Of course, even assessments that do not mean much outside of the classroom can be valuable tools for informing day-to-day instruction. In fact, a teacher will need to frequently use this kind of formative classroom assessment along the way toward a more authentic assessment.

In one well-known approach to lesson planning, the starting point for planning is the end goal. Backward design encourages teachers to start their plans from the summative assessment to make sure that learning activities give students' the opportunities and support they need to build their knowledge and skills to that end.[1] With this approach in mind, a group of my colleagues created an authentic assessment to act as a capstone at the end of students' senior year. They called this assessment the "Fire Project," a name meant to evoke a burning desire that students feel about a particular issue in their community or in the world. The Fire Project was originally envisioned by Angela Sangha-Gadsden and Jackson Potter, who developed it as a cross-curricular project between English and history and then expanded it to several other content areas with several other colleagues around 2010. One of those colleagues, David Hernandez, has been central in its ongoing evolution and implementation. Along with David, Amy Levingston, and several others have sustained the Fire Project for more than 10 graduating classes. The Fire Project has several components that ask students to bring together academic skills with sociopolitical action on an issue about which they are passionate. It is meant as an assessment of students' learning trajectory across four years of high school. Like the soil project mentioned above, it is an end goal, which, in the spirit of backward design, is also a starting point. And in that same spirit, the remainder of this chapter is organized to trace backward from the Fire Project to successively smaller assessments and activities designed to build toward it.

THE SOPHOMORE CAPSTONE

When the Fire Project was created by the teachers at our school who taught seniors, I was a member of the tenth grade team. As a member of this team, I helped to design the sophomore capstone project as a formative assessment marking the halfway point to the Fire Project. In the sophomore capstone project, students choose an item that has substantial meaning, importance, or utility in their life and create a museum exhibit about that item. The idea is for each student to conceptualize a speculative museum exhibit that teaches subsequent generations about our society through key cultural artifacts. Museums can be problematic institutions that celebrate colonialism by unethically displaying stolen colonial artifacts. Just like other educational institutions, they can instead be more critically conscious about the stories they tell and ethical about how they collect, represent, or return artifacts and engage with the public. In this project, we chose to embrace the potential for students to have fun with a speculative future where they positioned themselves to examine an item that was important in their present life.

Whereas students are encouraged to apply the most relevant disciplinary lenses to complete their Fire Project, the sophomore capstone project is shared across most tenth grade classes and therefore has components that focus on each of the content areas. For science teachers, projects in which students choose their topic present a challenge because there often are not obvious connections between students' interests and our content areas. In my curriculum planning, I have found three processes to be helpful in meeting this challenge. The first process, illustrated in the next section, is to reconsider how our content areas are useful in the world to open a wider range of possible authentic assessments. The section after that uses the chemistry component of the sophomore capstone project as an example of the second process, which is to use learning standards to focus the design of an original assessment. The third process is to repurpose published or widely used science activities to build toward the authentic assessment. The latter half of this chapter illustrates this process with a unit that built toward the sophomore capstone project where the unit assessment asked students to write both a conventional lab report and a letter to an elected official. In other words, this chapter illustrates planning for the lofty goal of a senior-year project that weaves together academics and activism by tracing back to repurposing common tenth grade chemistry activities (see Figure 4.1).

FIGURE 4.1 Backward mapping from assessments.

Fire Project:
As a graduation capstone, students choose an issue about which they are passionate, study that issue across disciplines, and take some kind of action to address it.

Sophomore Capstone Project:
At the halfway mark to the Fire Project, students create a speculative museum exhibit analyzing an item that is important to them. For chemistry class, students complete two assignments that become part of the exhibit:
1. Chemical Composition Analysis
2. Environmental Impact Study

Unit X

SJSI Unit: Metal Extraction for Technological Use:
Students write a letter to an elected official about regulations in the materials economy and a lab report about an experiment with copper.

Unit Y

Unit Z

RECONCEPTUALIZING CONTENT AREAS

A year or two before the creation of the sophomore capstone project, I was co-leading an advisory lesson in a homeroom setting with ninth graders. The daily lesson my co-teacher and I were given by school counselors asked students to imagine who they wanted to be in five or ten years and express their answer in the form of a collage. We gave students a stack of magazines and construction paper for the task. As students' collages started to take shape, I was troubled by what I saw. Students were defining their future selves by the cars they wanted to drive and the clothes and accessories they wanted to wear. I was disturbed by the idea that students were defining their future selves by their consumption of luxury goods. Some might attribute the results of this activity to the fact that almost all the students came from financially challenging situations. It is easy to understand why youth from economically dispossessed communities might imagine futures of material prosperity. On the other hand, it is dishonest to suggest that affluent students are any less enraptured by the lure of materialism. In fact, they are more immersed in it as a fundamental part of the dominant culture in society. When I was in ninth grade myself, I was neither affluent nor enduring hardship, and I daydreamed about material wealth and the things I could buy as an adult. Even though my parents explicitly and regularly challenged materialism, I (like other young people) was inundated with advertisements and messaging that encouraged consumerism.

Reflecting on the advisory activity with students helped me understand that the future-looking collage assignment guided students in the direction of material consumption. Magazines are chock full of advertisements for consumer goods like cars, jewelry, designer clothes, and fragrances. I suspected that, given these starting materials, groups of people from various economic positions would likely produce similar collages. Aspiring to break free from economic hardship is different from defining our future selves by the consumer goods we own, but these two are conflated in an economic system built around never-ending consumption. My observations that day led me to realize that my content area, chemistry, could play a role in disrupting the problematic ways in which our society connects our value as humans and our happiness in life to the consumption of goods. Indeed, Sara Tolbert and Alexandra Schindel have argued that science teaching can challenge pervasive consumerism.[2]

Chemistry is often depicted in popular culture as the mixing of colorful bubbly solutions in oddly shaped glassware. In school, students associate chemistry with the periodic table and Bunsen burners and dreaded stoichiometry problems. Some chemists refer to their discipline as the "central science" for the ways in which viewing the world at the molecular or atomic level can be a link between physical and biological phenomena. Chemical educators refer to a triangle of connections between macroscopic observations of materials, submicroscopic particles, and symbolic representations of the latter to explain the former.[3] But reflecting on the collage activity helped me to expand (and in some ways, simplify) my understanding of chemistry: fundamentally, chemistry deals with the material world. With this perspective, I came to view part of my work as getting students to think critically about their interactions with the Earth and its materials—which included problematizing extraction and the consumption of goods. I began to frame my classes as a challenge to DuPont's famous slogan, "Better things, for better living…through chemistry." Instead, I wanted students to consider the Latin American concept of *buen vivir* or living well.[4] There are three obvious distinctions between the values reflected by *buen vivir* versus those implied by DuPont's slogan. Dupont's slogan emphasizes the notion of "better" and it connects better living to "things" and to "chemistry." In contrast, *buen vivir* does not imply that we seek never-ending improvement or comparison. It also does not suggest that things nor chemistry are what make life good. *Buen vivir* emphasizes collective well-being of human and more-than-human communities. It is a cooperative, rather than competitive view. It seeks good relationships with the places, people, and communities we share life with.[5]

My realization that learning chemistry could play a role in challenging rampant materialism helped me see the potential for my class to contribute to the sophomore capstone project. The sophomore capstone project begins with students selecting an item that is important to their daily life. The range of students' choices was wide; some selected their favorite sneakers or other clothing items, cell phones or other electronic devices, jewelry, or cosmetic products. Other students selected tools, instruments, or items related to food or cooking or to their practice of a particular artform or sport. Reconceiving chemistry as an opportunity to challenge students to think about their relationship with the Earth's materials, my colleagues and I set out to design an assignment that could inspire thinking of that kind while also aligning with learning standards. I encourage teachers of physics, biology, or other disciplines to take up a process like this to rethink your content area. Some starting points for this exercise are suggested in the next chapter.

AUTHENTIC ASSESSMENTS USE STANDARDS AS GUIDEPOSTS

One reason that the sophomore capstone project has been sustained for more than a decade is that teachers have been able to show administrators that the learning activities are standards-aligned. Even as chapter 1 critiques the NGSS, standards can be a helpful tool for focusing multifaceted curriculum to enable the design of lesson plans with more well-defined goals. The original sophomore capstone project was designed before the adoption of the NGSS, but the two assignments we designed turned out to be amenable to alignment in some ways. Specifically, the chemistry class contribution to the sophomore capstone project had two components that aligned nicely with performance expectations (PE) constructed from the three strands of the NGSS (see table 4.1). Readers familiar with the NGSS might notice that these two PE are unfamiliar. Rather than selecting from the enumerated performance expectations included on the standards website (like HS-PS1-1 or HS-ESS3-2), I wove together one science and engineering practice (underlined in table 4.1) with a disciplinary core idea (in bold), and a cross cutting concept (italicized). This fits with the intention behind

TABLE 4.1 NGSS performance expectations written for sophomore capstone project

Assignment	Assignment description	NGSS performance expectations (PE)*
Chemical composition analysis	Students choose one component material of their item for the sophomore capstone project and (1) explain which of the material's properties make it suitable for application in their chosen item, and (2) explain how the chemical composition and structures of the material (including bonds and intermolecular forces) give rise to those particular properties.	Construct and revise an explanation of how the **properties of materials are determined by their composition and structures** *at the atomic and molecular levels, including electrical forces within and between atoms.*
Environmental impact study	Students describe the lifecycle of the material they analyzed in the chemical composition analysis. They use the phases of the materials economy including extraction, production, distribution, consumption, and disposal to assess the environmental impact of consuming this material in consideration of its entire life cycle.	Obtain and communicate information about the **use and conservation of materials and energy** *to evaluate the sustainability of a process or technology.*

* Note: These are not taken from the example PE included in the NGSS. They are built from grade-level progression statements of the three strands, with science and engineering practices underlined, **disciplinary core ideas in bold**, and *cross-cutting concepts italicized*.

the NGSS: to encourage teachers to creatively take up the three dimensions together. The standards were not meant to limit teachers only to the exemplar PE that are published on the NGSS website.[6]

One of the most important changes between the NGSS and previous science education standards was the elevation of science and engineering practices to the same level of priority as disciplinary core ideas and cross cutting concepts. In fact, several prominent scholars in science education argue that the prioritization of teaching practices creates openings for equity-oriented teaching.[7] Indeed, for the sophomore capstone project, focusing on constructing explanations (NGSS Practice #6) and obtaining, evaluating, and communicating information (NGSS Practice #8) allowed us to design assessments that organized students' chemistry learning around an object that was meaningful to them. The articulation of these practices allowed us to focus. We were able to move from a wide range of possible assessments to something specific that allowed students to take up scientific ideas and practices in a context that was meaningful to them outside of class.

Advocates of the NGSS recommend bundling DCI like this to support students' ability to explain a phenomenon.[8] By "bundling" together a PE expectation that focused on a chemistry DCI (PS1.A) with a DCI from Earth and space sciences (ESS3.A), we also mitigated the tendency of the NGSS to separate the advantageous properties of designed materials from their negative consequences. The NGSS PE are not intended as lesson objectives, but instead, they provide guidance, at a broad level, for the kinds of competencies students can develop across grade-level bands of science education. This fits with a backward mapping approach because planning for instruction begins with designs for what teachers want students to be able to do at the end of a unit or school year. Then teachers sequence activities that can lead students toward those pursuits. With this approach in mind, we had to consider how sophomore students could be prepared to write up the two chemistry components of the capstone project (the chemical composition analysis and environmental impact study) across their tenth grade year.

The sophomore capstone project represents an authentic assignment because it creates opportunities for students to think deeply about an artifact that they identify as important to their life outside of the classroom, while also giving teachers an opportunity to assess the ways in which students are taking up scientific practices and ideas. Given that this assessment is responsive to students' choices and positions chemistry as an opportunity to rethink our relationship to the material world, there was no published curriculum I could find to build effectively toward these specific goals. At the same time, it was not feasible for my colleagues and me to design an entire year of chemistry learning activities from scratch. To reconcile goals that prioritize context with curricula that prioritize standards, teachers can take up backward planning in ways that thoughtfully situate existing (published) science learning activities within historical, political, and cultural context. Science learning activities focused on the co-construction of practices and ideas are designed to teach students to *do* science. This is a good thing. What are often missing from published curricula are opportunities for students to consider how doing science is relevant to their lives and communities or how the enterprise of science operates in the world.[9] Furthermore, curricula that try to build in relevance almost always fail to place scenarios in realistic historical and political context.

To be fair, it can be difficult for science curriculum to address context in sufficient depth without veering too far into the realm of social studies lessons. One of the ways to address context while remaining focused on teaching the sciences is to emphasize the consideration of what values, assumptions, and methods are implicit in *doing* science.[10] This approach shifts the goals of the curriculum away from enculturating students into the disciplines of science. Instead, the goal is to give students opportunities to appreciate scientific contributions, critique the enterprise of science, and try-out/try-on approaches to science that seem useful in their lives. The idea is to teach from within the constraints of school science toward alternative futures.

The sophomore capstone project was originally conceived as a midway point that built toward the senior capstone Fire Project. Correspondingly, tenth grade chemistry needed a sequence of learning activities that would prepare students to successfully complete chemical composition analyses and environmental impact reports that constituted the chemistry portion of the sophomore capstone. I anticipated that several students would choose electronic items for their sophomore capstone project, and science standards tend to focus on the properties and reactions of elements. At the intersection of those two ideas, I designed a unit focused on the metals that are used in devices like mobile phones and video game consoles. I knew a substantial number of my students were interested in mobile phones and video games, and the materials from which those technologies are built raises a number of important geopolitical issues. The SJSI for this unit was the extraction of metals from the Earth for technological use.

I relied on the newly developed NGSS to focus my planning while at the same time keeping critiques of standards at the front of my mind. The following discussion shows how lessons can challenge the ideologies embedded in disciplinary core ideas from table 4.1 while still supporting students to meet the associated performance expectation. Consider this excerpt from the framework that served as the basis for the NGSS:

> Materials important to modern technological societies are not uniformly distributed across the planet (e.g., oil in the Middle East, gold in California). Most elements exist in Earth's crust at concentrations too low to be extracted, but in some locations—where geological processes have concentrated them—extraction is economically viable (NRC, 2012, p. 191).

Though this statement provides a clear example of how standards are not visionary for teachers who prioritize issues of justice, it may still be helpful in focusing planning within the constraints of school science. The statement suggests that the decision about whether to extract materials from the Earth is a geologic-economic calculation and takes for granted that whoever decides to extract materials has the right to do so. But the examples they reference tell a different story. Petroleum extraction in the Middle East has been at the heart of violent US imperialism in regional political struggles for decades.[11] And the famous gold rush in California began on the lands of the Indigenous Nisenan peoples in the immediate aftermath of the US claiming these lands in an unjust war against Mexico.[12] Despite this problematic lack of context, the framework acknowledges that these purportedly economic and geologic decisions have social and political consequences, if not also causes. The statement referenced in table 4.1 above is followed with an example:

> All forms of energy production and other resource extraction have associated economic, social, environmental, and geopolitical costs and risks, as well as benefits. New technologies and regulations can change the balance of these factors—for example, scientific modeling of the long-term environmental impacts of resource use can help identify potential problems and suggest desirable changes in the patterns of use (NRC, 2012, p. 191).

One of the key considerations missing from this statement is who bears the risks, pays the costs, or who benefits from the extraction of Earth's materials. There is no consideration of how political power creates (or removes) new regulations or how values determine the design of scientific models and inform what constitutes "desirable changes in the patterns of use." The very notion of "desirable changes" indicates that values and politics are inseparable from the actual practice of science and the application of scientific modeling to make decisions.

The principles for defining SJSI articulated in the previous chapter can be helpful in posing the topics described by this DCI in ways that are connected with students' interests (for example in mobile phones and video game consoles). In defining the SJSI as the extraction of metals for technological use, the aim was to interrogate systems (the politics of the materials economy), challenge problematic ideologies (colonialism, extractive capitalism), and imagine justice (fair trade, rematriation of Indigenous land, just transition). But existing curricula do not frame the phenomena this way, so how can teachers plan units around SJSI without the time or autonomy to build their curriculum from scratch?

REPURPOSING PUBLISHED ACTIVITIES

The principles in this chapter suggest that this process can begin by designing an authentic assessment and then mapping backward. In planning learning activities to build skills and understanding related to the assessment, teachers can use a mixture of published activities that they adapt with some supplemental or complementary activities that they design. Here I share an example of what this can look like from a unit on extracting metals for technological use. One year when I was teaching this unit, one of the US Senators from our state proposed a bill that would require the US Securities and Exchange Commission to regulate how publicly traded companies reported the sources of the mineral resources they used to manufacture their products.[13] The legislation's goal was to increase transparency in supply chains and to discourage human rights abuses that often accompany mineral extraction. The news of the legislation inspired an authentic assessment that asked students to write a letter to this senator expressing their point of view about the underlying issues. Student letters were required to share their chemical and political understandings of extracting metals from the Earth. The politics of this issue are complex. More regulation of the materials economy generally offers some protection against the most egregious examples of exploitation and pollution. And yet this regulation generally does nothing to fundamentally change the exploitative relationships between wealthy mining companies and the lands and peoples from whom they extract their wealth. Given this already complicated context, I was worried that the letter assignment would not provide enough space for students to elaborate their understandings of the chemistry phenomena involved. So, I also planned for them to write a more conventional laboratory report to form a two-part assessment. Together these two parts fulfilled my two criteria for authentic assessments. The letter connected students' science learning with meaningful issues outside of our class, and the lab report gave me an extra opportunity to understand and provide feedback on how they were taking up scientific skills and practices.

Supporting students to be successful on assessments like the metal extraction lab report and letter to an elected official also requires careful planning across the preceding unit. In my first few years in the classroom, I made the mistake of assigning challenging writing assignments as homework. Difficult assignments—especially those that are highly schooled or less applicable outside of academic settings (like lab reports)—should be done in school with teacher and peer support. With my colleagues, we figured out how to scaffold practices and concepts across the unit in ways that allowed us to reflect on the values, assumptions, and methods of the sciences (see table 4.2).

To plan activities to support student success with the letter and lab report, we looked to published chemistry and Earth science curricula that addressed the phenomena of metal mining or refining. For example, *ChemCom*, published by the American Chemical Society, has a unit where students consider the merits of using coins versus paper currency to focus on the properties of metal materials.[14] In one version of that unit, there are several laboratory activities that prompt students to construct understandings of the properties of metallic elements as they relate to their atomic structures, the periodic table, and the reactions they undergo. I noticed that students found these activities engaging, even as they consistently found the larger question driving the unit to be painfully boring. There are also several curricula that include laboratory activities to model the extraction of copper metal from the ore malachite. I adapted one from the *Science and Sustainability* textbook written by the Science Education for Public Understanding Program (SEPUP) and published by Lab-Aids.[15] Both published curricula include some social context and encourage environmental considerations. Even still, supporting students to meet the goals of the assessment required cobbling activities from various published curricula with substantial reframing and adaptation. It also required designing additional activities to address histories of colonialism and current disparities in political and economic power—themes that are not commonly found in science curricula or standards.

Starting from the two final assessments, I decided to modify an activity from *Science and Sustainability* in which students chemically reduced malachite, a copper ore, to isolate copper metal. This served as the laboratory activity for the final lab report because it focused our inquiry into the chemical byproducts and reactions involved in isolating a technologically important metallic element from its naturally occurring form. Being a textbook that emphasized sustainability, the activity in *Science and Sustainability* included accompanying analysis questions that prompted students to notice the relatively large amount of solution phase waste produced compared to the tiny amount of copper recovered. The readings and prompts that surrounded this activity also pointed toward global inequities and connecting those with overconsumption in affluent countries.[16] But the analysis questions asked students to consider the viewpoint of executives from the copper refining industry, rather than the impacted communities, as is often the case in mass-produced curricula. The activity itself could also be described as what science teachers often call a "cookbook activity," in which students are asked to carefully follow prescribed steps to achieve an expected result.

In customizing the activity for my students, I made several changes. To encourage students to think first about the environmental impact on the surrounding communities, I paired the activity with excerpts from non-governmental reports about environmental injustices and metal mining around the world. These class readings would be valuable background information for students as they wrote their letters to our elected official. I wrote new analysis questions to prompt students to consider how the laboratory model they were creating was a safe microscale version of processes that happen at much larger scales and with much harsher chemicals and byproducts. The goal was for students to understand the chemical reactions involved in the context of the materials economy and environmental justice. Rather than considering the perspective of mining company executives, the customized prompts drew on their perspective as consumers of electronic goods and asked them to think about how to act in solidarity with the workers and community members in mining communities. To mitigate the overly determined procedural character of the activity, I decided not to perform the suggested teacher-led demonstration to verify the identity of the final copper product. Instead, students could design their own experiments to gather evidence about the identity of their final product, a goal that required more scaffolding and backward mapping.

This scaffolding began with an activity from the *ChemCom* textbook that I adapted by stretching from a single laboratory activity into a series of activities, surrounding them with historical context, and building in practice for the writing involved in the final assessments. The activity in the *ChemCom* textbook is called "Striking it Rich" and involves treating the copper surface of a penny with zinc solution and heat to make a brass alloy with a golden color. The *ChemCom* curriculum placed it toward the end of their unit focused on designing coins to introduce alloying as a method of manipulating the properties of metals. In isolation, it is a cookbook activity. But I repurposed the activity to introduce a phenomenon within the larger thematic unit organized around the SJSI of extracting metals for technological use. It became a way to engage students around the notion of manipulation—a mini-storyline within the unit. Alluding to fake gold jewelry, I asked students to construct an explanation about the material composition of the brass-coated penny and then planned a series of activities where they investigated two properties of metals: density and reactivity. Here again, I drew on existing curriculum materials. There are lots of available activities about density, but most of them need to be adapted to push high school students' thinking a little deeper. I describe how I did that in more detail below. With respect to metal reactivity, I modified another *ChemCom* activity from the same unit to focus more on scientific practices. Students were asked to adapt the methods they learned in these activities to collect data that would facilitate revising their explanation about the composition of the penny. Ultimately, this series of lessons would be the scaffolding for students to design their own procedures to collect evidence about the identity of their final product in the copper from malachite activity. For each activity, the class practiced writing a single section of a lab report (structured like one part of a scientific journal article) with important context about the enterprise of science and an important piece of historical context. For example, with the initial "Striking it Rich" activity, students wrote only the experimental design section of the lab report.

Focusing on what we did during that first activity was a way to emphasize which chemicals and processes were involved in treating the penny so that students might see that information as evidence about the composition of the penny. This writing activity built toward the final assessment. Even more, this small, isolated section of a laboratory report was an opportunity to discuss technical writing and the ways it communicates the values espoused by scientific communities—all while having a little fun. I started this lesson by asking students to write a paragraph describing a recent series of events or an activity in some out-of-school context. I encouraged them to choose a funny event or an activity that was meaningful to them. Then, we practiced rewriting these paragraphs in the past tense and passive voice. I modeled this process by converting sentences like "I ate pizza for lunch" to "Pizza was for lunch" or "I walked to school" to "Walking was the mode of transportation to school." After converting their own sentences, students shared some of the silliest passive voice mutations with each other. We laughed together at how ridiculous these converted sentences sounded. I joked that I would feign ignorance if my colleagues became upset if they carried these writing practices into their English class. Then we looked at a few experimental sections from journal articles in chemistry and noticed the prevalence of this kind of sentence construction, which was the opening to discuss how values can be encoded in writing styles. This was an opportunity to talk about the importance of replication and transparency in scientific knowledge production but also about more elusive values like objectivity and neutrality. We discussed how removing the actors from scientific procedures may communicate these goals. We also considered how the passive voice can obscure the role of scientists' beliefs, viewpoints, and sociopolitical commitments in deciding what kinds of questions to ask, what kinds of experiments to conduct, and how to interpret the data. We talked about how there is a recent trend among scientists to write papers with more personal pronouns and active voice than in previous generations.[17] In each of the laboratory activities that followed, we practiced writing a different component of a laboratory report with corresponding NGSS practices like analyzing and interpreting data and constructing explanations. We practiced writing introduction and conclusion sections that focused on making arguments about the societal relevance of the experiment and the results, respectively.

Our discussions in this unit about the connections between technical writing and the values of the scientific enterprise was not a one-off, but an ongoing feature of class. My goal in teaching students how to write lab reports was to introduce them to scientific communication—not as the best way to share information—but as a set of practices established by groups of people to reflect and project their values. We often discussed the power of scientific practices to reveal insights and conceal oversights. Lessons like these give students the opportunity to develop the skills assessed by schools without positioning their own ways of communicating as inferior.[18] These lessons accurately communicate how the sciences are pluralistic and socially embedded, disrupting the dominant and misleading narrative that science is a singular, universal way for seeking truth that emerged from Europe.

One of the canonical stories of the dominant narrative in school science is the story of Archimedes investigating whether a king's crown was pure gold by measuring its density. In fact, I was introduced to the concept of density with this story when I was in middle school. There are many versions that blend different pieces of the legend involving a bathtub, the word "eureka" and Archimedes principle of buoyancy. The familiarity of these legends reminds us that the practices and concepts of science are sometimes divorced from historical context and other times placed in a romanticized history that communicates a Eurocentric narrative.

With the final unit assessment aimed at challenging the imperial relationships that shape the extraction and trade of technologically important metals, it was important to add historical context that was both accurate and helpful for understanding the status quo. With those goals in mind, I designed an assignment that focused on density, as an important property of metals. Instead of using historical context to perpetuate Eurocentric origin stories of science, I wanted to help students think about the scale of plunder of precious metals during the Spanish colonization of Latin America. I began from the following quote in Eduardo Galeano's classic book *The Open Veins of Latin America*:[19]

> Between 1503 and 1660, 185,000 kilograms of gold and 16,000,000 kilograms of silver arrived at the Spanish port of Sanlúcar de Barrameda. Silver shipped to Spain in a little more than a century and a half exceeded three times the total European reserves—and it must be remembered that these official figures are not complete (p. 23).

Leaning into the importance of unit analysis in high school science, the problem set prompted students to put these huge numbers into context using the density of the metal elements to think about the volume of metals looted by conquistadors. I asked them to compare the masses and volumes of silver and gold in the quote above with the sizes and weight capacities of modern 18-wheel semi-trucks. This was one way to use skills valued in high school science to wrap our heads around the scale of the theft. The assignment asked them to compare the current day value of these metals with the GDP of the Latin American countries where the metals were extracted and then consider how those amounts could have been invested over the intervening centuries to understand the reverberations of the historical theft. In terms of contextualization, this activity (combined with others described below) helped students understand modern mineral extraction in terms of colonization and imperialism. History helps to explain how mining companies from the global North continue to exploit workers and lands in Indigenous communities and in the global South. In terms of chemistry, this assignment gave students practice with the important skill of dimensional analysis and opportunities to think about the meaning of density in context. In terms of the NGSS, this assignment helped students to think beyond the narrow geologic-economic reasoning in the standards.

Readers might also note that I included density in a high school chemistry unit, even though it typically taught in middle grades science classes. Indeed, density is mentioned in the clarification statement of NGSS PE MS-PS1-2 and included in countless middle grades curricular materials. As discussed in chapter 1, the organization of the canon can be somewhat arbitrary, but it is also important to afford students intellectual respect and maintain high expectations. Density turned out to be a useful concept as I mapped backward my teaching about the properties of metal in this unit. So, I found ways to extend the concept in ways that challenged students academically. After the problem set that problematized the colonial theft of precious metals from Latin America, I wrote a follow-up assignment to encourage students thinking about density as a periodic property of metals, a topic that deals with density in ways that extend the complexity of this concept to challenge students. The density of metal elements is determined by complex interactions of atomic radius, cohesion, and metallic bonding – which is illustrated by a phenomenon called the lanthanide contraction.[20] Density of chemical elements peaks with osmium in the lower middle section of the periodic table. Osmium is a precious metal that is more expensive and yet, much less visible in popular culture than gold, platinum, or silver. This assignment was therefore another opportunity for us to discuss the relationships between the properties of materials, their applications, and

TABLE 4.2 Backward mapping of activities in metal extraction unit building toward final assessments

Activity	Description (teacher modifications or design noted in bold text)	Source
Assessment Part 2: Letter to elected official	Students write a letter supporting or critiquing legislation intended to increase transparency and ethics in the extraction and international trade of metal elements that are important for electronic technologies they consume.	**Teacher designed**
Assessment Part 1: Lab report	Students write a laboratory report structured like a scientific journal article describing the process by which they modeled the reduction of malachite ore and identified the final product as copper metal. **Follow-up to activity #8**	**Teacher designed**
8. Copper from malachite lab	Students use acidic solution and iron filings to isolate elemental copper from malachite. **Teacher modified activity to ask students to determine a method for identifying final product.**	Science & Sustainability
7. Environmental justice & metal mining	Students read excerpts of non-governmental reports. **Teacher curated excerpts.**	Multiple reports
6. Making claims about metals (return to striking it rich)	Students design their own method for gathering evidence about the composition of a treated penny. **Follow-up to activity #1**	**Teacher designed**
5. Metal reactivity lab and periodic reactivity	Students use experimentation to construct a metal activity series. **Teacher modified activity to increase focus on scientific practices.**	ChemCom Multiple sources exist
4. Periodic density: osmium	Students work through a series of prompts to construct an understanding of density as periodic and related to atomic structure and metallic bonding.	**Teacher created**
3. Stolen treasure	Students use unit analysis and density to think about the scale of precious metals stolen during Spanish colonization of Latin America. **Teacher designed problem set extrapolating from the source text.**	Open Veins of Latin America
2. Density lab	Students explore and calculate the density of different metal objects. **Teacher modified to extend from hands-on to minds-on activity.**	Multiple sources exist
1. "Striking it Rich"	Students treat the copper surface of a penny with Zn^{2+} solution and heat to create a brass coating **Teacher extended from hands-on activity to explaining a phenomenon across multiple activities**	ChemCom

their value within the political context of the materials economy. Conceptually, understanding density as a periodic property of elements makes connections with ideas about atomic structure, including electron configurations, atomic radius, and atomic mass. So, this assignment connected the ways our class was learning about properties like metal reactivity, oxidation, and conductivity (as explained by metallic bonding) with their use in technological applications like the circuitry of video game consoles and mobile phones.

The series of learning activities described here prepared students to design procedures for identifying their final product in the copper from malachite lab, to write a 5-section lab report for that activity, and to write a letter to the senator commenting on his legislation about transparency in metal sourcing. Careful planning allowed me to open more space for students to make sense of phenomena on their own terms and within larger thematic contexts. I still remember one student who connected the dots between this unit and an activity from a previous unit to independently propose putting her final copper product in a flame to look for the characteristic green light emission as evidence of its identity. This was a demonstration suggested by the textbook from which I adapted the activity, but this student was drawing on her experience from earlier in the course to apply and justify a particular scientific procedure. This served as an excellent accidental assessment of how she was taking up scientific practices and ideas.

The series of learning activities also built toward the sophomore capstone project beyond this unit. For students who needed substantial scaffolding for that project, the technological metals unit laid very specific groundwork for a project that focused on an electronic item. For students who were more prepared to extrapolate from this unit on their own, it provided a more general process for making conceptual connections between a material's sourcing, structure, properties, and applications and the associated issues of history, political power, and environmental justice. Moreover, it served as practice with two different genres of writing.

BEYOND THIS EXAMPLE: REINVENTION IN NEW CONTEXTS

Beyond the specific examples that have been the focus of this chapter, colleagues and I have taken up some of the ideas, themes, and principles articulated here in several other ways. I hope the following examples and extensions inspire more creative authentic science assessments in readers' classrooms. While the authentic assessment from the technological metals unit asked students to write letters about a particular piece of legislation with a connection to our state, there are numerous other directions that units like these have taken or could take. For example, the Trump administration tried to roll back the SEC regulations prompted by a particular piece of legislation, which created a new context for students to engage.[21] Teachers could also take up the related issue of electronic waste or e-waste, the obsolete electronic devices that are often disposed in problematic ways by exploiting labor in US prisons or in situations around the world where people experience economic desperation.[22] There are regulations in many places that require electronics manufacturers to take more responsibility for the recycling of their obsolete products or government recycling programs for e-waste in many locales. Teachers have designed authentic assessments that focus on promoting responsible versions of these kinds of initiatives. Indeed, I have seen learning about the extractive materials economy inspire a newfound appreciation for recycling among students. Conversely, it has been the entry point for students (and their teachers) to problematize the recycling industry itself. For example, on the Southeast side of Chicago, science teachers like Chuck Stark and Adilene Aguilera taught about e-waste and associated recycling programs. They later became intimately involved with a successful struggle to block the relocation of a metal recycler who frequently violated environmental regulations to the mostly Latine community surrounding their school.[23]

For science teachers who are already involved in their students' communities in deep ways, this chapter included ideas about adapting existing curricula to offer insight into issues that matter in their contexts. For science teachers who are just beginning to think about the connections between SJSI and their content areas, this chapter introduced some ideas about where to begin. Across this continuum, the examples in this chapter show how teachers need not choose whether to be attentive to standards or responsive to context, nor do teachers need to create their curriculum from scratch to take up issues of justice and challenge dominant ideologies. Continuing with the theme of negotiating the tensions of school science, in the next chapter, I describe how teachers also need not choose between teaching that inspires wonder and joy versus teaching that engages students with dissenting against injustice.

CHAPTER 5

Teaching for the Love of Life, Not Biology

A few years ago, I received a picture message: the program for the varsity baseball team of the public high school where I live on the South Side of Chicago. This was not unusual because my children have played organized baseball and softball in the area since preschool tee-ball. So, I have dozens of friends and contacts who are members of the local community of baseball coaches, parents, and volunteers. Surprisingly, this text came from a colleague in the local science education community instead. A chemistry teacher at the school, Tomasz Rajski, sent me the program because he noticed one of the team's sponsors. There, alongside the team roster, was an advertisement for an industrial chemical plant that is located about a mile down the street from the school. The ad explained that this plant:

> produces inorganic chemical catalysts that are used in the petroleum refining and specialty petrochemical industries. These products are used in removing sulfur, nitrogen, and other impurities from crude oil streams that are emitted as atmospheric pollutants during the refining and consumption of gasoline and other petroleum-based products.

This advertisement captures the problems and possibilities of science teaching that are the focus of this book. This plant is a local manifestation of the STEM pipeline, a place where my children or my neighbors' children could one day be employed within walking distance of their homes by pursuing careers in chemistry or chemical engineering. As part of the petrochemical industry, this plant is also implicated in the global climate crisis. In fact, I originally became aware of this plant because the EPA's toxic release inventory identified it as the top industrial polluter in my neighborhood. The teacher who sent me this advertisement ultimately posed this plant as a problem for his students to consider in their chemistry class. For several years, students in Mr. Rajski's class have studied the impact of the plant on the local environment *and* considered its impact on the global environment. In doing so, they have provided an excellent example of what this book calls problem-posing or justice-centered science pedagogy.

Studying a local chemical plant in this way makes the thrust of science class turning a critical lens on science itself. This is a departure from how science is typically taught that raises several dilemmas about the relationships students are cultivating with the sciences. These dilemmas have shown up implicitly throughout the book: in the critique of the pipeline in the Introduction and the canon in chapter 1, as a consideration of student standpoints in chapter 2, as recommendations for defining SJSI in chapter 3, and in terms of how teachers conceptualize their content areas in chapter 4. This chapter takes up these dilemmas more explicitly in terms of the following questions: What are the sciences? How do they make us feel? What do our definitions and feelings about the sciences mean for how we think about equity in science education? In addressing these questions, this chapter confronts questions of equity as access to the STEM pipeline versus more expansive ways of thinking about equity. This chapter deals with tensions between hope versus despair, critique versus imagination, and questions about the place for feelings like joy, wonder, pride, and fun in science class. As in other chapters, the answers to these questions are illustrated with concrete examples of lessons that I have taught, researched, observed, or that teachers can find in other books or resources.

WHAT ARE THE SCIENCES?

The sciences are commonly understood as bodies of knowledge developed empirically by professional scientists. This understanding was reinforced by generations of science curricula that treated science as a set of important concepts that students should understand. Reforms of the last decade or so (like the NGSS) emphasize that science is just as much composed of the set of practices that continue to augment, revise, and even radically change those bodies of knowledge. Some equity-minded science educators view this shift as an opening to embrace students' sense-making practices in science class.[1] Returning to the example that began this chapter helps us think about a few examples of what it means to think expansively about scientific practices.

Whereas the ad in the baseball program immediately turned my attention toward the neighborhood chemical plant, an alternate approach may have embraced baseball as an entry point to the sciences. In *Science in the City*, Bryan Brown explains how baseball players and coaches use the language and concepts of physics to understand how to manipulate the ball to their advantage. This is an example of the kinds of everyday sense-making that good science teachers try to draw out and build upon in their classes.[2] It takes up a context that many students will find fun and engaging. It also expands what kind of sense-making is considered scientific, which is one important way that science educators think about equity.[3]

Following this line of reasoning, it becomes easy to see that people in my neighborhood engage in scientific practices and with scientific phenomena in all kinds of diverse ways every day—most of which have nothing to do with the chemical plant or baseball. A young person might think about the processes of condensation or evaporation while observing a cold glass of water on a hot summer day or while stepping over a persistent puddle in a low-lying street corner days after the last rain. A parent might think about the right dose of medicine for a sick child. A neighbor might think about where heat is escaping through drafty windows while trying to figure out how to reduce their utility bills. A community member might watch night herons or turtles in the restored prairie in the neighborhood park, or they may notice how the migration patterns of geese have shifted with climate change. A grandparent might pass down a family recipe to a grandchild while explaining how the right level of heat or amount of moisture helps the food come out just right. Expanding what counts as scientific to include students' everyday ways of knowing is necessary, and it can be the starting point and the focus for myriad equitable and engaging science learning activities.

I argue that expanding what counts as scientific practices is also a view of equity that, by itself, is insufficient for teaching toward justice in our current context. An honest examination of where and how the practices and ideas of chemistry are taken up in my neighborhood cannot ignore the chemical plant—even if we encourage students to think about chemistry in broader ways. To ignore the realities of how chemistry is practiced and defined in industrial settings would be misleading students about the discipline of chemistry, which they are required to study for graduation. In the case of my neighborhood, it would also risk denying students an opportunity to understand their local context. In what other part of their schooling would they be encouraged to consider the meaning of the ad in their baseball program or to think about what happens inside the industrial building that casts an afternoon shadow over one of the most popular local taquerias?

BEYOND 'NATURE OF SCIENCE'

Proponents of teaching explicitly about the nature of science (NOS) remind teachers that the sciences are not only bodies of knowledge and sets of practices. The sciences are also composed of communities of practitioners, who are members of other communities too, thus deeply situating the whole enterprise in social context. But what NOS enthusiasts often miss is that the enterprise of science is not just a loose collection of scientific communities, it is also a set of highly structured institutions, which, by their design, are exclusionary, aligned with powerful political forces (like the military or the petroleum industry), and resistant to change. Therefore, champions of emphasizing NOS in schools often glorify, promote, or explain the enterprise of science without allowing for teachers or students to critique the scientific enterprise as it exists in institutions.

The chemical plant in my neighborhood provides an excellent example. It is owned by W.R. Grace, a multinational corporation that has paid hundreds of millions of dollars in fines to the US EPA for the environmental damages it has caused.[4] The same multinational corporation has also settled multiple lawsuits for its involvement in the tragedy of asbestos, the mineral used as a building material that is responsible for countless cases of deadly and preventable cancers.[5] W.R. Grace lost another, very different, lawsuit over the corporation's attempts to patent neem oil, a natural substance that has been used as an agricultural pest repellent by people in India for centuries.[6] This company therefore illustrates the ways in which the enterprise of science has often failed to account for the consequences of its products and inventions *and* how it has co-opted Indigenous knowledges and tried to patent and profit from them.[7]

W.R. Grace is named after its founder, the son of a wealthy Irish landowner who, during the infamous potato famine, led a failed attempt to bring desperate laborers from Ireland to settle land in Peru. Pivoting from his father's version of colonialism to another, W.R. Grace built a fortune by exporting *guano* (bat and bird feces) back to Europe as fertilizer.[8] The agricultural application of guano was a practice developed by the Indigenous peoples of the Andean region centuries prior in the Incan Empire.[9] In a way that harkens to the corporation's recent attempt to patent neem oil in India, W.R. Grace co-opted this Indigenous scientific knowledge to build a fortune. With Tomasz Rajski, I have argued that the significance of the chemical plant owned by W.R. Grace is its normalcy and banality. It is not an aberration or an exception. Instead, it is more accurately described as a representative example of the institutions that make up the enterprise of science. Even just in the handful of neighborhoods where I have lived and taught, this plant is added to a list that includes the coal power plant and the medical waste incinerators discussed in chapter 1. I have certainly not sought to live by polluters, but in working class communities of color, sources of industrial contamination are often nearby.

In the racial reckoning that followed the murder of George Floyd in 2020, institutions like universities and banks in the US and in many other places around the world were forced to confront the racist colonial roots of their founding. If teachers investigate the history of science with a critical lens, they will find the same kinds of stories again and again.[10] Simply put, this is one way to understand why models of "diversity, equity, and *inclusion*" or "science for all" are often misguided.[11] Is this the science we want for all? Are these the institutions into which marginalized people deserve to be included?

In referring to NOS, it is worth considering that by using the word "nature," proponents of NOS seem to suggest a few assumptions. First, the connotations of NOS suggest that science has arrived at its status quo by some organic process, unsullied by social or political projects. Secondly, by referring to science as a singular term, NOS scholars presume that there is only one universal science. Together, these two assumptions would mean that there are no alternatives to the current status quo of the STEM enterprise. Some NOS scholars go so far as to argue that teachers are barely capable of understanding NOS, let alone whether they could have any role in changing it.[12] I strongly disagree. Therefore, I prefer to use more specific terms, referring to the STEM enterprise, if I mean the institutional structures like the chemical plant in my neighborhood or the university where I work. Or, if I refer to the practices valued by communities of biologists, I use the term *culture of the field of biology*. This greater specificity leaves open that science is not singular and can, in fact, be changed. Science education as a catalyst for alternative futures offers an otherwise for teachers—a different way to think about our role *vis-à-vis* the enterprise of science. This starts with affirming and cultivating students' wonder about the Earth, love for life, and awe about the universe without tying these deep feelings to our content areas. In the three sections that follow, I describe what this kind of distinction can look like in the different science content areas with example lessons.

HOW DO SCIENCES MAKE US FEEL?

Biology teachers might consider the difference between inspiring curiosity about the phenomena of life versus enculturating students into their discipline. In my research with colleagues about science teacher education, we learned how a new biology teacher named Mariana grappled with this difference.[13] Early in our teacher licensure program, Mariana critiqued fellow teachers for not taking advantage of what she saw as the clear connections between biology and students' lives:

> I feel like science is very relevant, but sometimes it's taught in a way that it kind of takes you away from that … Science, I think, is just very connectable, and you could think about it every day because you're a living being, and science is part of our everyday lives. But sometimes it's taught in a way where they don't connect it, and you can't make that connection either.… [There are] bigger pictures that sometimes I feel teachers miss.

But when Mariana tried teaching a series of lessons in her placement school, she began to see how the biology curriculum was organized around the big ideas in the discipline instead of these connections to students' lives:

> My whole issue right now that I have with curriculum—even with what I taught that week, about cell structure and function: Why is this important? And how is this going to help [students] in the long run and outside of this classroom? How or what aspects of this do I want them to know that after one science class is going to stick with them? And, I don't know. That's what I'm struggling with, and I don't think I did that during that week.

In our teacher education program, students like Mariana read about the ways in which prominent biologists have been central in inventing and reinventing scientific racism, again and again.[14] For example, in an excellent chapter in the

1987 book *Anti-Racist Science Teaching*, biology teacher Michael Vance shows how scientists like Nobel-prize winner Konrad Lorenz were lauded by both the British secondary biology curriculum and white supremacist youth groups. As Mariana learned and read about the entanglements of her discipline of biology and colonialism, she became more conflicted about her role as a science teacher.

> I'm caught somewhere between wanting to deliver appreciation and love for the science content, but also in a way that doesn't—science in general has not always been fair in its history, so trying to tie that into students' lives, but also seeing what students could get out of it.

Mariana's dilemma is common among science teachers. By "queering dissection," Sara Tolbert provides another compelling example.[15] Tolbert explains how some students, especially those with feminist commitments to care or those who reject the objectification and exploitation of more-than-human species, are disgusted by the traditional biology exercise of dissecting animals like cats or fetal pigs. At the same time, other students are fascinated and enthralled by the opportunity to partake in dissection as a sort of rite-of-passage into the medical or scientific career pathways to which they aspire. This latter group also includes marginalized students who deserve such pathways. Ultimately, these tensions led Tolbert to the conclusion that: "the students' perspectives, then, challenge us to consider how science educators can be differently prepared NOT as representatives of scientific communities but to develop a role as interlocutors of/within more critical, multilogical socioscientific practices."[16] This challenge suggests a possible resolution to Mariana's dilemma of being "…caught in between wanting to deliver an appreciation and love for the science…" Rather than teaching students to love science, we can reframe our responsibility as sustaining students' natural love, wonder, and curiosities for the Earth, our fellow inhabitants, and outer space beyond. At the same time, we can teach students to appreciate and critique the benefits, harms, insights, and oversights of scientific ways of knowing. For science teachers, this implies expanding our views of our disciplines while remaining honest about the associated institutions. One increasingly common example of this kind of teaching is taken up by biology teachers whose lessons about HeLa cells provide students with opportunities to critique the scientists and institutions who exploited Henrietta Lacks. Both the National Science Teaching Association and *Rethinking Schools* have published examples that may inspire teachers to create lessons that problematize scientific institutions.[17]

NEITHER CHEMOPHOBIA, NOR CHEMOPHILIA

As argued in previous chapters, teaching students to be critical of the STEM enterprise can be scary for teachers in an era of climate change deniers and anti-vaxxers. Even before these organized campaigns of misinformation gained steam, some chemistry teachers feared inducing what they call chemophobia, or the irrational fear of chemicals. There is even a popular activity that has long been used by chemistry teachers to guard against this fear while reminding students that all materials are made of chemicals. This activity begins by introducing a dangerous substance called dihydrogen monoxide (DHMO) and various problems it can cause. Teachers often reference dhmo.org, which explains that problems associated with this colorless, odorless chemical include tissue damage caused by prolonged exposure to its solid phase, deaths caused by accidental inhalation of its liquid phase, and massive amounts of property damage each year. Teachers typically inform students that DHMO is also a component of many more dangerous chemical mixtures before asking the class whether the government should ban this chemical. After what is usually an affirmative vote by the class to ban DHMO, chemistry teachers lead students through deconstructing the name dihydrogen monoxide to reveal that they were talking about H_2O all along.

Like the mining activity discussed in chapter 3, this exercise can communicate a few different principles, depending on how teachers and students debrief it. For example, reflecting on the ease of deconstructing the name dihydrogen monoxide may encourage students not to be intimidated by long chemical names. This version of the lesson is often used by teachers as an introduction to chemical nomenclature. On the other hand, in an episode of a cable TV comedy show, the hosts used this activity to demean environmental activists and argue that movements to regulate the chemical industry are misinformed. In fact, regulating or even banning dangerous chemicals is an important and effective policy approach.[18] For example, in the decades after lead was banned from paint, gasoline, and water pipes, childhood lead poisoning dropped precipitously overall, even as it remained a serious problem of environmental racism.[19] In another example, banning the use of chlorofluorocarbons (CFCs) as refrigerants halted the growth of the hole in the ozone layer.[20] Whereas the ozone hole was a major global environmental concern when I was a high school chemistry student, as a high school chemistry teacher, I was able to use it as a hopeful example. Mario Molina, the first Mexican-born chemist to win a Nobel prize received the award for the work he did to elucidate the role of CFCs in the ozone hole. Through this example, students could see how the discipline of chemistry was responsible for creating this catastrophe and then later, undertaken differently, providing the evidence that led to the prohibition of the synthetic chemical responsible. Lessons that take up these examples may guard against both chemophobia and also chemophilia so that students have opportunities to develop healthy skepticism while learning how to ask thoughtful questions about the chemical industry.

AWE ABOUT SPACE, WONDER ABOUT EARTH

I had a conversation recently with a young astronomer who spoke enthusiastically about his interest in space. At the same time, he was considering leaving his field because of the ways it remains entangled with Euro-American settler colonialism. He referenced his objection to the construction of telescopes in Hawaii despite protests by local Indigenous peoples and how observatories in Chile continue unequal relationships between powerful scientific institutions in the global North and their partners in the global South.[21] Rampant colonial ideology in astronomy is visible in science curriculum. For example, a quick online search reveals several versions of a popular curriculum that asks students to construct a plan for colonizing Mars. Some versions ask students to question the ethics of this endeavor while others leave the so-called mission as unproblematic. Previous chapters have discussed how scholars who are fascinated by physical phenomena may object to the long historical entanglement between the field of physics and the development of military technologies, including nuclear weapons and other weapons of mass destruction.[22] But other kinds of astronomy and other ways of studying the physical phenomena of the universe are possible – and indeed have long existed. I have seen student teachers develop exciting lessons about astronomical traditions in various societies around the world. Similarly, a recent episode of NOVA on PBS documented astronomer Maram Kaire's investigation of the long history of space science in his homeland of Senegal.[23] This documentary emphasizes the sophistication of ancient African astronomies and traces them to the present. With thoughtfully prepared questions, students might critically analyze some aspects of the film too. Rather than thinking of showing documentaries as a break from teaching, teachers can use a film like this as part of a critical multicultural astronomy unit where students considered anti-colonial possibilities for space science.

The interdisciplinary character of Earth and environmental sciences often means that teachers of these content areas are less dogmatic about promoting their discipline than some other science teachers. Even so, students who pursue these fields in college and career pathways often encounter a rude awakening about the difference between loving the disciplines of Earth and environmental sciences versus loving the Earth and the environment. For example, many graduates of geology programs quickly find that their best opportunities for employment are with the mining or petroleum industries. Companies seek their expertise to exploit, rather than protect, the Earth. Teachers could assemble a lesson or even a unit interrogating how Exxon-Mobil has funded campaigns to incite doubt about climate change, even as scientists on their payroll have known for decades about the relationship between their product and climate change.[24] In my classes, I have asked students to analyze leaked memos from the company. I have also shown students the film, *Merchants of Doubt*, which documents how consultants for corporations in the chemical, fossil fuel, and tobacco industries have undermined public acceptance of scientific consensus. In lessons like these, students are able to grapple with the sciences as bodies of knowledge, as a set of practices, as communities of practitioners, and a set of institutions. The latter opens opportunities to openly discuss the political and ethical forces that permeate all aspects of the sciences.

BEYOND ACCESS OR RIGOR: EQUITY AS INTELLECTUAL RESPECT

Transgressing disciplinary boundaries and encouraging students to critique the scientific enterprise is a responsibility that should not be taken lightly. One of the primary concerns that teachers raise is diluting the academic richness of the curriculum, or what is often referred to as *rigor*. Indeed, research documents how science curriculum designed to address issues of public health in marginalized communities has historically been patronizing rather than responsive or respectful.[25] Whereas privileged students learn from curricula designed to prepare them for pathways into universities, marginalized students are expected to comply with rote learning about basic health concepts. In Chicago Public Schools, district officials observed a similar pattern where some schools tracked students who were labeled as "underprepared" into classes like environmental science, physical sciences, or Earth science in ninth grade as a remedial option. Meanwhile their more privileged peers took biology or physics. In 2017, the district tried to address this problem by swapping out more flexible high school graduation requirements for a strict regimen of one year each in biology, chemistry, and physics.

Unfortunately, the barrier to equity was not a lack of disciplinary rigidity, but instead a rigid commitment to the idea of tracking, or segregating students based on their perceived abilities. Tracking is driven by racism while it also reinforces false racial hierarchies.[26] It is borne out of a lack of intellectual respect for students and a narrow ableist view of human capacities. Interdisciplinary teaching does not imply compromising academic richness. In fact, crossing disciplinary boundaries encourages students to view real problems with more complexity. Extending beyond interdisciplinarity to transdisciplinary science teaching implies not only taking up multiple practices and ideas from several disciplines, but also prioritizing engagement with SJSI ahead of emphasizing content area conventions. Transdisciplinary science teaching encourages students to consider the insights and oversights associated with disciplinary practices and bodies of knowledge. In the second half of this chapter, I describe several lessons that push disciplinary boundaries while affording students intellectual respect and even encouraging joy, fun, or wonder. These sorts of activities breathe life into the curriculum and remind me of a saying that I first heard from a colleague, Cynthia Nambo: We want curriculum with vigor, associated with the energy of life, rather than rigor, associated with the stiffness of death.[27]

LOVE IN AN ASSESSMENT?

If fun and love are to have a place in the science classroom, science teachers cannot limit the ways they assess students' writing to canonical genres like lab reports. Giving students opportunities to write for different audiences, purposes, and styles can be fun, academically vigorous, and even healing or liberating.[28] Moreover, most science classes do not provide students with enough opportunities to write, consider feedback (from peers and the teacher), and then revise their writing. Building toward more complex writing tasks requires backward mapping, as discussed in chapter 4. The metal extraction unit described in that chapter was often preceded in my curriculum by another unit in which students had opportunities to develop ideas about the properties of materials and the connections between their extraction and colonialism. The final assessment for that unit was an unorthodox genre of writing for school. Students were assigned to write a speculative love letter to their imagined future partner that made an argument about whether they wanted a diamond ring to represent their love for each other. I encouraged students to have fun with this letter and to be creative.

This unit assessment, first mentioned in the chapter 3, was meant to draw on students' understandings of the chemical composition and properties of diamonds while also weaving information into their arguments about the political and historical contexts of European colonial oppression and diamond cartels in Africa. Weaving together chemical reasoning with political and historical analysis—all within the genre of a personal letter to a loved one—is a very complicated writing task. This illustrates how pushing beyond disciplinary boundaries and past canonical genres of writing can enhance, rather than compromise, academic expectations. But the first several times that I tried to use this assignment as an assessment at the end of a unit, I quickly saw that I had not provided enough scaffolding or practice for students to be able to construct rich explanations of the chemistry concepts—let alone successfully weave together all these complex ideas. A few students who were experienced writers in each class were able to write beautiful letters, but even these often did not include the depth of scientific reasoning that I hoped. For most students, the insights I heard them discuss in class did not come through in their writing.

The quality of student work was hindered by my curricular planning. Rather than giving up on the promise of this fun, and potentially meaningful assessment, I worked with colleagues to add scaffolding and use backward mapping to improve my plans. I started by creating a rubric for the final love letter. Standards like the NGSS can be helpful in efforts like these to refocus or more tightly align a unit. For example, the rubric for the love letter articulated clear expectations for students: engage practices of *constructing explanations* and *engaging in argument from evidence* while discussing the disciplinary core idea of *structure and properties of matter* as well as the cross-cutting concept of *structure and function*. Specifically, I provided students with a rubric that asked them to describe diamonds in terms of their atomic structure and molecular bonding and to write explanations connecting those submicroscopic structures with their unique physical and chemical properties. The rubric also asked for letters to compare the properties and cost of natural diamonds with other comparable materials like synthetic diamonds, moissanite, and cubic zirconia. This comparison was meant to undergird an argument about whether diamonds' special properties made them better suited for jewelry or perhaps industrial or technological applications like saw blades and microprocessors. But the rubric was not limited to these chemical concepts. There were also criteria that invited students to construct arguments about the political economy and historical context of the diamond cartel. Students wrote about the De Beers corporation, whose advertising campaign made diamonds synonymous with engagement rings and whose rise was predicated on brutal European colonialism and apartheid in Africa.

Using backward design, I started from the love letter rubric to decide which activities were important, which were unnecessary, and what new activities were needed. The goal was to move students gradually toward writing love letters that expressed their complex thinking about diamonds as a fascinating material of Earth. In this process, I identified and improved shortcomings in my instructional planning by evaluating student work. This illustrates how teachers can use assessment to improve teaching rather than to punish or rank students. Like with phenomenon-centered science curricula, the learning activities in the diamond unit were organized to support students building gradually toward deeper understandings and more sophisticated scientific practices. In this way, my process resembled popular story lining approaches to planning for science teaching that are intended to increase coherence for students.[29] But the primary difference between the thematic curriculum described here and storyline approaches are that a justice-centered approach embraces the "gaps" that inevitably arise in constructing explanations about the world using scientific ideas. What this means is that students are explicitly engaged with the limitations of scientific knowledge systems as a necessary part of connecting their science learning to its usefulness in their lives and communities. Students needed to weave historical and political knowledge with chemical concepts to make an argument to their future partner about diamonds. In this case, utility to life outside of the classroom is less concrete than in some other authentic assessments. But students have said that this unit assessment caused them to rethink their approach to giving gifts in their personal relationships or reconsider the values and purposes of jewelry or precious gems and metals. The goal was not to demonize consumption, jewelry, or precious metals but to inspire more thinking about relationships between the Earth's materials, aesthetics, and ethics in our personal and public lives. In this unit, students showed their expansive and critical thinking in contrast with the artifacts they produced during the magazine collage activity recounted at the start of the previous chapter. For me, this illustrated how different curricula can elicit very different kinds of engagement and teach different lessons about what matters.

HOPE, JOY, AND FUN IN A SERIOUS SCIENCE CLASS

This section draws on examples from throughout the book to highlight how hope, joy, and fun are part of a justice-centered science curriculum. These concepts can be challenging to define and will not be experienced in the same ways by all students. For example, while writing love letters about the very serious issue of the diamond cartel, some students had fun with the genre by including playful pet names and funny one-liners. Similarly, in another activity, my students and I enjoyed playing around with language by poking fun at the passive voice constructions common in the experimental sections of chemistry manuscripts. While written in a "cookbook" format, the activity from the *ChemCom* textbook where students coated pennies with a brass alloy elicited the kinds of "oohs" and "aahs" from students that make science teachers smile. The motion detector dance battles and athlete profile videos described in chapter 1 gave students opportunities to show how a range of talents could challenge the boundaries of physics in fun and expressive ways. Even if we have deeper goals for our teaching, it does not hurt to also build in opportunities for these more light-hearted forms of engagement, awe, or wonder.

In chapter 4, I described a problem set about density that emphasized unit analysis, a technique that relies on using conversion factors to solve problems. Before introducing unit analysis in chemistry or physics class, teachers might consider introducing the metric system with another light-hearted activity aimed at considering the values, assumptions, and methods of the sciences. The idea for this activity was brought to me and fellow teachers by Tomasz Rajski, the colleague of mine who sent the photo of the baseball program that began this chapter. The activity begins by asking students to think of qualities that, to the best of their knowledge, have not yet been quantified effectively by humans. In small groups, students choose one of these qualities and invent an imaginary unit and an instrument to measure it. For more advanced courses (e.g., twelfth grade science electives), these units might be compound units, like Newtons (which are $\frac{kg \cdot m}{s^2}$) or Watts (Joules per second). This activity makes space for fun and creativity—even while it can also challenge Eurocentric and androcentric naming conventions. One of the best examples I have seen is that several groups have decided to imagine measuring love. Some groups focus on romantic love, whereas the scale devised by one group allowed for different types of love (e.g., romantic, platonic, familial, etc.). One proposed unit of measurement for love was the "Heart," with the shorthand being the heart emoji in the same way that a kilogram is represented by kg. Another group chose the "Cupid" as their unit of measurement (which, time permitting, could have prompted a classroom conversation about whether that is a Eurocentric choice). Indeed, this activity allows for class discussions about the values and practices of the sciences to mingle with silliness. Whenever I lead this activity, I ask groups of students to brainstorm and discuss some of the societal pros and cons that might emerge from their newfound ability to quantify something that was previously immeasurable. Continuing with the love example, students have speculated that measuring love could lead to lots of hurt feelings, jealousy, resentment, and even problematic applications of their proposed technology in courtrooms involving divorce cases or custody battles. Conversations about imaginary units of measurement are often sprinkled with jokes and laughter, even as they open opportunities to explore the problematics of scientizing and quantifying aspects of nature and culture. This underscores that science classrooms can be places where students experience whimsical, playful kinds of fun *and* the more profound feelings like joy or wonder.

In chapter 3, I described a unit organized around the SJSI of drug development. Versions of this unit have prompted students to reflect on a range of feelings from pride in their writing to wonder about their ancestors' lives. In the first part of the two-part authentic assessment for the unit, students worked in pairs to measure the amount of acetylsalicylic acid in one pill of brand name aspirin using titration. In part two of the assessment, students wrote a question that would be helpful to ask the next time they were issued a prescription. We compiled and edited these questions as a whole class to create a list of ten prescription questions that students could take with them to the doctor or pharmacist. In AP chemistry, instead of titrating a commercial aspirin tablet, students synthesized aspirin first and then analyzed their own aspirin product. They completed a lab write-up which reported on their own synthesis and analysis of aspirin. Students found this combination of assessments useful in both practical and academic ways. For example, Jade wrote in her lab report that understanding the chemical equivalence of brand name and generic drugs was an important point that she would share with her family and community. She worried that people she cared about might otherwise be manipulated by drug companies overcharging for brand name products. At the same time, the more canonical part of the assessment showed students that they can develop sophisticated academic skills within this meaningful context. For example, Curtis wrote the following self-assessment about his scientific writing while reflecting on the aspirin lab report as compared with writing from previous classes across three years of high school:

> I have definitely improved on my scientific writing.... My recent lab reports show much more formal, scientific diction and knowledge as I become more conscious of issues by researching them more thoroughly. The content shown in lab reports is much more sophisticated than first reports. I learned to make claims that are supported by evidence through quantitative practices in a lab, not claims that are irrelevant to the topic being written on. I learned not to be vague when describing a concept, what was used in an experiment, how it was used, etc.

As with the unit described in the previous chapter, the activities that prepared students for this assessment were largely drawn from published chemistry activities like titration experiments, stoichiometry problems, and molecular modeling activities. But I also included scaffolded literacy activities where our class read Science-Technology-Society literature that had informed my understanding of drug development and medicinal plants. For example, students read an excerpt from a 1975 article in *Science* where Mexican chemist Bernard Ortiz de Montellano described how he used organic chemistry techniques to compare medicinal plants catalogued by the Aztec empire with compounds used in modern Western medicine.[30] A student named Cristina reflected on learning about the example of the arroyo willow, which has been used by Indigenous peoples in Mexico as a treatment for fever and contains the chemical precursor to aspirin: "It gave me an incentive to really understand the science behind synthesizing [acetyl]salicylic acid and trying to imagine ways of how my ancestors cured their aches and pains."[31] Cristina's quote connects her motivation with feelings of imagination and wonder.

Profound feelings like this can also be inspired by opportunities to think about the vastness of the universe or the quantum mechanics of electrons. Even as this book consistently argues for connecting science learning with students' lives and concrete realities, science class can also offer momentary escape into the wonder of the Earth and the cosmos. Whether informally in class or during interviews for research projects, students have shared with me that immersion, even in the minutia of scientific concepts, can provide temporary relief from other drama or worries in their lives or in the school. Conversely, studying a seemingly arbitrary scientific phenomenon can feel like the height of irrelevance to a stressed-out teenager, not to mention a student dealing with trauma. As a result, this kind of wonder cannot always be the driving force for a required class that students did not choose to take, but teachers can, nonetheless, look for opportunities to create these moments.

Or sometimes, these moments happen unexpectedly. The osmium assignment mentioned above was the result of me following an idea down a metaphorical rabbit hole while planning a lesson about gold, platinum, and silver. I ended up learning about the phenomenon called the lanthanide contraction and got lost in the excitement of learning something that was totally new to me even though I had studied and taught chemistry for years. I like to think that I brought my wonder into the classroom during the osmium lesson and modeled those feelings for students. In one of the first conversations I had with friend and colleague, Enrique Lopez, we discussed how teaching students to be critical of the STEM enterprise does not mean we have to abandon the notion that science can inspire wonder and feed students' curiosity. The key, as described above, is encouraging students' natural love for life and wonder about the universe as opposed to cultivating a love for the field of biology or awe about the discipline of physics.

Just as critiquing the STEM enterprise does not preclude scientific inquiry inspiring joy, learning about oppression and the roots of inequality need not be a path toward despair. In fact, when we can see how our current reality has been created, it can become easier for us to imagine other possibilities. We can see that the social world that humans have constructed could be dismantled, changed, and built differently. To draw on an example from the previous chapter, learning about the life cycle of metal materials in technological applications gave students who live in environmental justice communities in Chicago an opportunity to think about their place in the global materials economy differently. While bearing an unequal share of pollution in their city, they were also consumers of products whose manufacture brought environmental injustice on communities elsewhere. Rather than viewing these relationships in simple right and wrong terms, these lessons can inspire students to think about interdependence and solidarity.

The group of teachers I work with in Chicago, the Youth Participatory Science Collective, found that learning about environmental justice victories—locally and internationally—can be a source of hope.[32] Students working on a community solar project in Jasmine Jones's classes in 2022 learned about the successful effort to shut down two coal fired power plants not too far from their school a decade before. Right down the street, Nina Hike teaches her students about Hazel Johnson, known as the mother of environmental justice. Ms. Johnson was organizing in the Altgeld Gardens neighborhood when Ms. Hike lived there as a small child. When I teach about environmental justice, I often tell the story from chapter 1 of my childhood community's successful efforts to shut down the two medical waste incinerators in our neighborhood because that story continues to inspire hope for me. Many teachers in our group have recently begun telling the story of the successful campaign to keep a metal recycling facility from relocating from a predominately white north side area to a mostly Latine south side neighborhood, an effort in which several of our colleagues were involved. Beyond telling stories of successful campaigns for justice, science teachers who form relationships with community organizations can link students with opportunities to be involved in efforts that matter to them. Getting involved in a cause or organization that does meaningful change-making work is one of the best ways to inspire hope. When students know the stories of past grassroots successes and have a chance to become engaged themselves, they can start to see themselves as part of a tradition of struggle and part of building an alternative future.

The examples in this chapter show how science teachers do not need to choose between taking on injustice and cultivating hope. Similarly, academic sophistication is not in conflict with practical relevance. Nor does encouraging students to critique the STEM enterprise preclude engaging their senses of curiosity and wonder. Even in a classroom that confronts serious issues, there is room for fun and joy. Rejecting these binaries became easier for me when I also rejected the notion that science teachers should promote the sciences. Instead, teachers can choose to engage students in appropriating scientific practices, appreciating scientific insights, identifying scientific oversights and critiquing scientific institutions.

CHAPTER 6

Teaching Science as a Catalyst for Alternative Futures

Education—as a set of institutions, processes, and relationships—links the past, present, and future of our societies. Therefore, it can play a role in cultivating wisdom and maintaining important practices. But it is often conservative to the point of reproducing a romanticized and deeply unjust vision of society. Education can be dynamic, transformative, and imaginative. But it can also uncritically embrace innovation to the point of driving a wedge between young people and their elders. The curriculum and conditions within schools provide ample and indisputable evidence of vast social, racial, economic, and environmental injustices while also acting as a source and perpetuator of inequities. On the other hand, schools are among the most promising places to continue the work of eradicating oppression and building strong, healthy, and sustainable communities. These are the central contradictions of education, which are visible in every part of schooling. Teaching involves navigating the tensions between these oppositional functions of schooling, which makes it complex work. One way to distill this complexity is to think about teaching for equity as fundamentally about equipping students to thrive in the world as it currently exists while simultaneously building capacities to struggle for more just and sustainable worlds.

Science—if we understand it as a set of institutions, processes, and relationships (in addition to bodies of knowledge)—is also complex and contradictory. Like education, the sciences reflect and contribute to profound social injustice while they simultaneously represent immense transformative potential. By putting these two important social processes and institutions together, *science education* multiplies contradictions of inertia and inequity versus transformation and justice. Looking between these tensions, science education can offer glimpses of more just and sustainable futures. The goal of this book is to move from those glimpses to principles and possibilities. The first chapter critiqued the common STEM pipeline metaphor to highlight the problems and limitations with the status quo. Chapters 1 and 2 encouraged readers to consider why they teach science and to think of their students as transformative intellectuals. Chapter 3 introduced processes for identifying and defining SJSI, in dialogue with students. Chapter 4 shared strategies for designing authentic assessments that address SJSI and to plan curriculum that builds towards them. Chapter 5 described how changing our relationships with our disciplines can make space for feelings like joy and wonder even while taking up weighty issues in science classes.

This final chapter offers a different metaphor for thinking about the transformative potential of science education: a *catalyst for alterative futures*. "Catalyst for change" is a common metaphor for something that sparks a new and different social process. In chemistry, a catalyst creates an alternative pathway for a reaction, so it can happen under conditions that are less harsh. A catalyst can also improve chemists' ability to achieve a desired set of outcomes from the reaction. Together, these two features are analogous to the potential for science education as a catalyst. Creating conditions that are less harsh involves making space for students to thrive in the present while achieving our desired outcomes of building more just and sustainable worlds.

BETTER CONDITIONS IN SCHOOL, SCIENCE, AND SOCIETY

The conditions of many science classrooms can be described metaphorically as high pressure, high temperature—and even corrosive—environments. Minoritized students experience threats to their dignity and identities in interactions with their teachers or peers. Many students feel deep anxiety about high stakes exams and grades. Unfortunately, there are science educators who view these conditions as necessary and even beneficial. They view their classrooms as crucibles wherein the next generation of rigorous scientists are formed. In contrast, science education as a catalyst creates classroom conditions that are less harsh by rejecting harmful and limiting notions of rigor and by welcoming students' whole selves into science classrooms. For teachers, this involves more expansive views of what constitutes sophisticated scientific thinking, but it does not imply lowering expectations. To view youth as transformative intellectuals represents a higher set of expectations than to enforce the rigor of an outdated and irrelevant curriculum.

Despite railing against the pipeline metaphor and the ways in which science educators are positioned as promoters of the STEM enterprise, this book also argues that providing marginalized students with pathways into STEM careers remains an important goal in science teaching. Access to opportunities in STEM can be part of creating conditions that are less harsh for students and their families. Providing increased access to opportunities in STEM is a necessary, but wholly insufficient strategy, for slowly changing the STEM enterprise itself. Pedagogies of access imply challenging students to engage with sophisticated practices and ideas that afford them the intellectual respect they deserve—regardless of their career aspirations. Equally important are opportunities for students to consider their values *vis-à-vis* those they will encounter in the STEM enterprise. This includes planning lessons that explicitly interrogate the values communicated and espoused by communities of scientists. Creating alternate pathways for science careers implies framing students' appropriation of scientific practices and ideas as additive, heterogeneous, and reflective. Inviting students to try out and get better at using scientific practices and ideas should not require them to assimilate into the status quo of scientific communities. Teachers should avoid communicating notions of success in science as opportunities for students to escape their communities, even if conditions there may sometimes be harsh too. Instead, teachers can position scientific pathways as opportunities for students to serve their communities and advocate for them. Teachers may encourage students to pursue careers in medicine or education or to attend to community concerns through careers like engineering that typically eschew those kinds of considerations.

This is especially true for students who have been excluded from these opportunities by racism, sexism, and economic hardship. As Ebony McGee incisively documents in her book *Black, Brown, Bruised,* college STEM environments are racialized in ways that replicate harsh conditions for students of color.[1] While high school teachers have little control over the conditions students will find at universities or other STEM settings after they graduate, they should know that experiencing similar conditions in high school classes is *not* good preparation. Instead, students can benefit from an alternative environment that is nurturing, responsive, and actively anti-racist and anti-sexist. In this kind of environment, they can even learn to anticipate, understand, and resist some of the problematic features they are likely to encounter in STEM institutions as adults.

Whether or not students pursue pathways into the sciences beyond high school, they will encounter SJSI in their lives. The everyday relevance and political character of scientific knowledge has arguably never been more apparent than in the current era of climate crisis, pandemic, and artificial intelligence. Science curriculum that shies away from these realities seems unlikely to prepare students to deal with it.[2] The complexity of these politics presents an opportunity to support students to grapple with contradictions. Teachers can model being critical of the pharmaceutical industry while still trusting vaccines they produce. Teachers can affirm the indisputable evidence of anthropogenic climate change while challenging the notion that the sciences have the solutions. Instead of implying that humans might tinker or engineer their way out of these complex problems, teachers can help students think about how there are multiple paths forward that require us to consider science, politics, culture, and other ways of knowing together.

Still, it is a scary time to teach about controversial topics in some localities. With right-wing attacks on teaching about everything from racism to sexuality to mental health, it is not easy to be a teacher in this moment. These conditions highlight the importance of brave teachers who engage their students in examining both their own values and the scientific enterprise. Indeed, a generation of students educated to consider these topics thoughtfully in their science classes may create a set of political conditions that are less harsh than the present. In the meantime, what allows teachers to be courageous are their relationships and solidarities with colleagues and others who are pushing back against these attacks. These relationships are also the basis for forming groups in which teachers can do the learning that justice-centered curriculum requires of them. In the final few sections, I describe some ways in which science teachers might work with each other and with colleagues and communities outside of science education to create alternative pathways for futures that are more just and sustainable.

ALTERNATIVE OUTCOMES: PRIORITIZING OUR COLLECTIVE WELL-BEING

Besides accelerating change under conditions that are less harsh, the alternate pathways created by catalysts allow for chemists to be more selective about the outcomes of those changes. When I write about outcomes, I am not referring to students' readiness for college or work but to the relationship between schools, science, and society. In this metaphor, science education as a catalyst for alternative futures implies democratizing or redistributing who determines these outcomes. The suggestions I share in this section are meant to inspire teachers' imaginations about what is possible in science education.

Imagine how science education may look if the workforce needs of corporate or military interests did not have undue influence on what students learn in school. Imagine an educational system that was responsive instead to the hopes and aspirations of students, parents, and communities. Consider whether biology, chemistry, and physics are the courses that deserve to be prioritized. If we dislodged these disciplines as the gold standard of college preparatory curriculum, it could open space for other ideas, concepts, and practices. Science education as a catalyst for alternative futures foregrounds our collective well-being as inhabitants of Earth and emphasizes that this pursuit requires self-determination for communities who have been dispossessed and marginalized by racial capitalism and settler colonialism. In this section, I argue that an alternative series of courses could connect school science more tightly with the former goal, but that we can nevertheless pursue this work in our current courses. In the next section I explain how an SJSI approach to curriculum may contribute to the latter condition.

Two major global issues at the intersection of science and society have dominated our collective consciousness in recent years: climate change and pandemic. The rapid development of artificial intelligence and its many implications may constitute a third major challenge in this regard. And the specter of nuclear warfare always looms in the background of conversations about science, technology, and threats to thriving life on Earth. If we foreground our collective well-being as inhabitants of Earth, then requiring that all students take one course each in biology, chemistry, and physics does not align with our most pressing issues. The hallowed place of these three disciplines is the result of inertia in educational politics and false notions of intellectual rigor; it is not responsive to our current reality.[3] In fact, the status quo of science education has contributed to the creation of the current crises.

The structure of middle and high schools could benefit from all sorts of restructuring and rethinking—including what some educators call *abolition*.[4] But even within the existing structures, changing the conventional series of high school science courses could align the goals of learning more clearly with our collective well-being. Courses in environmental sciences, public health, and STS are more aligned with the education that young people deserve as they navigate their present and future circumstances in informed and thoughtful ways (see Table 6.1).[5] If we changed the courses students take in high schools, many students would still decide to pursue majors in biology, chemistry, and physics in college. In fact, the transdisciplinary perspectives they considered in high school would better equip them to be thoughtful practitioners of these disciplines. The alternative course sequence would provide everybody who attends high school with more opportunities to learn about issues like climate change, pandemic, and interactions with technology within their social and political context. If we truly value community engagement and sociopolitical agency as outcomes of our school systems, this kind of alternative pathway makes sense.

In a radical vision of science education, teachers could partner directly with grassroots organizations dedicated to environmental justice and public health equity to align science learning with social movements.[6] Indeed, a group of teachers and organizers has done exactly that over several years in Chicago.[7] STS courses could help students problematize their engagement with artificial intelligence, social media, and other communication technologies. These interfaces that already inspire youth engagement become topics to problematize and study rather than distractions from (or shortcuts through) their schoolwork. With the rapid expansion of computer science requirements and data science curriculum in high schools, STS courses could teach these skills while explicitly considering their social implications. Partnerships between grassroots organizations and technology educators, like the Young People's Race Power and Technology

TABLE 6.1 Reimagining high school science course sequence

	Canonical science education	*Science education as a catalyst for alternative futures*
9th Grade	Biology	Public Health
10th Grade	Chemistry	Environmental Sciences
11th Grade	Physics	Science, Technology, & Society
12th Grade	Advanced Science Elective	Community-Engaged Capstone Project

Project and Fresh Supply in Chicago, provide some excellent examples of what this can look like.[8] This kind of teaching encourages youth to engage with technologies in ways that challenge injustice rather than reproduce it.[9]

For teachers who are more inclined to pursue change within institutions, this alternative course sequence would also create opportunities for partnerships with governmental agencies to cultivate more sanctioned forms of civic engagement.[10] Required high school courses in environmental sciences could work with regional chapters of the EPA or municipal environmental departments to facilitate student voice in local environmental policies. High school public health courses might connect with the CDC or local agencies to similarly amplify the voice of the youth in issues of public health. Even as these agencies currently embody many of the same contradictions as schools and science, they too could be transformed to be more democratic and responsive to marginalized communities.

The fields of public health, environmental science, and STS have an inherent interdisciplinary character that differentiates them from the more rigid fields of biology, chemistry, and physics. For this reason, they lend themselves to curriculum organized around SJSI. With such a curriculum, this change in required courses would be more than simply swapping one set of content areas for another. Beyond even the inherent interdisciplinarity of these fields, the goal would be *trans*disciplinary courses. There are important distinctions between these words that are sometimes used interchangeably, including two that I highlight here. First, transdisciplinary teaching prioritizes addressing issues or problems ahead of communicating disciplinary ideas or developing disciplinary practices.[11] For example, teachers in southern Chile have taken up local impacts of the climate crisis as a generative theme to design curricula across all of their content areas.[12] Or an STS class could take up the ways in which social media and search engine algorithms reinforce problematic ideologies.[13] Second, transdisciplinary approaches include explicit reflection on the strengths and limitations of disciplinary ways of knowing.[14] In other words, the scientific disciplines themselves become objects of inquiry and critique. Therefore, it is important to emphasize that transdisciplinary teaching characterized by these distinctions does not need to wait for a new set of core courses.

The SJSI curriculum examples throughout this book illustrate that transdisciplinary teaching is possible in biology, chemistry, and physics classes too.

Even without changing high school graduation requirements, we can shift from organizing curricula around scientific phenomena to curricula that prioritize addressing SJSI in our current courses. In these transdisciplinary approaches, teachers ask themselves how their content area can be useful in themes that matter locally and globally. This question is the converse of asking how to connect the canon of school science with students' lives or interests.[15] The subtle difference between these converse approaches to curriculum represent the difference between a conventional pathway and an alternative one. Metaphorically, this is how catalysts allow us to choose between multiple possible outcomes of a reaction.

SCIENCE EDUCATION TOWARD MANY FUTURES

Changing the sequence of high school science courses would create opportunities to change other parts of school systems that interact with graduation requirements, like college admissions requirements and teacher preparation and licensure requirements. As a longtime chemistry teacher, a teacher educator, and somebody who has moved between high school and university teaching, I am sensitive to the ripple effects that changing any one of these pieces will have. Change can be difficult, but each of these policies is a site to intervene to create conditions that are less harsh, while we also plan radically different paths forward. We have an opportunity to reimagine all of the ways that we engage with education and the sciences because shifting toward transdisciplinary science courses that explicitly include more social, historical, and political context is neither a panacea nor a precondition for taking up the principles and possibilities described in this book.

This book focuses on principles and possibilities rather than "best practices," and it includes illustrative examples not ready-made lessons because there are no one-size-fits-all approaches. Teaching is always deeply contextual. Different peoples and communities have, what Eve Tuck and K. Wayne Yang call, "diverse dreams of justice in education."[16] For that reason, the alternative pathways created through science education as a catalyst for alternative futures should be determined locally by groups that include educators, students, parents, community elders, organizers, and scientists. Under ideal conditions, these constituencies would work together to determine the priorities for science education and then co-design curricula to meet their goals and aspirations. As I write this, I am cognizant of the ways in which concepts like local control and parents' rights have been co-opted by well-funded reactionary groups that seek to prohibit education from confronting issues like oppression and climate change. And yet, I still believe deeply in the importance of education being determined democratically and in ways that honor the rights of marginalized communities to educate their own children.

With the tension between local control and science education for our collective wellbeing, rethinking policies, like graduation requirements and standards, may be helpful to make space for more transformational grassroots change efforts. They may also guard against distortions of local place-based science education initiatives. For example, the increased emphasis on climate change in the NGSS, as compared with previous standards, is a barrier against the fossil fuel lobby's efforts to corrupt science education to meet their interests. At the same time, the underlying ideologies of the standards do not align with climate justice nor education for a just transition away from extractive economic systems. Science education toward transformational goals is more likely to be taken up in grassroots contexts. In another example from Chicago, a district-wide graduation requirement for service-learning projects in content area classes created space for projects that addressed environmental racism in chemistry classes. The policy created space for small groups of teachers, scientists, community organizers, and young people to work together at the school and neighborhood level. For science education to enhance the self-determination of marginalized communities, teachers need time, resources, and support to reimagine science classes alongside young people, parents, and other community members. This means infusing more resources into schools; while most schools need more physical resources like textbooks, technology, or even lab supplies, those are not what are needed most. What we need most is smaller class sizes, more time for teacher learning, and enhanced services for students' physical, mental, and emotional wellbeing.

One of the things that happens when teachers have more time and support to learn is that they can think about their work and their content areas differently. This includes imagining alternate pathways and dreaming of different futures. These possibilities can include distant utopian visions and more immediate changes. In the teacher collectives in which I have participated, we build in opportunities for teachers to envision and imagine aspirational lessons and projects. This type of activity translates well for pre-service teachers too. In my courses for teacher candidates, students spend time writing and talking about projects they envision implementing at some point in their careers. I encourage readers, upon finishing this book, to spend some time drawing up a science curriculum project that you dream about pulling off in your classes next year or five years from now. This should be the kind of classroom undertaking that would make you proud—a unit or project that embodies your values and the values of the community where you teach. You can share this dream lesson with a friend. You can write it down. You can begin reaching out to colleagues and community members who can help you make it happen. In one of our summer planning institutes for teacher collectives, after doing this lesson-dreaming activity, teachers co-wrote "problem-posing letters" with local community activists or youth. These letters articulated a charge to their next group of students to take up a justice-oriented project in science class that mattered in the local community. The letters were signed by their teacher, community members, and in some cases, students from previous years. Teachers could work with parents or other elders to write these letters too. This kind of community charge represents a much different way to set the learning goals for a science class than standardized benchmarks, grades, or exams.

For a long time, the soil project that has been described in this book was an aspirational project for me. The most important factor in being able to implement several versions of that project has been my ongoing engagement with small groups of colleagues that included community organizers, scientists, and fellow science teachers. Facilitating and participating in collectives like this has been the most effective driver of my development as a teacher, and other teachers with whom I have collaborated say the same thing. Our small groups of teachers from different schools have met in living rooms over summer break, in classrooms on teacher institute days, or even on Saturdays in university or community spaces. There are four commitments shared by these teacher collectives that I briefly emphasize here, with the hope that this book will seed the formation of more such groups. The first commitment is that we have not limited these groups to science teachers, even though science teachers often comprise the majority of the group. We have been fortunate enough to work with scientists, community organizers, and young people in ways that amplify their voices about what matters in science teaching. Even though members who occupy other roles are oftentimes also parents, one direction for growth for our groups is to account more explicitly for parents' voices. The second commitment is humility, which is not just a recognition of what we do not know or cannot do, but a recognition of our interconnectedness and interdependence.[17] These first two principles are therefore related. Teachers, scientists, organizers, youth, and parents all have expertise, which is interrelated and complementary in the development of science education as a catalyst for change. We believe it is important to acknowledge our formal roles so that we hear each other across perspectives while also consciously flattening hierarchies. Another manifestation of our commitment to humility is a commitment to transdisciplinary teaching, which is connected to our recognition of the limitations and interdependence of the sciences and other ways of knowing. One example of this commitment has been dedicating large segments of our science teacher institutes to studying the historical contexts of SJSI and the communities where we teach. Our third commitment is to praxis, defined as theory and practice or practice and reflection. In other words, we treat teaching itself as a learning opportunity, recognizing that we only learn from our experience teaching if we dedicate time and space to reflecting on it. Finally, a commitment to hope has been a consistent theme articulated by my colleagues in these collectives.[18] In other words, we believe in the potential of science education to inform the power of organized people to build different worlds.

Hope is at the heart of science education as a catalyst for alternative futures. Using the plural of the word *futures* is an intentional choice indicating belief in self-determination for communities whose pasts and presents have been overdetermined by oppression and domination. This is an acknowledgement of sovereignty and heterogeneity even within profound interdependence. All the Earth's inhabitants are connected by our shared dependence on the planet's land, water, air, and the cycles of materials that move through them. Our interconnection is deepened and further complicated by human-created food systems, transportation systems, school systems, and so on. These are the relationships and systems that science education should be asking students to consider and radically reimagine.

Referring to futures is a recognition that our interconnectedness as inhabitants of Earth does not imply a singular path forward. There is not one correct formation of human community. There is not one right way to understand the Earth's systems or the universe beyond. There is no single universal science. If nothing else, science education as a catalyst for alternative futures engages students with concepts of interdependence through difference. As a metaphoric catalyst, the role of science education is subtle, limited, small—and yet still vitally important. Science education as a catalyst for alternative futures can help to orient our social systems in directions that accelerate change under conditions that are less harsh, toward multiple outcomes that are more just and sustainable.

Notes

Introduction

1. Glen S. Aikenhead, *Science Education for Everyday Life: Evidence-Based Practice* (New York: Teachers College Press, 2006); The Committee on Equal Opportunities in Science and Engineering, *Biennial Report to Congress: Investing in Diverse Community Voices* (Alexandria, VA: National Science Foundation, 2018).
2. National Research Council, *A Framework for K–12 Science Education: Practices, Crosscutting Concepts, and Core Ideas* (Washington, DC: National Academies, 2012), 278.
3. Jeannie Oakes, *Multiplying Inequalities: The Effects of Race, Social Class, and Tracking on Opportunities to Learn Mathematics and Science* (Santa Monica, CA: RAND, 1990); William Tate, "Science Education as a Civil Right: Urban Schools and Opportunity-to-Learn Considerations," *Journal of Research in Science Teaching* 38, no. 9 (2001), http://doi.org/10.1002/tea.1045; Peggy J. Trygstad, Kristen A. Malzahn, Eric R. Banilower, Courtney L. Plumley, and Anna D. Bruce, "Are All Students Getting Equal Access to High-Quality Science Education? Data from the 2018 NSSME+" (Chapel Hill, NC: Horizon Research, 2020), https://files.eric.ed.gov/fulltext/ED614661.pdf.
4. Megan Bang, Beth Warren, Ann S. Rosebery, and Douglas Medin, "Desettling Expectations in Science Education," *Human Development* 55, no. 5–6 (2013), http://doi.org/10.1159/000345322; Na'ilah Suad Nasir and Sepehr Vakil, "STEM-Focused Academies in Urban Schools: Tensions and Possibilities," *Journal of the Learning Sciences* 26, no. 3 (2017), http://doi.org/10.1080/10508406.2017.1314215; Ebony O. McGee, *Black, Brown, Bruised: How Racialized STEM Education Stifles Innovation* (Cambridge, MA: Harvard Education Press, 2020).
5. Bryan A. Brown, *Science in the City: Culturally Relevant STEM Education* (Cambridge, MA: Harvard Education Press, 2019); Angela Calabrese Barton and Edna Tan, "Funds of Knowledge and Discourses and Hybrid Space," *Journal of Research in Science Teaching* 46, no. 1 (2009), http://doi.org/10.1002/tea.20269; Christopher Emdin, *Urban Science Education for the Hip-Hop Generation: Essential Tools for the Urban Science Educator and Researcher* (Boston: Sense, 2010); Maria Varelas, ed., *Identity Construction and Science Education Research: Learning, Teaching, and Being in Multiple Contexts (Vol. 35)* (Boston: Sense, 2012).
6. Maria González-Howard and Enrique Suárez, "Retiring the Term English Language Learners: Moving Toward Linguistic Justice Through Asset-Oriented Framing," *Journal of Research in Science Teaching* 58, no. 5 (2021): 749–752, http://doi.org/10.1002/tea.21684.
7. Daniel Morales-Doyle and Eric "Rico" Gutstein, "Racial Capitalism and STEM Education in the Chicago Public Schools," *Race, Ethnicity, and Education* 22, no. 4 (2019), http://doi.org/10.1080/13613324.2019.1592840.
8. Antonia Darder, *Reinventing Paulo Freire: A Pedagogy of Love* (Boulder, CO: Westview, 2002).
9. Joel Spring, *Deculturalization and the Struggle for Equality: A Brief History of the Education of Dominated Cultures in the United States* (New York: Routledge, 1994).

10. Megan Bang, Ananda Marin, and Douglas Medin, "If Indigenous Peoples Stand with the Sciences, Will Scientists Stand with Us?," *Dædalus, Journal of the American Academy of Arts and Sciences* 147, no. 2 (2018), http://doi.org/10.1162/DAED_a_00498.
11. Juan C. Garibay, "STEM Students' Social Agency and Views on Working for Social Change: Are STEM Disciplines Developing Socially and Civically Responsible Students?," *Journal of Research in Science Teaching* 52, no. 5 (2015), http://doi.org/10.1002/tea.21203.
12. Kristen L. Gunckel and Sara Tolbert, "The Imperative to Move Toward a Dimension of Care in Engineering Education," *Journal of Research in Science Teaching* 55, no. 7 (2018), http://doi.org/10.1002/tea.21458.
13. Sandra Harding, *The Science Question in Feminism* (Ithica, NY: Cornell University Press, 1986).
14. Daniel Morales-Doyle and Kenneth Booker, "Transforming the Extractive Politics of STEM Education and CTE," in *Handbook of Critical Approaches to the Politics and Policy of Education*, ed. K. Saltman and N. Nguyen (New York: Routledge, forthcoming).
15. Bettina L. Love, *We Want to Do More Than Survive: Abolitionist Teaching and the Pursuit of Educational Freedom* (Boston: Beacon, 2019).
16. Maxine Greene, *Releasing the Imagination: Essays on Education, the Arts, and Social Change* (San Francisco: Jossey-Bass, 2000).
17. Paulo Freire, *Pedagogy of Hope* (New York: Continuum, 2004), 65.
18. Daniel Morales-Doyle, Maria Varelas, David Segura, and Marcela Bernal-Munera, "Access, Dissent, Ethics, Politics: Pre-Service Teachers Negotiating Conceptions of the Work of Teaching Science for Equity," *Cognition and Instruction* 39, no. 1 (2021): 35–64, http://doi.org/10.1080/07370008.2020.1828421.
19. Manali J. Sheth, "Grappling with Racism as Foundational Practice of Science Teaching," *Science Education* 103, no. 1 (2019): 37–60, http://doi.org/10.1002/sce.21450.
20. Django Paris and H. Samy Alim, eds., *Culturally Sustaining Pedagogies: Teaching and Learning for Justice in a Changing World* (New York: Teachers College Press, 2017); Gloria Ladson-Billings, "But That's Just Good Teaching! The Case for Culturally Relevant Pedagogy," *Theory Into Practice* 34, no. 3 (1995), http://doi.org/10.1080/00405849509543675.
21. Eve Tuck and K. Wayne Yang, eds., *Toward What Justice? Describing Diverse Dreams of Justice in Education* (New York: Routledge, 2018).
22. Daniel Morales-Doyle, Alejandra Frausto Aceves, Tiffany L. Childress-Price, and Mindy J. Chappell, "History, Hope, and Humility in Praxis: Co-Determining Priorities for Professional Learning with Content Area Teachers" (unpublished manuscript).

Chapter 1
1. Robert D. Bullard, *The Quest for Environmental Justice: Human Rights and the Politics of Pollution* (San Francisco: Sierra Club, 2005).
2. Christine E. Sleeter and Carl A. Grant, *Making Choices for Multicultural Education: Five Approaches to Race, Class, and Gender* (Hoboken, NJ: Wiley, 2007).
3. John L. Rudolph, *How We Teach Science: What's Changed and Why It Matters* (Cambridge, MA: Harvard University Press, 2019).
4. Glen S. Aikenhead, *Science Education for Everyday Life: Evidence-Based Practice* (New York: Teachers College Press, 2006).
5. Carl von Linné, Systema Naturae, ed. 10 (facsimile downloaded from https://www.biodiversitylibrary.org/item/10277#page/12/mode/1up, 1759).
6. Richard Levins, "Ten Propositions on Science and Antiscience," in *Biology Under the Influence: Dialectical Essays on Ecology, Agriculture, and Health* (New York: Monthly Review), 91.

7. Jonathan Marks, "Long Shadow of Linnaeus's Human Taxonomy," *Nature* 447, no. 28 (May 2007), https://doi.org/10.1038/447028a; Jonathan Marks, *Is Science Racist?* (Cambridge: Polity, 2017).
8. "Linnaeus and Race," The Linnean Society of London, September 3, 2020, https://www.linnean.org/learning/who-was-linnaeus/linnaeus-and-race.
9. Kathryn L. Kirchgasler and Diego Román, "Historicizing Language-as-Resource: Why Science Education's Raciolinguistic Histories Matter for Translanguaging Today," *Journal of Research in Science Teaching* (under revision); Kathryn L. Kirchgasler, "Tracking Disparities: How Schools Make Up Scientific Americans and Pathologized Others" (PhD diss., University of Wisconsin-Madison, 2018).
10. Peter Loyson, "Chemistry in the Time of the Pharoahs," *Journal of Chemical Education* 88, no. 2 (2011): 146–150, http://www.doi.org/10.1021/ed100492a.
11. Clifford D. Conner, *A People's History of Science: Miners, Midwives, and Low Mechanicks* (New York: Nation Books, 2005).
12. Luis Ortiz-Franco, "Chicanos Have Math in Their Blood: Pre-Columbian Mathematics," *Radical Teacher*, no. 43 (1993): 10–14, https://www.jstor.org/stable/20709756.
13. la paperson, *A Third University Is Possible* (Minneapolis: University of Minnesota Press, 2017).
14. Craig Steven Wilder, *Ebony and Ivy: Race, Slavery and the Troubled History of America's Universities* (New York: Bloomsbury, 2013).
15. Linda Tuhiwai Smith, *Decolonizing Methodologies: Research and Indigenous Peoples* (New York: Zed, 1999).
16. Emory D. Keoke and Kay M. Porterfield, *American Indian Contributions to the World: 15,000 Years of Inventions and Innovations* (New York: Checkmark, 2003).
17. Aikenhead, *Science Education for Everyday Life*.
18. Liliana Valladares, "Post-Truth and Education: STS Vaccines to Re-Establish Science in the Public Sphere," *Science and Education* (2021); http://www.doi.org/10.1007/s11191-021-00239-0.
19. Arthur Boylston, "The Origins of Inoculation," *Journal of the Royal Society of Medicine* 105, no. 7 (2012): 309–313, http://www.doi.org/10.1258/jrsm.2012.12k044.
20. Ainissa Ramírez, *The Alchemy of Us: How Humans and Matter Transformed One Another* (Cambridge, MA: MIT Press, 2020); Ainissa Ramirez, "Hidden Black Scientists Proved the Polio Vaccine Worked," *Scientific American* (June 17, 2021), https://www.scientificamerican.com/article/hidden-black-scientists-proved-the-polio-vaccine-worked/.
21. Lisa Thomas, *Homeland: Four Portraits of Native Action*, directed by Roberta Grossman (Berkeley, CA: Katahdin Productions, 2005), DVD.
22. Southwest Research and Information Center, http://www.sric.org/voices/2002/v3n3/navajo.php.
23. Martin Luther King, Jr., "The Quest for Peace and Justice," Nobel Lecture (December 11, 1964), https://www.nobelprize.org/prizes/peace/1964/king/lecture/.
24. Neil deGrasse Tyson and Avis Lang, *Accessory to War: The Unspoken Alliance Between Astrophysics and the Military* (New York: W. W. Norton, 2018).
25. Shirin Vossoughi and Sepehr Vakil, "Towards What Ends? A Critical Analysis of Militarism, Equity, and STEM Education," in *At War: The Fight for Students of Color in America's Public Schools*, ed. Arshad I. Ali and Tracy L. Buenavista (New York: Fordham University Press, 2018), 117–140.
26. Thomas M. Philip, Ayush Gupta, Andrew Elby, and Chandra Turpen, "Why Ideology Matters for Learning: A Case of Ideological Convergence in an Engineering Ethics Classroom Discussion on Drone Warfare," *Journal of the Learning Sciences* 27, no. 2 (2018): 183–223, http://www.doi.org/10.1080/10508406.2017.1381964.

27. Manali J. Sheth, "Grappling with Racism as Foundational Practice of Science Teaching," *Science Education* 103, no. 1 (2019): 37–60, http://www.doi.org/10.1002/sce.21450.
28. Mark Windschitl, Jessica Thompson, and Melissa Braaten, *Ambitious Science Teaching* (Cambridge, MA: Harvard Education Press, 2018).
29. Aikenhead, *Science Education for Everyday Life*.
30. David Segura, Daniel Morales-Doyle, Susan Nelson, Amy Levingston, and Karen Canales, "Sustaining Community-School Relationships Around Shared Visions of Climate Justice and Science Teaching," *Connected Science Learning* 3, no. 5 (2021), https://www.nsta.org/connected-science-learning/connected-science-learning-september-october-2021/sustaining-community.
31. Paul Mohai, Byoung-Suk Kweon, Sangyun Lee, and Kerry Ard, "Air Pollution Around Schools Is Linked to Poorer Student Health and Academic Performance," *Health Affairs* 30, no. 5 (2011): 852–862, http://www.doi.org/10.1377/hlthaff.2011.0077.
32. Images of original student work and more analysis available in Daniel Morales-Doyle, "Justice-Centered Science Pedagogy: A Catalyst for Academic Achievement and Social Transformation," *Science Education* 101, no. 6 (2017): 1034–1060, https://doi.org/10.1002/sce.21305.
33. Antonia Darder, *Reinventing Paulo Freire: A Pedagogy of Love* (Boulder, CO: Westview, 2002).
34. Bill Bigelow, "Scholastic Inc – Pushing Coal," *Rethinking Schools* 25, no. 4 (2011), https://rethinkingschools.org/articles/scholastic-inc-pushing-coal-2/.
35. Katie Worth, "Climate Change Skeptic Group Seeks to Influence 200,000 Teachers," *Frontline* (March 28, 2017), https://www.pbs.org/wgbh/frontline/article/climate-change-skeptic-group-seeks-to-influence-200000-teachers/.
36. Jie Jenny Zou, "Oil's Pipeline to America's Schools: Inside the Fossil-Fuel Industry's Not-So-Subtle Push Into K–12 Education," https://apps.publicintegrity.org/oil-education/ (Washington, DC: Center for Public Integrity, 2017).
37. Alberto J. Rodriguez, "What About a Dimension of Engagement, Equity, and Diversity Practices? A Critique of the Next Generation Science Standards," *Journal of Research in Science Teaching* 52, no. 7 (2015): 1031–1051, http://www.doi.org/10.1002/tea.21232.
38. Kristen L. Gunckel and Sara Tolbert, "The Imperative to Move Toward a Dimension of Care in Engineering Education," *Journal of Research in Science Teaching* 55, no. 7 (2018): 938–961, http://www.doi.org/10.1002/tea.21458; Darren G. Hoeg and John L. Bencze, "Values Underpinning STEM Education in the USA: An Analysis of the Next Generation Science Standards," *Science Education* 101, no. 2 (2017): 278–301, http://www.doi.org/10.1002/sce.21260; Matthew Weinstein, "NGSS, Disposability, and the Ambivalence of Science in/under Neoliberalism," *Cultural Studies of Science Education* 12, no. 4 (2017): 821–834, http://www.doi.org/10.1007/s11422-017-9844-y.
39. Max Liboiron, *Pollution Is Colonialism* (Durham, NC: Duke University Press, 2021).

Chapter 2

1. G. Cristina Mora, *Making Hispanics: How Activists, Bureaucrats, and Media Constructed a New American* (Chicago: University of Chicago Press, 2014).
2. Lázaro Lima, "Latino Louisiana," in *Latino America: A State-by-State Encyclopedia, Volume 1: Alabama-Missouri*, ed. Mark Overmyer-Velázquez (Santa Barbara, CA: ABC-CLIO, 2008), 347–361; Gilbert C. Din, *The Canary Islanders of Louisiana* (Baton Rouge: Louisiana State University Press, 1988).
3. Daniel Morales-Doyle, Shirin Vossoughi, Sepehr Vakil, and Megan Bang, "In an Era of Pandemic and Protest, STEM Education Can't Pretend to Be Apolitical," *Truthout*,

August 19, 2020, https://truthout.org/articles/in-an-era-of-pandemic-and-protest-stem-education-cant-pretend-to-be-apolitical/.
4. Decoteau J. Irby, "I Am, We Are Somebodies: An Introduction to the Idea of Dignity," in *Dignitiy Affirming Education: Cultivating the Somebodiness of Students and Educators,* ed. Decoteau J. Irby, Charity Anderson, and Charles Payne (New York: Teachers College Press, 2022), 1–20.
5. Daniel Morales-Doyle and David O. Stovall, "Contradictions and the Dignity of Resistance: Truth and Reckoning at a Social Justice School," in *Dignity Affirming Education: Cultivating the Somebodiness of Students and Educators,* ed. Decoteau J. Irby, Charity Anderson, and Charles Payne (New York: Teachers College Press, 2022), 42–58.
6. Django Paris and H. Samy Alim, eds., *Culturally Sustaining Pedagogies: Teaching and Learning for Justice in a Changing World* (New York: Teachers College Press, 2017).
7. Thomas M. Philip, "An 'Ideology in Pieces' Approach to Studying Change in Teachers' Sensemaking About Race, Racism, and Racial Justice," *Cognition and Instruction* 29, no. 3 (2011): 297–329, http://www.doi.org/10.1080/07370008.2011.583369.
8. Daniel Morales-Doyle, "Students as Curriculum Critics: Standpoints with Respect to Relevance, Goals, and Science," *Journal of Research in Science Teaching* 55, no. 5 (2018): 749–773, http://www.doi.org/10.1002/tea.21438.
9. Richard R. Valencia, *Dismantling Contemporary Deficit Thinking: Educational Thought and Practice* (New York: Routledge, 2010).
10. Philip, "An 'Ideology in Pieces' Approach."
11. Daniel Morales-Doyle, Maria Varelas, David Segura, and Marcela Bernal-Munera, "Access, Dissent, Ethics, Politics: Pre-Service Teachers Negotiating Conceptions of the Work of Teaching Science for Equity," *Cognition and Instruction* 39, no. 1 (2021): 35–64, http://www.doi.org/10.1080/07370008.2020.1828421.
12. Valencia, *Dismantling Contemporary Deficit Thinking.*
13. Norma Gonzalez, Luis C. Moll, Martha Floyd Tenery, Anna Rivera, Patricia Rendon, Raquel Gonzales, and Cathy Amanti, "Funds of Knowledge for Teaching in Latino Households," *Urban Education* 29, no. 4 (1995): 443–470, http://www.doi.org/10.1177/0042085995029004005; Luis C. Moll, Cathy Amanti, Deborah Neff, and Norma Gonzalez, "Funds of Knowledge for Teaching: Using a Qualitative Approach to Connect Homes and Classrooms," *Theory Into Practice* 31, no. 2 (1992): 132–141, http://www.doi.org/10.1080/00405849209543534.
14. Angela Calabrese Barton and Edna Tan, "Funds of Knowledge and Discourses and Hybrid Space," *Journal of Research in Science Teaching* 46, no. 1 (2009), http://www.doi.org/10.1002/tea.20269.
15. Gerald Markowitz and David Rosner, *Lead Wars: The Politics of Science and the Fate of America's Children* (Berkeley, CA: University of California Press, 2013).
16. Shirin Vossoughi, Natalie R. Davis, Ava Jackson, Ruben Echevarria, Arturo Muñoz, and Meg Escudé, "Beyond the Binary of Adult Versus Child Centered Learning: Pedagogies of Joint Activity in the Context of Making," *Cognition and Instruction* 39, no. 4 (2021): 211–241, http://www.doi.org/10.1080/07370008.2020.1860052.
17. Natalie R. Davis, Shirin Vossoughi, and John F. Smith, "Learning from Below: A Micro-Ethnographic Account of Children's Self-Determination as Sociopolitical and Intellectual Action," *Learning, Culture and Social Interaction* 24 (2020): 100373, http://www.doi.org10.1016/j.lcsi.2019.100373.
18. Glen S. Aikenhead, *Science Education for Everyday Life: Evidence-Based Practice* (New York: Teachers College Press, 2006).

19. Patricia Hill Collins, "Learning from the Outsider Within: The Sociological Significance of Black Feminist Thought," *Social Problems* 33, no. 6 (1986): 14–32, http://doi.org/10.2307/800672.
20. Sandra Harding, "Rethinking Standpoint Epistemology: What Is 'Strong Objectivity'?," *Centennial Review* 36, no. 3 (1992): 437–470, https://www.jstor.org/stable/23739232; William F. McComas, "Considering a Consensus View of Nature of Science Content for School Science Purposes," in *Nature of Science in Science Instruction: Rationales and Strategies*, ed. William F. McComas (Cham: Springer, 2020), https://doi.org/10.1007/978-3-030-57239-6_2.
21. Gregory Cajete, *Native Science: Natural Laws of Interdependence* (Santa Fe, NM: Clear Light, 2000).
22. Thomas M. Philip, Megan Bang, and Kara Jackson, "Articulating the 'How,' the 'For What,' the 'For Whom,' and the 'With Whom' in Concert: A Call to Broaden the Benchmarks of Our Scholarship," *Cognition and Instruction* 36, no. 2 (2018): 83–88, http://www.doi.org/10.1080/07370008.2018.1413530.
23. Alberto J. Rodriguez, "Strategies for Counterresistance: Toward Sociotransformative Constructivism and Learning to Teach Science for Diversity and for Understanding," *Journal of Research in Science Teaching* 35, no. 6 (1998): 589–622.
24. Henry A. Giroux, *Teachers as Intellectuals: Toward a Critical Pedagogy of Learning* (Westport, CT: Bergin and Garvey, 1988).
25. Jeffrey M. R. Duncan-Andrade and Ernest Morrell, *The Art of Critical Pedagogy: Possibilities for Moving from Theory to Practice in Urban Schools* (New York: Peter Lang, 2008); Augustine Romero, "Critically Compassionate Intellectualism: The Pedagogy of Barriorganic Intellectualism," in *Raza Studies: The Public Option for Educational Revolution*, ed. Julio Cammarota and Augustine Romero (Tucson, AZ: University of Arizona Press, 2014).
26. Michael W. Sjoding, Robert P. Dickson, Theodore J. Iwashyna, Steven E. Gay, and Thomas S. Valley, "Racial Bias in Pulse Oximetry Measurement," *New England Journal of Medicine* 383 (2020): 2477–2478, http://www.doi.org/10.1056/NEJMc2029240; Martin J. Tobin and Amal Jubran, "Pulse Oximetry, Racial Bias and Statistical Bias," *Annals of Intensive Care* 12, no. 2 (2022), http://www.doi.org/10.1186/s13613-021-00974-7.
27. Jomo W. Mutegi, Demetrice Smith-Mutegi, and Nicole Lewis, "Fostering Critical Perspectives of Science Among Preservice Elementary Teachers: An Empirical Identification of Affordances and Hindrances," *Journal of Science Teacher Education* 33, no. 8 (2022), http://www.doi.org/10.1080/1046560X.2021.2015531.
28. Lundy Braun, *Breathing Race Into the Machine: The Surprising Career of the Spirometer from Plantation to Genetics* (Minneapolis: University of Minnesota Press, 2014).
29. Dorothy E. Roberts, "Abolish Race Correction," *Lancet* 397, no. 10268 (2021): 17–18, http://www.doi.org/10.1016/S0140-6736(20)32716-1.
30. Alice B. Popejoy, "Too Many Scientists Still Say Caucasian," *Nature* 596 (2021): 463, http://www.doi.org/10.1038/d41586-021-02288-x.
31. Dorothy E. Roberts, *Fatal Invention: How Science, Politics, and Big Business Re-Create Race in the Twenty-First Century* (New York: New Press, 2011).
32. Michael Omi and Howard Winant, *Racial Formation in the United States*, 3rd ed. (New York: Routledge, 2014).

Chapter 3

1. Alexis D. Riley and Felicia Moore Mensah, "'My Curriculum Has No Soul!': A Case Study of the Experiences of Black Women Science Teachers Working at Charter Schools," *Journal

of Science Teacher Education 34, no. 1 (2023): 86–103, https://doi.org/10.1080/1046560X.2022.2028710.
2. Daniel Morales-Doyle, "Putting Science Education in Its Place: The Science Question in Social Justice Education," *Cultural Studies of Science Education* 18, no. 1 (2023): 81–94, http://www.doi.org/10.1007/s11422-023-10151-w.
3. Mark Windschitl, Jessica Thompson, and Melissa Braaten, *Ambitious Science Teaching* (Cambridge, MA: Harvard Education Press, 2018).
4. Paulo Freire, *Pedagogy of the Oppressed* (New York: Continuum, 1970/2001).
5. Michael Apple, *Ideology and Curriculum*, 3rd ed. (New York: Routledge Farmer, 2004).
6. Mindy Chappell and Tiffany Childress Price, "Tiffany Childress-Price and Dr. Mindy Chappell: Youth Participatory Science and Student Power," interview by Nina Hike and Celeste Ramovic, *Pushing Praxis*, podcast audio, February 13, 2022, https://pushingpraxis.org/2022/02/13/tiffany-childress-price-and-dr-mindy-chappell-youth-participatory-science-amp-student-power/.
7. Jeffrey M. R. Duncan-Andrade, *What a Coach Can Teach a Teacher: Lessons Urban Schools Can Learn from a Successful Sports Program* (New York: Peter Lang, 2010).
8. Shirin Vossoughi, Natalie R. Davis, Ava Jackson, Ruben Echevarria, Arturo Muñoz, and Meg Escudé, "Beyond the Binary of Adult Versus Child Centered Learning: Pedagogies of Joint Activity in the Context of Making," *Cognition and Instruction* 39, no. 4 (2021): 211–241, http://www.doi.org/10.1080/07370008.2020.1860052.
9. American Chemical Society, *Chemistry in the Community*, 4th ed. (New York: W. H. Freeman, 2002).
10. Deborah Spar, "Markets: Continuity and Change in the International Diamond Market," *Journal of Economic Perspectives* 20, no. 3 (2006): 195–208, http://www.doi.org/10.1257/jep.20.3.195.
11. Sepehr Vakil, "'I've Always Been Scared That Someday I'm Going to Sell Out': Exploring the Relationship Between Political Identity and Learning in Computer Science Education," *Cognition and Instruction* 38, no. 2 (2020): 103, http://www.doi.org/10.1080/07370008.2020.1730374.
12. Marjorie Faulstich Orellana, Lisa Dorner, and Lucila Pulido, "Accessing Assets: Immigrant Youth's Work as Family Translators or 'Para-Phrasers,'" *Social Problems* 50, no. 4 (2003): 505–524, http://www.doi.org/10.1525/sp.2003.50.4.505.
13. Marc Mauer, "Addressing Racial Disparities in Incarceration," *Prison Journal* 91, no. 3 (2011): 87S–101S, http://www.doi.org/10.1177/0032885511415227.
14. Megan Bang, "Learning on the Move Toward Just, Sustainable, and Culturally Thriving Futures," *Cognition and Instruction* 38, no. 3 (2020): 434–444, http://www.doi.org/10.1080/07370008.2020.1777999.
15. Joel Spring, *Deculturalization and the Struggle for Equality: A Brief History of the Education of Dominated Cultures in the United States* (New York: McGraw-Hill, 2003).
16. Daniel Morales-Doyle and David O. Stovall, "Contradictions and the Dignity of Resistance: Truth and Reckoning at a Social Justice School," in *Somebodiness: Theory and Methods of Dignity-Based Education,* ed. Decoteau J. Irby, Charles Payne, and Charity Anderson (New York: Teachers College Press, 2022).
17. Sara Tolbert, Alexa Schindel, and Alberto J. Rodriguez, "Relevance and Relational Responsibility in Justice-Oriented Science Education Research," *Science Education* 102, no. 4 (2018): 796–819, http://www.doi.org/10.1002/sce.21446.
18. Freire, *Pedagogy of the Oppressed*.

19. Pilar O'Cádiz, Pia Lindquist Wong, and Carlos Alberto Torres, *Education and Democracy: Paulo Freire, Social Movements and Educational Reform in São Paulo* (Boulder, CO: Westview, 1998).
20. Alejandra Frausto, "Coaching Teachers to Construct Critical Science Pedagogies with Marginalized Urban Youth," paper presented at the Annual International Conference of NARST, Chicago, Illinois (April 2015).
21. Ole Skovsmose, "Mathematical Literacy and Globalisation," in *Internationalisation and Globalisation in Mathematics and Science Education*, ed. Bill Atweh, Angela Calabrese Barton, Marcelo C. Borba, Noel Gough, Christine Keitel-Kreidt, Catherine Vistro-Yu, and Renuka Vithal (Dordrecht: Springer, 2008), 3–18.
22. Joan Solomon and Glen Aikenhead, eds., *STS Education: International Perspectives on Reform* (New York: Teachers College Press, 1994).
23. Penny LeCouteur and Jay Burreson, *Napoleon's Buttons: 17 Molecules That Changed History* (New York: Penguin, 2003).
24. Gregory Cajete, *Native Science: Natural Laws of Interdependence* (Santa Fe, NM: Clear Light); Clifford D. Conner, *A People's History of Science: Miners, Midwives, and Low Mechanicks* (New York: Nation Books, 2005).
25. Conner, *A People's History of Science*; Robert DeKosky and Douglas Allchin, eds., *An Introduction to the History of Science in Non-Western Traditions*, 2nd ed. (Seattle: History of Science Society, 2008).
26. Ruha Benjamin, *Race After Technology* (Medford, MA: Polity, 2009); Robin Wall Kimmerer, *Braiding Sweetgrass: Indigenous Wisdom, Scientific Knowledge, and the Teachings of Plants* (Minneapolis: Milkweed Editions, 2013); Ainissa Ramirez, *The Alchemy of Us: How Humans and Matter Transformed One Another* (Cambridge, MA: MIT Press, 2020).
27. Kishonna L. Gray, *Intersectional Tech: Black Users in Digital Gaming* (Baton Rouge: Louisiana State University Press, 2020).
28. William A. Sandoval, Jarod Kawasaki, and Heather F. Clark, "Characterizing Classroom Discourse Across Scales," *Research in Science Education* 51, no. 1 (2021): 35–49, http://www.doi.org/10.1007/s11165-020-09953-7.
29. Windschitl, Thompson, and Braaten, *Ambitious Science Teaching*.
30. These two practices are the first two phases of what Alejandra Frausto Aceves and I have called Youth Participatory Science, but they also can be applied separately from the rest of that framework. Daniel Morales-Doyle and Alejandra Frausto, "Youth Participatory Science: A Grassroots Curriculum Framework," *Educational Action Research* 29, no. 1 (2021): 60–78, https://doi.org/10.1080/09650792.2019.1706598.
31. Manning Marable, "Katrina's Unnatural Disaster: A Tragedy of Black Suffering and White Denial," *Souls* 8, no. 1 (2006): 1–8, http://www.doi.org/10.1080/10999940500516942.
32. Britt Russert, *Fugitive Science: Empiricism and Freedom in Early African American Culture* (New York: New York University Press, 2017).
33. Bryan A. Brown and Jomo W. Mutegi, "A Paradigm of Contradictions: Racism and Science Education," in *International Encyclopedia of Education*, 3rd ed., ed. Eva Baker, Penelope Peterson, and Barry McGaw (Cambridge, MA: Elsevier, 2010), 554–564, http://www.doi.org/10.1016/B978-0-08-044894-7.00124-X.
34. Dorothy Roberts, *Fatal Invention: How Science, Politics, and Big Business Re-Create Race in the Twenty-First Century* (New York: New Press, 2012).
35. Ann Morning, Hannah Brückner, and Alondra Nelson, "Socially Desirable Reporting and the Expression of Biological Concepts of Race," *Du Bois Review: Social Science Research on Race* 16, no. 2 (2019): 439–455, http://www.doi.org/10.1017/S1742058X19000195.

36. Brian M. Donovan, "Learned Inequality: Racial Labels in the Biology Curriculum Can Affect the Development of Racial Prejudice," *Journal of Research in Science Teaching* 54, no. 3 (2017): 379–411, http://www.doi.org/10.1002/tea.21370.
37. Kelly M. Hoffman, Sophie Trawalter, Jordan R. Axt, and M. Norman Oliver, "Racial Bias in Pain Assessment and Treatment Recommendations, and False Beliefs About Biological Differences Between Blacks and Whites," *Proceedings of the National Academy of Sciences* 113, no. 16 (2016): 4296–4301, http://www.doi.org/10.1073/pnas.1516047113.
38. Dawn Gill and Les Levidow, eds., *Anti-Racist Science Teaching* (London: Free Association, 1987).
39. Michael Vance, "Biology Teaching in a Racist Society," in *Anti-Racist Science Teaching*, ed. Dawn Gill and Les Levidow (London: Free Association, 1987).
40. Alpana K. Gupta, Mausumi Bharadwaj, and Ravi Mehrotra, "Skin Cancer Concerns in People of Color: Risk Factors and Prevention," *Asian Pacific Journal of Cancer Prevention* 17, no. 12 (2016): 5257–5264, http://www.doi.org/10.22034/APJCP.2016.17.12.5257.
41. Marcela Bernal-Munera, "Integrating Social Justice Issues in the Biology Curriculum to Strengthen Community College Students' Critical Consciousness," *Cultural Studies of Science Education* (2022).
42. Joseph L. Graves and Alan H. Goodman, *Racism, Not Race: Answers to Frequently Asked Questions* (New York: Columbia University Press, 2021); David Upegui, "Review of *Racism, Not Race*," *American Biology Teacher* 84, no. 8 (2022): 508–509, http://www.doi.org/10.1525/abt.2021.84.8.508.
43. David Upegui, Julie Coiro, Stefan Battle, Rudolf Kraus, and David Fastovsky, "Integration of the Topic of Social Justice Into High School Biology Curricula," *Science and Education* (2021): 1–19, http://www.doi.org/10.1007/s11191-021-00287-y; David Segura, Maria Varelas, Daniel Morales-Doyle, Brezhnev Batres, Phillip Cantor, Diana Bonilla, Angela Frausto, Carolina Salinas, and Lynette Gayden Thomas, "Negotiating Structures and Agency in Learning to Teach Science for Equity and Social Justice," in *Recruiting, Preparing, and Retaining STEM Teachers for a Global Generation*, ed. Jacqueline Leonard, Andrea C. Burrows, and Richard Kitchen (Leiden, Netherlands: Brill, 2019), 241–261; David Upegui and David E. Fastovsky, *Integrating Racial Justice Into Your High-School Biology Classroom: Using Evolution to Understand Diversity* (New York: Taylor and Francis, 2024).
44. Melissa Braaten, Danelle Foster, Jason Foster, Rae Jing Han, Déana Scipio, and Enrique Suárez, "How Can We Confront and Dismantle Systemic Racism Through Science Learning?," in *STEM Teaching Tools*, ed. Phillip Bell and Deb Morrison, https://stemteachingtools.org/brief/79.
45. Kristin L. Gunckel, "Repairing Elementary School Science," *Theory Into Practice* 58, no. 1 (2019): 71–79, http://www.doi.org/10.1080/00405841.2018.1536918.
46. Joan Roughgarden, *Evolution's Rainbow: Diversity, Gender, and Sexuality in Nature and People* (Berkeley: University of California Press, 2013).
47. Anne Fausto-Sterling, "Why Sex Is Not Binary," *New York Times*, October 25, 2018, https://www.nytimes.com/2018/10/25/opinion/sex-biology-binary.html.
48. Subini A. Annamma, David Connor, and Beth Ferri, "Dis/ability Critical Race Studies (DisCrit): Theorizing at the Intersections of Race and Dis/ability," *Race Ethnicity and Education* 16, no. 1 (2013): 1–31, http://www.doi.org/10.1080/13613324.2012.730511.
49. Phillip A. Boda, "The Conceptual and Disciplinary Segregation of Disability: A Phenomenography of Science Education Graduate Student Learning," *Research in Science Education* 51, no. 6 (2021): 1725–1758, http://www.doi.org/10.1007/s11165-019-9828-x.
50. Kristen L. Gunckel and Sara Tolbert, "The Imperative to Move Toward a Dimension of Care in Engineering Education," *Journal of Research in Science Teaching* 55, no. 7 (2018),

http://www.doi.org/10.1002/tea.21458; Alejandra Frausto Aceves and Daniel Morales-Doyle, "More Than Civil Engineering and Civic Reasoning: World-Building in Middle School STEM" (under review).
51. Bill Bigelow and Tim Swinehart, eds., *A People's Curriculum for the Earth* (Milwaukee, WI: Rethinking Schools, 2015).
52. Carrie Tzou, Megan Bang, and Leah Bricker, "Commentary: Designing Science Instructional Materials That Contribute to More Just, Equitable, and Culturally Thriving Learning and Teaching in Science Education," *Journal of Science Teacher Education* 32, no. 7 (2021): 858–864, http://www.doi.org/10.1080/1046560X.2021.1964786.
53. Megan Bang, Beth Warren, Ann S. Rosebery, and Douglas Medin, "Desettling Expectations in Science Education," *Human Development* 55, no. 5–6 (2013): 302–318, http://www.doi.org/10.1159/000345322.
54. Bang, Warren, Rosebery, and Medin, "Desettling Expectations in Science Education."
55. Erin A. Cech, "The (Mis)Framing of Social Justice: Why Ideologies of Depoliticization and Meritocracy Hinder Engineers' Ability to Think About Social Injustices," in *Engineering Education for Social Justice*, ed. Juan Lucena (Dordrecht: Springer, 2013), 67–84, http://www.doi.org/10.1007/978-94-007-6350-0_4.
56. Erin B. Godfrey, Carlos E. Santos, and Esther Burson, "For Better or Worse? System-Justifying Beliefs in Sixth-Grade Predict Trajectories of Self-Esteem and Behavior Across Early Adolescence," *Child Development* 90, no. 1 (2019): 180–195, http://www.doi.org/10.1111/cdev.12854.
57. Juan C. Garibay, "STEM Students' Social Agency and Views on Working for Social Change: Are STEM Disciplines Developing Socially and Civically Responsible Students?," *Journal of Research in Science Teaching* 52, no. 5 (2015): 610–632, http://www.doi.org/10.1002/tea.21203.
58. Ginevra Clark, "Cultivating Connection in the Classroom," *Nature Reviews Chemistry* (2022): 1–2, https://doi.org/10.1038/s41570-022-00370-0.
59. Performance Expectation HS-LS1-7 in Lead States, *Next Generation Science Standards: For States, By States* (Washington, DC: National Academies, 2013).
60. Kathryn L. Kirchgasler, "Moving the Lab Into the Field: The Making of Pathologized (Non)Citizens in US Science Education," *Curriculum Inquiry* 48, no. 1 (2018): 115–137, http://www.doi.org/10.1080/03626784.2017.1409595.
61. Jomo Mutegi, "The Inadequacies of 'Science for All' and the Necessity and Nature of a Socially Transformative Curriculum Approach for African American Science Education," *Journal of Research in Science Teaching* 48, no. 3 (2011): 301–316, http;//www.doi.org/10.1002/tea.20410.
62. "Karen Washington: It's Not a Food Desert, It's Food Apartheid," interview by Anna Brones, *Guernica*, May 7, 2018, https://www.guernicamag.com/karen-washington-its-not-a-food-desert-its-food-apartheid.
63. Luz Calvo and Catriona Rueda Esquibel, *Decolonize Your Diet* (Vancouver, BC: Arsenal Pulp, 2015); Sean Sherman and Beth Dooley, *The Sioux Chef's Indigenous Kitchen* (Minneapolis: University of Minnesota Press, 2017); Bryant Terry, *Vegan Soul Kitchen* (Cambridge, MA: Da Capo, 2009).
64. Vossoughi et al., "Beyond the Binary."
65. Jeffrey M. R. Duncan-Andrade, "Note to Educators: Hope Required When Growing Roses in Concrete," *Harvard Education Review* 79, no. 2 (2009): 181–194, http://www.doi.org/10.17763/haer.79.2.nu3436017730384w.

66. Daniel Morales-Doyle, Alejandra Frausto Aceves, Tiffany L. Childress-Price, and Mindy J. Chappell, "History, Hope, and Humility in Praxis: Co-Determining Priorities for Professional Learning with Content Area Teachers" (unpublished manuscript).

Chapter 4

1. Grant Wiggins and Jay McTighe, *Understanding by Design* (Alexandria, VA: Association for Supervision and Curriculum Development, 2005).
2. Sara Tolbert and Alexa Schindel, "Altering the Ideology of Consumerism: Caring for Land and People Through School Science," in *Sociocultural Perspectives on Youth Ethical Consumerism*, ed. Giuliano Reis, Michael Mueller, Rachel Gisewhite, Luiz Siveres, and Renato Brito (London: Springer, 2018), 115–129, http://www.doi.org/10.1007/978-3-319-65608-3_8.
3. Jesper Sjöström and Vicente Talanquer, "Humanizing Chemistry Education: From Simple Contextualization to Multifaceted Problematization," *Journal of Chemical Education* 91, no. 8 (2014): 1125–1131, http://www.doi.org/10.1021/ed5000718.
4. Eduardo Gudynas, "Buen Vivir: Today's Tomorrow," *Development* 54 (2011): 441–447, http://www.doi.org/10.1057/dev.2011.86.
5. Unai Villalba, "Buen Vivir vs Development: A Paradigm Shift in the Andes?," *Third World Quarterly* 34, no. 8 (2013): 1427–1442, http://www.doi.org/10.1080/01436597.2013.831594.
6. Joseph Krajcik, Susan Codere, Chanyah Dahsah, Renee Bayer, and Kongju Mun, "Planning Instruction to Meet the Intent of the Next Generation Science Standards," *Journal of Science Teacher Education* 25, no. 2 (2014): 157–175, http://www.doi.org/10.1007/s10972-014-9383-2.
7. Megan Bang, Ann Rosebery, Angela Calabrese Barton, Beth Warren, and Bryan Brown, "Toward More Equitable Learning in Science," in *Helping Students Make Sense of the World Using Next Generation Science and Engineering Practices,* ed. Christina V. Schwarz, Cynthia Passmore, and Brian J. Reiser (Arlington, VA: National Science Teachers Association, 2017), 33–58.
8. Krajcik et al., "Planning Instruction."
9. Alberto J. Rodriguez, "Strategies for Counterresistance: Toward Sociotransformative Constructivism and Learning to Teach Science for Diversity and for Understanding," *Journal of Research in Science Teaching* 35, no. 6 (1998): 589–622, http://www.doi.org/10.1002/(SICI)1098-2736(199808)35:6<589::AID-TEA2>3.0.CO;2-I.
10. For a useful discussion of the philosophical components of knowledge systems (like the science disciplines), see Bryan McKinley Jones Brayboy and Emma Maughan, "Indigenous Knowledges and the Story of the Bean," *Harvard Educational Review* 79, no. 1 (2009): 1–21, http://www.doi.org/10.17763/haer.79.1.l0u6435086352229.
11. Timothy Mitchell, *Carbon Democracy: Political Power in the Age of Oil* (Brooklyn, NY: Verso, 2011).
12. Benjamin Madley, *An American Genocide: The United States and the California Indian Catastrophe, 1846–1873* (New Haven, CT: Yale University Press, 2016).
13. Jeff Schwartz, "The Conflict Minerals Experiment," *Harvard Business Law Review* 6 (2016): 129.
14. American Chemical Society, *Chemistry in the Community*, 6th ed. (New York: W. H. Freeman, 2012).
15. Science Education for Public Understanding, *Science and Sustainability* (Ronkonkoma, NY: Lab Aids, 2005).

16. SEPUP has since published another relevant module on e-waste for middle school: https://sepuplhs.org/middle/modules/disposal/index.html.
17. Leong Ping Alvin, "The Passive Voice in Science Writing: The Current Norm in Science Journals," *Journal of Science Communication* 13, no. 1 (2014): 1–16, http://www.doi.org/10.22323/2.13010203.
18. Nelson Flores and Jonathan Rosa, "Undoing Appropriateness: Raciolinguistic Ideologies and Language Diversity in Education," *Harvard Educational Review* 85, no. 2 (2015): 149–171.
19. Eduardo Galeano, *The Open Veins of Latin America: Five Centuries of the Pillage of a Continent*, 25th Anniversary Ed. (New York: Monthly Review, 1997).
20. R. N. Keller, "The Lanthanide Contraction as a Teaching Aid," *Journal of Chemical Education* 28, no. 6 (1951): 312–317.
21. Ed Pilkington, "Proposed Trump Executive Order Would Allow US Firms to Sell 'Conflict Minerals,'" *The Guardian*, February 8, 2017, https://www.theguardian.com/us-news/2017/feb/08/trump-administration-order-conflict-mineral-regulations.
22. US Department of Justice Office of the Inspector General, *A Review of Federal Prison Industries' Electronic-Waste Recycling Program* (October 2010), https://oig.justice.gov/reports/BOP/o1010.pdf; Brook Larmer, "E-Waste Offers an Economic Opportunity as Well as Toxicity," *New York Times Magazine*, July 5, 2018, https://www.nytimes.com/2018/07/05/magazine/e-waste-offers-an-economic-opportunity-as-well-as-toxicity.html.
23. Brett Chase, "Outspoken Teachers Who Urged Students to Join Environmental Protest Avert Firing by Chicago Board of Ed," *Chicago Sun Times*, July 27, 2022, https://chicago.suntimes.com/2022/7/27/23281221/general-iron-cps-public-school-ctu-teachers-union-george-washington-high-lauren-bianchi-chuck-stark.

Chapter 5

1. Megan Bang, Ann Rosebery, Angela Calabrese Barton, Beth Warren, and Bryan Brown, "Toward More Equitable Learning in Science," in *Helping Students Make Sense of the World Using Next Generation Science and Engineering Practices*, ed. Christina V. Schwarz, Cynthia Passmore, and Brian J. Reiser (Arlington, VA: National Science Teachers Association, 2017), 33–58.
2. Beth Warren, Cynthia Ballenger, Mark Ogonowski, Ann S. Rosebery, and Josiane Hudicourt-Barnes, "Rethinking Diversity in Learning Science: The Logic of Everyday Sense-Making," *Journal of Research in Science Teaching* 38, no. 5 (2001): 529–552.
3. Thomas M. Philip and Flávio S. Azevedo, "Everyday Science Learning and Equity: Mapping the Contested Terrain," *Science Education* 101, no. 4 (2017): 526–532.
4. EPA, "Case Summary: W. R. Grace and Co. Bankruptcy Settlement," US Environmental Protection Agency, last modified July 2023, https://www.epa.gov/enforcement/case-summary-w-r-grace-co-bankruptcy-settlement.
5. "W. R. Grace Offers $18.5M to Settle Montana Asbestos Claims," *AP News*, January 10, 2023, https://apnews.com/article/health-business-montana-public-greg-gianforte-3533fb7fb90e366ec0e8c99868ed0545.
6. M. Ahmed, "Neem Patent Turns Bitter for Europe's W. R. Grace," *Business Standard*, December 12, 1997, https://www.business-standard.com/article/specials/neem-patent-turns-bitter-for-europes-w-r-grace-197121301087_1.html.
7. Linda Tuhiwai Smith, *Decolonizing Methodologies: Research and Indigenous Peoples* (New York: Zed, 1999).

8. Stephen Abrecht and Barbara Durr, "Amazing Grace: The Story of W. R. Grace and Co.," *NACLA's Latin American and Empire Report* 10, no. 3 (1976): 3–14.
9. Francisca Santana-Sagredo et al., "'White Gold' Guano Fertilizer Drove Agricultural Intensification in the Atacama Desert from AD 1000," *Nature Plants* 7, no. 2 (2021): 152–158.
10. Jomo W. Mutegi, Demetrice Smith-Mutegi, and Nicole Lewis, "Fostering Critical Perspectives of Science Among Preservice Elementary Teachers: An Empirical Identification of Affordances and Hindrances," *Journal of Science Teacher Education* 33, no. 8 (2022): 888–909, http://www.doi.org/10.1080/1046560X.2021.2015531.
11. Jomo Mutegi, "The Inadequacies of 'Science for All' and the Necessity and Nature of a Socially Transformative Curriculum Approach for African American Science Education," *Journal of Research in Science Teaching* 48, no. 3 (2011): 301–316, http://www.doi.org/10.1002/tea.20410.
12. Fouad Abd-El-Khalick, "Nature of Science in Science Education: Toward a Coherent Framework for Synergistic Research and Development," in *Second International Handbook of Science Education*, ed. B. J. Fraser, Kenneth Tobin, and Campbell J. McRobbie (Dordrecht, Netherlands: Springer-Kluwer, 2012), 1041–1062.
13. Daniel Morales-Doyle, Maria Varelas, David Segura, and Marcela Bernal-Munera, "Access, Dissent, Ethics, Politics: Pre-Service Teachers Negotiating Conceptions of the Work of Teaching Science for Equity," *Cognition and Instruction* 39, no. 1 (2021): 35–64, http://www.doi.org/10.1080/07370008.2020.1828421.
14. Bryan A. Brown and Jomo W. Mutegi, "A Paradigm of Contradictions: Racism and Science Education," in *International Encyclopedia of Education*, 3rd ed., ed. Eva Baker, Penelope Peterson, and Barry McGaw (Cambridge, MA: Elsevier, 2010), 554–564, http://www.doi.org/10.1016/B978-0-08-044894-7.00124-X.
15. Sara Tolbert, "Queering Dissection: 'I Wanted to Bury Its Heart, at Least,'" in *Gender in Learning and Teaching*, ed. Carol Taylor, Chantal Amade-Escot, and Andrea Abbas (London: Routledge, 2019), 39–53.
16. Tolbert, "Queering Dissection," 10.
17. Gretchen Kraig-Turner, "Beyond Just a Cells Unit: What My Science Students Learned from the Story of Henrietta Lacks," Rethinking Schools, 2017, https://rethinkingschools.org/articles/beyond-just-a-cells-unit/; "Who Was Henrietta Lacks?," National Science Teaching Association, https://www.nsta.org/lesson-plan/who-was-henrietta-lacks.
18. Leonardo Trasande, "How Banning Dangerous Chemicals Could Save the US Billions," *The Guardian*, June 25, 2019, https://www.theguardian.com/commentisfree/2019/jun/25/banning-dangerous-chemicals-could-save-the-us-billions-iq.
19. Centers for Disease Control and Prevention, "Blood Lead Levels—United States, 1999–2002," *Morbidity and Mortality Weekly Report* (MMWR) 54, no. 20 (2005): 513–516.
20. World Meteorological Organization, *Scientific Assessment of Ozone Depletion* (Geneva, Switzerland: WMO, 2022).
21. David Maile, "Science, Time, and Mauna a Wākea: The Thirty-Meter Telescope's Capitalist-Colonialist Violence, Part I," *The Red Nation* (2015); Javiera Barandiaran, "Reaching for the Stars? Astronomy and Growth in Chile," *Minerva* 53 (2015): 141–164.
22. Neil deGrasse Tyson and Avis Lang, *Accessory to War: The Unspoken Alliance Between Astrophysics and the Military* (New York: W. W. Norton, 2018).
23. *NOVA*, "Star Chasers of Senegal," written and directed by Ruth Berry, aired February 8, 2023, on PBS, https://www.pbs.org/wgbh/nova/video/star-chasers-of-senegal/.

24. Geoffrey Supran and Naomi Oreskes, "Assessing ExxonMobil's Climate Change Communications (1977–2014)," *Environmental Research Letters* 12, no. 8 (2017): 084019.
25. Kathryn L. Kirchgasler, "Science Class as Clinic: Why Histories of Segregated Instruction Matter for Health Equity Reforms Today," *Science Education* 107, no. 1 (2023): 42–70, http://www.doi.org/10.1002/sce.21756.
26. Jeannie Oakes, *Keeping Track: How Schools Structure Inequality* (New Haven, CT: Yale University Press, 1986).
27. William G. Wraga, "What's the Problem with a 'Rigorous Academic Curriculum'? Setting New Terms for Students' School Experiences," *Clearing House* 84, no. 2 (2011): 59–64.
28. Ernest Morrell, *Critical Literacy and Urban Youth* (New York: Routledge, 2007).
29. Brian J. Reiser, Michael Novak, Tara A. W. McGill, and William R. Penuel, "Storyline Units: An Instructional Model to Support Coherence from the Students' Perspective," *Journal of Science Teacher Education* 32, no. 7 (2021): 805–829, http://www.doi.org/10.1080/1046560X.2021.1884784.
30. Bernard Ortiz de Montellano, "Empirical Aztec Medicine," *Science* (1975): 215–220.
31. Daniel Morales-Doyle, "The Aspirin Unit: Confronting a Hostile Political Climate Through the Chemistry Curriculum," *Cultural Studies of Science Education* 15, no. 3 (2020): 639–657, http://www.doi.org/10.1007/s11422-019-09932-z.
32. Daniel Morales-Doyle, Alejandra Frausto Aceves, Tiffany Childress Price, and Mindy J. Chappell, "History, Humility, and Hope in Praxis: Science Teachers' Expansive Professional Learning" (under revision).

Chapter 6

1. Ebony O. McGee, *Black, Brown, Bruised: How Racialized STEM Education Stifles Innovation* (Cambridge, MA: Harvard Education Press, 2020).
2. Liliana Valladares, "Post-Truth and Education: STS Vaccines to Re-Establish Science in the Public Sphere," *Science and Education* (2021), http://www.doi.org/10.1007/s11191-021-00239-0; Catarina Dutilh Novaes and Silvia Ivani, "The Inflated Promise of Science Education," Boston Review, September 6, 2022, https://www.bostonreview.net/articles/the-inflated-promise-of-science-education.
3. Glen S. Aikenhead, *Science Education for Everyday Life: Evidence-Based Practice* (New York: Teachers College Press, 2006).
4. Bettina L. Love, *We Want to Do More Than Survive: Abolitionist Teaching and the Pursuit of Educational Freedom* (Boston: Beacon, 2019); David Stovall, "Are We Ready for 'School' Abolition? Thoughts and Practices of Radical Imaginary in Education," *Taboo: Journal of Culture and Education* 17, no. 1 (2018): 6.
5. My colleagues and I have extended this argument to include rethinking mathematics courses, see Patricia Buenrostro, Tiffany Childress Price, and Daniel Morales-Doyle, "Ditching Chemistry and Calculus: An Axiological Shift Towards Alternative Futures in High School STEM" (under review).
6. Thomas M. Philip and Flávio S. Azevedo, "Everyday Science Learning and Equity: Mapping the Contested Terrain," *Science Education* 101, no. 4 (2017): 526–532.
7. David Segura, Daniel Morales-Doyle, Susan Nelson, Amy Levingston, and Karen Canales, "Sustaining Community-School Relationships Around Shared Visions of Climate Justice and Science Teaching," *Connected Science Learning* 3, no. 5 (2021), https://www.nsta.org/connected-science-learning/connected-science-learning-september-october-2021/sustaining-community.

8. Sepehr Vakil, Alisa Reith, and Natalie Araujo Melo, "Jamming Power: Youth Agency and Community-Driven Science in a Critical Technology Learning Program," *Journal of Research in Science Teaching* 60, no. 8 (2022), http://www.doi.org/10.1002/tea.21843.
9. Sepehr Vakil, "Ethics, Identity, and Political Vision: Toward a Justice-Centered Approach to Equity in Computer Science Education," *Harvard Educational Review* 88, no. 1 (2018): 26–52, http://www.doi.org/10.17763/1943-5045-88.1.26; Sepehr Vakil and Maxine McKinney de Royston, "Youth as Philosophers of Technology," *Mind, Culture, and Activity* (2022), http://www.doi.org/10.1080/10749039.2022.2066134; Ruha Benjamin, *Race After Technology* (Medford, MA: Polity, 2009).
10. Marcia Linn and Korah Wiley, eds., *Opportunities for Engaging Students in Science Through Civic Reasoning, Discourse, and Action: A Brief for Practitioners* (Washington, DC: National Academy of Education, forthcoming).
11. Miwa Takeuchi, Pratim Sengupta, Marie-Claire Shanahan, Jennifer D. Adams, and Maryam Hachem, "Transdisciplinarity in STEM Education: A Critical Review," *Studies in Science Education* 56, no. 2 (2020): 213–253, http://www. doi.org/10.1080/03057267.2020.1755802.
12. Ivan Salinas, M. Beatriz Fernández, Daniel Johnson, and Nataly Bastías, "Freire's Hope in Radically Changing Times: A Dialogue for Curriculum Integration from Science Education to Face the Climate Crisis," *Cultural Studies of Science Education* (2023), http://www.doi.org/10.1007/s11422-023-10157-4.
13. Safiya Umoja Noble, *Algorithms of Oppression* (New York: New York University Press, 2018).
14. Lila Finch, Celeste Moreno, and R. Benjamin Shapiro, "Luminous Science: Teachers Designing for and Developing Transdisciplinary Thinking and Learning," *Cognition and Instruction* 39, no. 4 (2021): 512–560, http://www.doi.org/10.1080/07370008.2021.1945064.
15. Daniel Morales-Doyle, "Putting Science Education in Its Place: The Science Question in Social Justice Education," *Cultural Studies of Science Education* 18, no. 1 (2023): 81–94, http://www.doi.org/10.1007/s11422-023-10151-w.
16. Eve Tuck and K. Wayne Yang, eds., *Toward What Justice? Describing Diverse Dreams of Justice in Education* (New York: Routledge, 2018).
17. Max Liboiron, *Pollution Is Colonialism* (Durham, NC: Duke University Press, 2021).
18. For more, see Daniel Morales-Doyle, Alejandra Frausto Aceves, Tiffany L. Childress-Price, and Mindy J. Chappell, "History, Humility, and Hope in Praxis: Co-Determining Priorities for Professional Learning with Content Area Teachers" (under review).

Acknowledgments

This book is my best attempt to share, in writing, what I have learned in more than 20 years as a science educator. Across these two decades—and even before that—I have been taught by many brilliant teachers, students, colleagues, and comrades who have informed the ideas in this book. I have been the recipient of generous care, support, and encouragement that I needed to write it. I feel a deep sense of gratitude to those who I mention here, and I acknowledge that there are many others who contributed to my learning and well-being along the way. No matter what I write, these acknowledgements are insufficient to communicate the depth and breadth of my appreciation, so I keep them brief and chronological.

Thank you to Loretta Morales and Michael Doyle for being my first and wisest teachers. Thank you to my three brothers Sean, Patrick, and Brendan for always being willing thought partners.

When I was a teenager studying engineering, Jeff Duncan-Andrade and K. Wayne Yang showed me the power of transformative teaching. They also encouraged me to reach out to David O. Stovall, whose mentorship and friendship has been central to my learning and development throughout my career and adult life. Thank you, Stove.

Thank you, Keilan and Lauren Bonner, for making sure I made it through my first few years in the classroom. Thank you, Rico Gutstein, for helping me to understand the collective power of organized teachers, and thanks to countless CTU comrades for making it concrete. Thank you, Sue Nelson and David Segura, for being the best science department colleagues I could have ever had. Thank you, Rito Martinez, for hiring me and helping me grow into the best job of my life. Thank you, Kim Wasserman Nieto, for teaching me so much about environmental justice and forging such meaningful relationships between organizing and teaching. Thank you, Amy Levingston, for picking up the torch and taking it further.

Thank you to Brian Cabral and Diana Bonilla for showing me different ways to think about education.

Thank you to Maria Varelas and Alberto Rodriguez for mentoring me into the world of science education scholarship.

Thank you to colleagues and comrades in the Youth Participatory Science Collective and several antecedents. Tiffany Childress Price has taught me things all along the way. I have learned a so much from Alanah Fitch, Shelby Hatch, and Kathryn Nagy. I want to give Mindy Chappell her flowers for making the path a little easier. Thank you to Adilene Aguilera, Darrin Collins, Maribel Cortez, Abel Farias, Nina Hike, Jasmine Jones, Tammy Pheuphong, and Tomasz Rajski. The wisdom of Karen Canales has been essential, and I appreciate you.

Thank you to Natasha Singh, Faven Habte, Anna MacKinnon, Alex Gordon, Paul Khairallah, Annelise Brandel-Tanis, and Shanna Surena-Mattson for helpful feedback.

Thank you, Jayne Fargnoli for your feedback, patience, and encouragement. Thank you to my friend and colleague, Decoteau Irby, for advice and support and for continually including me in writing groups, even when my attendance was spotty.

Most of all, thank you to Alejandra Frausto Aceves for being a partner in every sense of the word. Your name belongs in every one of the lists above. Your support, influence, brilliance, and love defy description.

About the Author

Daniel Morales-Doyle is an associate professor in the Department of Curriculum and Instruction at the University of Illinois Chicago (UIC). Before joining the faculty at UIC, Daniel was a high school teacher in the Chicago Public Schools (CPS) for more than a decade. Daniel's work has been funded by the National Science Foundation and the Spencer Foundation as a 2020 National Academy of Education Postdoctoral Fellow. His work has been published in *Science Education; The Journal of Research in Science Teaching (JRST); Race, Ethnicity, and Education; Cognition and Instruction*, and other top journals. Daniel teaches courses on social justice and STEM education and coordinates a science teacher education program. He facilitates professional development for school districts, college faculty, and organizations who support science teaching. Daniel has appeared on National Public Radio and in podcasts commenting on issues of equity and sustainability in science education. He continues to be involved in public K–12 education, not only through research and collaborations with teachers, but also by serving on a local school council and as a parent of CPS students.

Index

Figures are indicated by *f*; Tables are indicated by *t*

ableism, 87–88, 131
Abolition Science (podcast), 11
abstraction, 70, 78, 86–87
access, 49, 63, 86, 130–131, 141
acetylsalicylic acid, 79, 135–136
Aceves, Alejandra Frausto, 30–31, 77, 158n30
acid-base chemistry, 26–28
activism, 19, 28–30, 38, 63, 74–75, 102
  fast-food chains and, 93–95
addiction, drug, 79
admissions policies
  college, 146
  high school, 146
Africa, 27, 72, 82, 129, 132–133
Aguilera, Adilene, 119
Aikenhead, Glen, 2
alternative futures, science education as a catalyst for, 12, 16, 126, 139–150, 144*t*
ammonia, 55, 59, 75
anchoring phenomenon in science curricula, 84, 86
anthropogenic climate change, 142
anti-racist science education, 24–25, 85, 87, 142
Anti-Racist Science Teaching (Vance), 126–127
anti-sexist science education, 24–25, 142
anti-vaccine sentiments, 27, 41
apartheid
  in Africa, 72, 133
  food, 92, 94, 96*t*

appropriation, 26, 138, 141
Arrhenius, Sven, 27
arroyo willow, 136
artificial intelligence, 143
'artificial turf' organizations, 76–77
asbestos, 124
aspirin, 79, 135–136
assessments, 117*t*, 7, 99, 112, 131–132, 134
  in aspirin lab activity, 135–136
  authentic, 14–15, 100–102, 105–111, 118–119, 133, 140
assimilation, 43, 50, 52*t*, 141
assumptions, 31, 44, 64, 91–92, 125
astronomy, 129–130
astrophysics, 61–62
atomic structure, 72, 111, 117*t*, 118, 132
Australia, 84, 86
authentic assessments, 14–15, 100–102, 105–111, 118–119, 133, 140

backward planning in curricula, 100–101 107–108, 103*f*, 110, 113, *116*, 117*t*
  in love letter writing activity, 131–133
Bang, Megan, 90
Barton, Angela Calabrese, 53
baseball, 121–123
Bayer, 79
Bernal-Munera, Marcela, 87
"best practices," 9, 41, 146
biases, racial, 63–65
Bigelow, Bill, 89

171

bilingualism, 4
biology, 11–12, 34, 87
   curricula, 21–22, 84, 88, 91, 126–127
   scientific racism and, 84–85
Black, Brown, Bruised (McGee), 141
Black people, African American and, 18, 54, 60, 62–63, 65, 81–82
   Black scientists, 27, 64, 84
boarding schools, Native American, 74
Boda, Phillip, 88
Boyle, Robert, 25
brain damage, 64–65
Brazil, 77–78
Brown, Bryan, 123
buen vivir (living well), 105

California, 109
Canary Islands, 46–47
cancer, 84, 86, 124
   carcinogenic incinerator pollution and, 18–19, 31–32, 138
canon in science education, 13, 17–23, 31, 97, 122, 144*t*
   exploitation in, 25–26
   learning standards enforcing, 100
   phenomena centered curricula and, 67
capitalism, 88–90, 93
   racial, 7, 63, 143
Capitan, Mitchell, 29, 35, 38
carcinogenic incinerator pollution, 18–19, 31–32, 138
cartels, diamond, 72, 82, 132–134
catalyst, science education as a
   for alternative futures, 12, 16, 126, 139–150, 144*t*
   for change, 13, 16, 140, 149
census, US, 45–46
Central America, 23, 26, 93
CFCs. *See* chlorofluorocarbons
change, science education as a catalyst for, 13, 16, 140, 149

Chappell, Mindy, 70
chattel slavery, 84
chemical industry, 121–125, 128–129
chemistry, 14–15, 99, 121–124, 128–129
   acid-base, 26–28
   AP chemistry class, 8, 32–39, 34*f*, 35*f*, 37*f*, 50, 135–136
   atomic structure in, 72, 111, 117*t*, 118, 132
   density assignment, 113, 115, 117*t*, 118
   environmental racism and, 147
   high school, 11, 22–23, 26–28, 36
   justice-centered science pedagogy, 14, 32–33
   laboratory activities, 111–114
   molecular structure in, 72, 83
   in sophomore capstone project, 102–106, 103*f*, 106*t*, 107–108
   utilizing popular culture in, 71–72
Chemistry of the Community textbook, 71–72, 111, 114, 117*t*, 134
chemophobia, 128–129
Chicago, Illinois, 32–33, 45, 121, 137, 144–145, 147
   e-waste in, 119
   Indigenous lands in, 47
   Instituto Justice and Leadership Academy, 77
   Police Department, 73
   Public Schools, 130–131
   Youth Participatory Science Collective, 99–100, 138, 158n30
child labor, 71–72
Chile, 129, 145
China, 27
chlorofluorocarbons (CFCs), 128–129
class
   middle class, 44, 93
   working, 53, 55, 74, 125

clichés, 43, 57, 63
climate change, 3, 6–7, 10, 97–98,
    142–143
    Chilean teachers on, 145
    denial, 40
    Exxon-Mobil campaigns around, 130
    natural disasters and, 81–82, 90–91
    in the NGSS, 147
    as scientific phenomena, 68
    STEM pipeline and, 121–122
coal-fired power plant, 14, 32–33,
    37–39, 99, 139
coal lobby, 39–40
Cold War, 30
collage activity, magazine,
    103–105, 133
collective, 25, 29, 94
    well-being, 105, 143–147
college, 49, 70, 79, 87, 91, 130, 144
    admissions, 146
    preparatory curriculum, 143
colonialism, 3–4, 26, 72, 74, 102, 112,
    125, 127
    historical context of, 47, 115–116,
        132–133
    resource extraction and, 82–83,
        115–116, 131–132
    scientific racism and, 85
    settler, 7, 25, 65, 86, 89, 129, 143
    by Spain, 46, 115
Columbus, Christopher, 6–7
communities, 1–2, 8–9, 41, 59–60, 99,
    105. *See also* Indigenous peoples
    of color, 18, 34, 45, 73–74,
        94, 125
    economically dispossessed,
        34, 73, 104
    engaging with, 69–70, 74–77
    environmental racism impacting,
        31–38
    health in, 18–19, 35
    Latine, 45–46, 50, 74
    marginalized, 3, 94, 130, 143, 147
    membership and, 44–48
    police impacting, 73
    scientific, 4, 124, 141
    self-determination for, 38, 76, 147
computer science, 72, 144
concerned scientists, 60–62
conspiracy theories, 27, 41–42
consumption, consumerism and, 4, 10,
    104–105, 112, 133, 137–138
    food systems and, 93
contamination, 91
    heavy metal, 15, 33–38, 34*f*, 35*f*,
        54–55, 99
context, 84, 96*t*, 146. *See also* historical
    context
    local, 15, 99, 124
    political, 20–21, 29–30, 68–69, 79,
        117–118, 144
    social, 12, 111, 124
cookie mining activity, 89–90
copper, 111–113, 117*t*, 118
corn, 26
COVID-19 pandemic, 62–63, 90
crayfish lesson, 87
cross-curricular projects,
    101–102, 103*f*
curricula, science, 1, 15, 39,
    122–123, 139. *See also*
    assessments; backward planning
    in curricula; canon in science
    education; science learning
    activities; standards, science
    education
    anchoring phenomenon in, 84, 86
    biology, 21–22, 84, 88, 91, 126–127
    college preparatory, 143
    colonialism in, 129
    computer science in, 144
    Earth science, 111
    elementary school, 39–40
    Eurocentric, 8, 13, 24–28, 115
    hidden, 69, 88
    limitations in, 4–5, 19–21

curricula, science (*continued*)
  phenomenon-centered, 40, 67–68, 80–81, 96*t*, 133
  problematic ideologies in, 3–4, 6–7, 13–14
  published, 100, 108, 111–112
  role of fun in, 30–31, 131–132, 134–138
  role of joy in, 30–31, 97, 134–138
  role of love in, 71–72, 131–134, 135
  SJSI and, 19, 145–146
  standards in, 100–101, 105–110, 106*t*
  students on, 48–49, 56–58, 72–73
curriculum planning, 1, 16, 39, 78, 102, 147–148. *See also* backward planning in curricula
  normativity problem in, 43–44
  SJSI in, 100, 140

Das, Atas, 11
data science, 144
Davis, Angela, 11
DCI. *See* disciplinary core ideas
De Beers corporation, 71–72, 133
deficit framing, 53, 70, 92–93, 96
demands of science curricula, 1, 21–22
demographics, US, 45–46
denial, climate change, 40
density, 113, 115, 117*t*, 118
design activities, 88–90
DHMO. *See* dihydrogen monoxide
diamonds, 14–15, 71–72, 82–83, 132–134
dignity, 48–49, 140
dihydrogen monoxide (DHMO) activity, 128
dis/ability, 43, 88
disciplinary boundaries, 69, 81, 86, 130–132
disciplinary core ideas (DCI), 65, 132
  of the NGSS, 41, 89–90, 106–107, 106*t*, 109–110

discrimination, 5–6, 43
disinterested scientists, 60–62
diversity, equity, and inclusion initiatives, 30, 59, 125
dominant perspectives in science education, 21–25, 52*t*, 81, 83–91, 115
  nixtamalization challenging, 26–28
  role of equity in, 2–3
drug
  development, 79, 135–136
  prescriptions, 73–74, 79
DuBois, W. E. B., 11
Duncan-Andrade, Jeff, 97
DuPont, 105

Earth science, 111, 130
Eastern Navajo Dine Against Uranium Mining (ENDAUM), 36
economically dispossession, 34, 73, 104
education, science. *See specific topics*
Einstein, Albert, 13
elementary school, 39–40, 44–45, 50, 87, 89–90
embodied learning, 30–32
empiricism, 20
ENDAUM. *See* Eastern Navajo Dine Against Uranium Mining
engineering, principles of, 10, 88–90
English (language), 4–5, 44, 73
enterprise, scientific, 3, 9, 17–18, 21, 25, 41, 124–125, 141–142. *See also* institutions, scientific
environmental
  justice, 18–19, 32–40, 97, 138, 144
  racism, 18, 31–39, 63, 91, 128, 147
  science, 28, 32–39, 34*f*, 35f, 37*f*, 48–49, 129–130
equity in science teaching, 1–2, 123, 130–131, 139
  standards and, 40–41, 107
  STEM and, 5

ethics, 29–30, 94–95, 133
  museums and, 102
etymology, 21–23
Eurocentric, 45–46, 67, 134–135
  curricula, 8, 13, 24–28, 115
  patriarchy, 21–24, 34
evidence, scientific, 18, 21, 38, 40, 129
  climate change and, 142
e-waste (electronic waste), 119
exclusionary culture, 60, 124
exploitation, 25–26, 41, 110–111,
    115–116, 127
  in food systems, 93
  in US prisons, 119
extraction, resource, 29, 41, 103f,
    105, 130
  colonialism and, 82–83, 115–116,
    131–132
  cookie mining activity, 89–90
  metals in, 108–113, 115–116, 117t,
    118–119, 131, 137
extractive economy, 89, 96t, 97–98,
    119, 147
Exxon-Mobil, 130

false beliefs, 4, 83–86
families, parents and, 48, 69–70,
    73–77, 104, 146–149
  funds of knowledge in, 53–55
fast-food chains, 93–95
feminism, 127
fertilizer, 125
financial aid, 49
"Fire project," capstone project, 101–
    106, 103f, 106t, 107–108
Floyd, George, 62, 125
food
  apartheid, 92, 94, 96t
  systems, 26, 91–95, 149
forced labor, 71–72
formative assessments, 101–102
fossil fuels, 7–8, 39–41, 147
France, 23, 46

Freire, Paulo, 11–12, 77, 81
Fresh Supply, 144–145
Frontline (PBS series), 82
Fukushima, Japan, 91
fun, role in science curricula of, 30–31,
    131–132, 134–138
funds of knowledge, 53–55

Galeano, Eduardo, 115
Garibay, Juan, 62
gaze, 81–83, 86
gender, 4, 20, 30–31, 44, 87, 90
generative themes, 77–78, 81
genetics, 4, 84–87
geology, 89, 109, 130
global North, global South and,
    116, 129
goals, 12, 15, 21, 76–77, 141, 144
  of science education, 2–3, 49, 101,
    107–108, 111–112, 114–115
gold, 109, 115–116
González, Norma, 53
Goodman, Alan, 87
Grace, W. R., 124–125
graduation requirements, high school,
    124, 130–131, 146–147
grassroots movements and
    organizations, 32–33, 45–46,
    75–77, 99, 138, 144–145
Graves, Joseph, 87
Greek (language), 22–23
Greene, Maxine, 11
ground-level ozone, 33
guano (bat and bird feces), 124–125
Gunckel, Kristen, 10, 87

Harding, Sandra, 11
Hawaii, 129
health, 63–66, 96t
  community, 18–19, 35
  food systems and, 91–94
  public, 1–2, 68, 86, 130,
    144–145, 144t

Heartland Institute, 40
heavy metal contamination, 15, 33–38, 34f, 35f, 54–55, 99
Hernandez, David, 101
heroin, 79
heteronormativity, 87–88
hidden curricula, 69, 88
hierarchies, 22, 31, 57, 65, 84
  racial, 82, 131
high school, 44–45, 89, 144–145. *See also* students, science; teachers, science; *specific science disciplines*
  graduation requirements, 123, 130–131, 146–147
  sophomore capstone project in, 101–106, 103f, 106t, 107–108
Hike, Nina, 138
Hill Collins, Patricia, 56
'Hispanic' ethnic category, 45–46
historical context, 6–8, 14–15, 31, 65, 113
  canon and, 20–23, 115
  of colonialism, 47, 115–116, 132–133
  SJSI in, 19, 68–69, 149
  of structural racism, 25
historical knowledge, 8, 15–16
history of science, 23, 25, 79, 125
Homeland (documentary), 28–29, 36–38
hope, role in science education of, 97–98, 134–138, 149
human rights, 110
humility, 77, 97, 149
Hurricane Katrina, 81–82, 90–91

identity, 4–5, 56, 63, 87–88, 140
ideologies, problematic, 3–4, 6–7, 13–14, 69, 83, 110, 145. *See also* dominant perspectives in science education
  ableism and, 87–88
  capitalism and, 88–90
  militaristic, 72
  nature-culture divide and, 90–91
  racism as, 64, 84–87
Illinois. *See* Chicago, Illinois
immigrants, 52, 93
imperialism, 3–4, 23–25, 109, 115
incinerator pollution, carcinogenic, 18–19, 31–32, 138
inclusion, 25, 30, 59, 125
India, 23, 27, 124–125
Indigenous peoples, 23, 47, 86, 89, 129
  gold rush impacting, 109
  knowledge, 26–27, 79, 124–125
  medicinal plants used by, 79, 136
  Navajo community as, 28–29, 35–38
individualism, 88, 91–92
industrial pollution, 34, 121–122, 125
inequities, 3–5, 52, 96, 112, 139–140
institutions, scientific, 3–4, 7, 20–22, 25, 31, 125, 139–142
  exclusionary culture of, 60, 124
  in the global North, 129
Instituto Justice and Leadership Academy, 77
intellectual respect for students, 95, 116, 130–131, 141
intellectuals, transformative, 14, 58–60, 62–66, 140
interdependence, 138, 149–150
Ireland, 47, 124–125

Japan, 91
Johnson, Hazel, 138
Jones, Jasmine, 138
joy, role in science curricula of, 30–31, 97, 134–138
justice-centered science pedagogy, 1–2, 7, 27–28, 52t, 80–83, 133–137
  in chemistry, 14, 32–33
  environmental justice and, 18–19, 32–40, 97, 138, 144
  individualism addressed by, 92

Kaire, Maram, 129
kinematics, 30, 62
King, Martin Luther, Jr., 29–30, 80
Kirchgasler, Katie, 92
knowledge, 74, 77–78, 95
　funds of, 53–55, 75
　historical, 8, 15–16
　Indigenous, 26–27, 79, 124–125
　production, 14, 24, 27, 114
　scientific, 8, 24, 28, 37–38, 114, 122–123, 133, 142

laboratory activities, 111–114, 117*t*
Lacks, Henrietta, 128
language, 20–21, 46, 50
　English, 4–5, 44, 73
　Greek, 22–23
　Portuguese, 77
Latin (language), 22–23
Latin America, 12, 45–46, 72, 115–116, *117t*
Latine communities, 45–46, 50, 74
lead poisoning, 34, 35*f*, 128
learning, 5, 15–16
　embodied, 30–32
learning standards, 5, 6, 10, 65, 88, 100, 102, 105
learn-to-earn ideology, 49, 59
Le Châtelier's principle, 34–35, 35*f*, 37*f*
Levingston, Amy, 101
Levins, Richard, 56
Lewis, Gilbert, 27
Liboiron, Max, 41
licensure, teacher, 78, 126–137
Linnaeus, Carolus (Carl von Linné), 22, 25, 84
literacy, scientific, 2–3, 21, 136
living well *(buen vivir)*, 105
local
　context, 15, 99, 124
　control, 146–147
Lopez, Enrique, 137
Lorenz, Konrad, 127

Louisiana, 45–47, 53, 81–82, 90–91
Love, Bettina, 11
love, role in science curricula of, 71–72, 131–134, 135

magazine collage activity, 103–105, 133
mainstream approaches. *See* dominant perspectives in science education
malachite, 111–112, 117*t*, 118
Marable, Manning, 81–82
marginalized, 30, 73, 81, 87
　communities, 3, 94, 130, 143, 147
　students, 4, 44, 88, 92–94, 130, 140–142
Mariana (biology teacher), 126–127
Mars, 129
materialism, 104–105
McGee, Ebony, 141
medical technology, 63–66, 85
medicinal plants, 79, 136
memory, 33, 81
Mensah, Felicia Moore, 67–68
Merchants of Doubt (film), 130
meritocracy, 88, 91
metals, extraction, 108–113, 115–116, 117*t*, 118–119, 131, 137
metric system, 23, 134
Mexico, 109
middle class, 44, 93
middle school, 84, 86, 89, 92, 116, 144
military, US, 30, 72, 129
mind and body, non-separation of, 30–32
mining, 28–29, 71–72, 89–90, 110–112, 117*t*, 130
minoritized students, 92, 140.
　See also marginalized
Molina, Mario, 128–129
Moll, Luis, 53
multiculturalism, 20, 28, 129
murder of Floyd, 62, 125
museums, 102, 103*f*

music videos, 71–72
Mutegi, Jomo, 92

Nambo, Cynthia, 131
National Football League (NFL), 64–65
National Science Teaching Association, 128
Native American boarding schools, 74
natural disasters, 81–82, 90–91
nature of science (NOS), 25, 29, 124–126
Navajo community, 28–29, 35–38
neem oil, 124–125
Nelson, Sue, 32
"Nerds and Jocks" teaching unit, 30–31
neutrality, political, 39–40, 62, 83–84, 114
New Mexico, 36
New Orleans, Louisiana, 81–82, 90–91
Newton, Isaac, 13
Next Generation Science Standards (NGSS), 2, 34–35, 40, 132, 147
  DCI, 41, 89–90, 106–107, 106*t*, 109–110
  design activities and, 88–89
  PE, 41, 89, 106–107, 106*nt*, 116
  sophomore capstone project and, 105–106, 106*t*, 107
NFL. *See* National Football League
NGSS. *See* Next Generation Science Standards
Nieto, Kimberly Wasserman, 32
nixtamalization, 26–28
Nobel prize, 128–129
'non-profit-industrial complex,' 77
non-proliferation, nuclear, 29–30
normativity, 43–44, 50
NOS. *See* nature of science
nuclear weapons, 29–30, 129, 143
nutrition, 26, 91–95

objectivity, 8, 20, 29–30, 39, 114
observatories, space, 129

Odette (former student), 27–28, 34–35, 34*f*, 35*f*, 36, 37*f*, 38
Oklahoma, 40
Open Veins of Latin America, The (Galeano), 115, 117*t*
oppression, 12, 48–49, 85–86, 88, 149
  perpetuated in science education, 4–5, 97
Ortiz de Montellano, Bernard, 136
osmium assignment, 116, 117*t*, 137
overdose, drug, 79
ozone layer, 128–129

painkillers, synthetic opioid, 79
parents, 48, 69–70, 73–77, 104, 146–149
  funds of knowledge in, 53–55
participatory processes, 70, 77
passive voice, 114, 134
patriarchy, paternalism and, 4–5, 13, 20, 92
  Eurocentric, 21–24, 34
PE. *See* performance expectations, NGSS
pedagogies, 12, 14–15, 24. *See also* justice-centered science pedagogy
  of access, 141
  SJSI and, 97–98
people of color, 24–25, 62–63, 86
  communities of, 18, 34, 45, 73–74, 94, 125
  students as, 53, 72–75, 141–142
People's Curriculum for the Earth, A (Bigelow), 89
performance expectations (PE), NGSS, 41, 89, 106–107, 106*t*, 116
Peru, 124–125
petrochemical industry, 121–122
petroleum industries, 109, 130
Petro Pete (pro-oil cartoon), 40
pharmaceutical industry, 4, 14, 27, 142

phenomena, scientific, 67, 81, 95, 110–111, 123, 126, 129, 146
  climate change as, 68
  nature-culture divide and, 90
phenomenon-centered curricula, 40, 67–68, 80–81, 96t, 133
phenotypes, 22, 84
physics, 4, 29–30, 61–62, 72–73, 83, 129
pipeline model of science education, STEM, 2–3, 10, 16, 19–21, 140–141
  climate change and, 121–122
  racism and sexism of, 4–5
  student thinking constrained by, 5–7
  unsustainability of, 7–9
police harassment and brutality, 62, 73–74
polio vaccine, 27
political, 39–40. *See also* neutrality, political
  context, 20–21, 29–30, 68–69, 79, 117–118, 144
  power, 11, 23–24
pollution, 10, 86, 110, 137–138
  coal power plant, 14, 32–33, 37–39
  incinerator, 18–19, 31–32
  industrial, 34, 121–122, 125
  radioactive, 28–30
popular culture, youth, 69–72, 82
Portuguese (language), 77
potato famine, Irish, 124–126
Potter, Jackson, 101
power, 39–40, 59, 76
  of activism, 38, 74–75
  of communities, 45
  of justice-centered science pedagogy, 27–28
  of patriarchal structures, 20
  political, 11, 23–24
  of science teachers, 19, 80
  of scientific institutions, 129
power plant, coal-fired, 14, 32–33, 37–39, 99, 138
prescription drugs, 73–74, 79

pre-service teachers, 44, 147–148
priorities of science teachers, 1–2, 4, 13, 33
prisons, US, 119
privilege, 3, 18, 46, 130
problematic, 71. *See also* ideologies, problematic
  assumptions, 31, 91–92
  institutions, 102, 127
problem-based learning, 80, 98
problem-posing education, 81, 96t, 96t, 122, 148. *See also* justice-centered science pedagogy
public
  health, 1–2, 68, 86, 130, 144–145, 144t
  schools, 44, 50, 76, 130–131
  transit, 49
published materials, 39–40, 79–80, 95, 136
  published curricula as, 100, 108, 111–112
  repurposing, 88–89, 100, 110–116, 117t, 118
pulse oximeters, 63–65

"Quest for Peace and Justice, The" (King), 29

race, 44–45, 69, 74, 84–86
  and privilege, 3, 18, 46
  social construction of, 45–46, 65, 86–87, 97–98
Race (PBS documentary), 87
racial, 73
  biases, 63–65
  capitalism, 7, 63, 143
  hierarchies, 82, 131
racialization, 30–31, 45–46, 63–64, 84, 86
racism, 20–23, 30, 64, 125
  environmental, 18, 31–39, 63, 91, 128, 147

racism (*continued*)
  in the pipeline model, 4–5
  scientific, 31, 84–87, 126–127
  structural, 12, 25
  students impacted by, 73–75, 131
  systemic, 86, 92
radioactive pollution, 28–30, 91
Rajski, Tomasz, 121–122, 125
Ramírez, Ainissa, 27
Rancel, Mariel, 88
recycling industry, 119
reflective questions, 70–71
remedial courses, 130
resistance, student, 48–53, 52*t*, 56–58, 70, 72
respect, intellectual, 95, 116, 130–131, 141
responsibilities, 91
  of science teachers, 19, 70–71, 73, 95–96, 130
Rhodes, Cecil, 82
rights, 146–147
  human, 110
rigor in science education, 130–131, 140–141, 143
Riley, Alexis, 67–68
Rodriguez, Alberto, 40
rubric for writing assignment, 132–133
Russia, 30

Sangha-Gadsden, Angela, 101
scaffolding practices, 15, 38, 95, 111, 113, 118, 132, 136
Schindel, Alexandra, 104
Scholastic, 39–40
Science (journal), 136
science, technology, engineering, and mathematics (STEM), 2–9, 38, 62, 91, 97–98. *See also* pipeline model of science education, STEM
  learn-to-earn ideology in, 49, 59
  marginalized students and, 141
  military funding in, 30
  stereotyping in, 72
Science and Sustainability (textbook), 111
Science Education for Public Understanding Program (SEPUP), 111
Science in the City (Brown), 123
science learning activities, 5, 15–16, 109
  aspirin lab activity as, 135–136
  "cookbook activities," 112–113
  design activities as, 88–90
  equitable, 1, 123
  laboratory, 111–114, 117*t*
  sophomore capstone project as, 101–106, 103*f*, 106*t*, 107–108
  writing based, 102, 110–111, 114–115, 117*t*, 131–134, 136
science teaching. *See specific topics*
Science Technology and Society (STS), 27, 31, 69, 136, 144–145
  SJSI and, 78–80
scientific. *See also* evidence, scientific; institutions, scientific; phenomena, scientific
  communities, 4, 124, 141
  enterprise, 3, 9, 17–18, 21, 25, 41, 141–142
  knowledge, 8, 24, 28, 37–38, 114, 122–123 133, 142
  literacy, 2–3, 21, 136
  racism, 31, 84–87, 126–127
  taxonomy, 22, 57
'scientific method,' 56
scientific practices, 40, 101, 107–108, 113–115, 117*t*, 118, 122–124
  appropriation of, 138, 141
scientists, 60–62, 122–123
  Black, 27, 64, 84
  scientist-as-hero trope, 25, 27
Securities and Exchange Commission, US, 110, 119

segregation, 44, 73, 131
self-determination, 38, 45, 76, 143, 147
Senegal, 129
sense-making, 67, 92, 123
SEPUP. *See* Science Education for Public Understanding Program
settler colonialism, 7, 25, 65, 86, 89, 129, 143
sex, biological, 87–88
sexism, 4–5, 20, 25, 29, 31
sickle-cell anemia, 84, 86
Sierra Leone, 82
silver, 115–116
SJSI. *See* "social justice science issues"
skin
 cancer, 84, 86
 color, 63–65, 84, 86–87
Skovsmose, Ole, 78
slavery, 25, 84–85
social construction, 44
 of gender, 87–88, 90
 of race, 45–46, 65, 86–87, 97–98
social context, 12, 111, 124
social justice education, 11–12, 14, 28, 48–49
"social justice science issues" (SJSI), 14, 19, 67–68, 78, 143, 145–146
 defining, 69, 80–98, 96*t*, 110, 122
 drug development, 79, 135–136
 food deserts as, 92–93
 identifying, 69–78, 140
 metal extraction as, 108–111, 113, 118–119
 pedagogies and, 97–98
 in sophomore capstone project, 103*f*
 transdisciplinarity and, 131
social media, 81, 145
social movements, 20, 97–98
sociopolitical contexts, 68–69, 71
soil, heavy metal contamination in, 33–38, 34*f*, 35*f*, 99
solubility of heavy metals, 34–36, 34*f*, 35*f*, 38

sophomore capstone project, "Fire Project," 101–106, 103*f*, 106*t*, 107–108
space science, 107, 129–130
Spain, 46, 115
Spanish (language), 46
standardization, 5, 44, 50, 57, 100
standards, science education, 34–35, 101, 106, 106*t*, 108–110. *See also* Next Generation Science Standards
 climate change and, 147
 equity and, 40–41, 107
 learning, 6, 10, 65, 88, 100, 102, 105
Stark, Chuck, 119
STEM. *See* science, technology, engineering, and mathematics
stereotypes, 4, 23, 30–31, 73
stoichiometry, 22–23
story line units, 80, 113, 133
Stovall, David, 49
Strong, LaToya, 11
structural racism, 12, 25
STS. *See* Science Technology and Society
students, science, 5, 11
 anxiety of, 140
 of color, 53, 72–75, 141–142
 on curricula, 48–49, 56–58, 72–73
 defining SJSI with, 69, 80–98, 96*t*, 110, 122
 dignity of, 48–49, 140
 gaze of, 81–83, 86
 immigrant, 28
 intellectual respect for, 95, 116, 130–131, 141
 listening to, 69–74
 marginalized, 4, 44, 88, 92–94, 130, 140–142
 pipeline model constraining, 5–7
 racism impacting, 73–75, 131
 resistance of, 48–53, 52*t*, 56–58, 70, 72

students, science (*continued*)
   responses to justice-centered science teaching, 14
   in STEM fields, 8–9
   stereotypes and, 30–31
   as transformative intellectuals, 14, 58–60, 62–66, 140–141
   voice of, 71, 145
study of reality, Freire, 77–78
summative assessment, 101
sustainability, 1–2, 10, 40, 89
synthetic opioids, 79
Systema Naturae (Linnaeus), 22, 84
systemic racism, 86, 92

Tan, Edna, 53
tar sands, 41
taxonomy, scientific, 22, 57
teacher collectives, 69, 87, 147–149
teacher learning, 13, 15–16, 69, 147
teachers, 45–47, 58–60, 139
   lesson-dreaming activity for, 147–149
   licensure for, 78, 126–137
   motivation of, 51–53, 52*t*
   pre-service, 44, 147–148
teachers, science, 99, 142, 147–149. *See also specific disciplines*
   accountability and, 14
   education programs, 126–127
   family and community engagement by, 69–70, 74–77
   high school, 13, 15, 17
   pipeline model limiting role of, 3–4, 19–21
   prevention of conspiracy theories by, 41–42
   priorities of, 1–2, 4, 13, 33
   responsibilities of, 19, 70–71, 73, 95–96, 130
   scaffolding practices of, 15, 38, 95, 111, 113, 118, 132, 136
   SJSI identification by, 14, 140
teaching, science. *See specific topics*

technical solutions to problems, 10, 61, 98
technology, 132–133, 143–145. *See also* Science Technology and Society
   medical, 63–66, 85
   metal extraction and, 108–109, 113, 115–116, 117*t*, 118–119, 131, 137
telescopes, 129
Texas, 39
textbooks, science, 7, 79–80, 112, 118
   Chemistry of the Community, 71–72, 111, 114, 117*t*, 134
   Eurocentrism in, 23, 26–27
titration experiments, 135–136
tokenism, 24–25, 27
Tolbert, Sara, 10, 104, 127
transdisciplinary science teaching, 131, 144–146, 149
transformative intellectuals, 14, 58–60, 62–66, 140–141
trauma, 137
Tuck, Eve, 13, 82, 146

"underprepared" students, 130
undocumented status, 49
unit analysis, 115–116, 117*t*, 134–135
United States (US), 6, 12, 39, 81–82, 93, 119
   demographic groups, 45–46
   immigrant students in, 28
   imperialism, 3–4, 25, 109
   military, 30, 129
   slavery in, 25, 84–85
universalism, 8, 48
Upegui, David, 87
uranium mining, 28–29, 35–38, 37*f*
US. *See* United States

vaccinations, 3–4, 6, 142
Vakil, Sepehr, 72
Valladares, Liliana, 27
Vance, Michael, 126–127

video game design, 72–73
violence, 73
voice, student, 71, 145

war on drugs, 74
water, heavy metal contamination in, 33, 36, 37–38, 37*f*
Wayne, K., 13
weapons of mass destruction, 29–30, 129
well-being, 45, 91, 105, 143–146
West, Cornell, 97
West Africa, 82
Western science, 25–26, 28, 90
white men, 3, 18–20, 24–26, 54
white privilege, 46
white supremacy, 4–5, 20, 22, 62, 64, 83–84, 127

women, 24–25, 27, 54, 60
workforce, 2, 5, 30, 143
working class, 53, 55, 74, 125
W.R. Grace, 124–125
writing activities, science, 102, 110–111, 131–134, 136
  in technological metals unit, 114–115, 117*t*, 118–119

Yang, K. Wayne, 146
You Can't Be Neutral on a Moving Train (Zinn), 83
Young People's Race Power and Technology Project, 144–145
Youth Participatory Science Collective, 99–100, 138, 158n30

Zinn, Howard, 83–84